PRÁTICAS FÍSICAS, DESPORTIVAS E ARTÍSTICAS

PRÁTICAS FÍSICAS, DESPORTIVAS E ARTÍSTICAS. UMA PERSPETIVA VYGOTSKIANA

AUTORES
Carlos Eduardo de Barros Gonçalves
Riller Silva Reverdito
Serge Éloi

EDITOR
EDIÇÕES ALMEDINA, S.A.
Rua Fernandes Tomás, n.os 76, 78 e 79 – 3000-167 Coimbra
Tel.: 239 851 904 • Fax: 239 851 901
www.almedina.net • editora@almedina.net

DESIGN DE CAPA
Joana Carvalho

PAGINAÇÃO
Aresta Criativa – Artes Gráficas

IMPRESSÃO E ACABAMENTO
Forma Certa

Maio 2022

ALMEDINA | GRUPOALMEDINA

BIBLIOTECA NACIONAL DE PORTUGAL – CATALOGAÇÃO NA PUBLICAÇÃO
GONÇALVES, Carlos

Práticas físicas, desportivas e artísticas. – 1ª ed. – (Fora de coleção)
ISBN 978-989-40-0382-3

CDU 796

PRÁTICAS FÍSICAS, DESPORTIVAS E ARTÍSTICAS

UMA PERSPECTIVA VYGOTSKIANA

CARLOS EDUARDO GONÇALVES
RILLER SILVA REVERDITO
SERGE ÉLOI
(ORGANIZADORES)

EDIÇÃO TRILINGUE

ALMEDINA

PRESENTATION

Riller Silva REVERDITO
Mato Grosso State University, Cáceres, MT, Brazil.

Vygotsky occupies some of the most important pages in the course of contemporary science. Despite the censorship placed on his works and prejudice to the philosophical and ideological bases, his ideas advanced over time, constituting a milestone of development for different areas. The creative capacity and innovation make his work current, even though more than 100 years have passed since his first work.

In Brazil, access to Vygotsky's works and ideas only took place in the 1980s, with the country's redemocratization process. However, access was still limited, based on some works translated from fragments of the original, and therefore loaded with distortions and misinterpretations. And, as presented in this work, the world is still discovering Vygotsky's contributions.

In the area of Sports Science and Physical Education we have a long way to go. Despite his work having addressed topics of interest and direct relationship with physical, sporting and artistic practices, works from a Vygotskian perspective are still incipient. Therefore, considering this point of view, we have the opportunity to glimpse something new and countless possibilities for discoveries.

From the Perspective of Vygotskian, the reader will find in this work some of the main concepts, as well as studies applied to physical, sports, and artistic practices. The interdisciplinary and contextual/ecological nature offers the reader a broad perspective, ranging from a pedagogical approach to training to the development of learning processes.

Finally, this work is an invitation to the reader interested in studies carried out in a Vygotskian perspective. Far from exhausting the theme, it seeks to share experiences and explore the challenges of research, in order to support other initiatives in the field of investigation and intervention in physical, sporting and artistic practices – an invitation to creative activity.

APRESENTAÇÃO

Riller Silva REVERDITO
Universidade do Estado de Mato Grosso, Cáceres, MT, Brasil.

Vygotsky ocupa algumas das páginas mais importantes do percurso da ciência contemporânea. Apesar da censura colocada as suas obras e do preconceito às bases filosóficas e ideológicas, suas ideias avançaram no tempo, constituindo-se como um marco de desenvolvimento para diferentes áreas. A capacidade criadora e inovação fazem da sua obra atual, mesmo tendo passados mais de 100 anos desde os seus primeiros trabalhos.

No Brasil, o acesso as obras e ideias de Vygotsky aconteceram de forma aberta somente a partir dos anos 1980, com o processo de redemocratização do país. Porém, o acesso ainda era de forma limitada, realizado a partir de algumas obras traduzidas de fragmentos do original, e, logo, carregadas de distorções e interpretações equivocadas. E, ao que é apresentado nessa obra, o mundo ainda está descobrindo as contribuições de Vygotsky.

Na área da Ciência do Esporte e da Educação Física temos um longo caminho para ser percorrido. Apesar da sua obra ter abordado temas de interesse e relação direta com as práticas físicas, esportivas e artísticas, trabalhos em uma perspectiva vygotskiana ainda são incipientes. Logo, assumindo esse ponto de vista, temos a oportunidade de vislumbrar algo novo e inúmeras possibilidades de descobertas.

Em uma perspectiva vygotskiana, o leitor irá encontrar nesta obra alguns dos principais conceitos, além de estudos aplicados às práticas físicas, esportivas e artísticas. A natureza interdisciplinar e contextual/ecológica oferece ao leitor uma perspectiva ampla, indo de uma abordagem pedagógica da formação ao desenvolvimento dos processos de aprendizagem.

Por fim, esta obra é um convite ao leitor interessado em estudos realizados em uma perspectiva vygotskiana. Longe de esgotar o tema, busca compartilhar experiências e explorar os desafios da pesquisa, com a finalidade de apoiar outras iniciativas no campo da investigação e intervenção nas práticas físicas, esportivas e artísticas – um convite à atividade criadora.

FOREWORD

Carlos Eduardo GONÇALVES
University of Coimbra, Faculty of Sport Sciences and Physical Education, Portugal.
Serge *ÉLOI*
Universidade Paris-Leste, França.

The last decade has witnessed a growing interest in the works by Lev Vygotsky (1896 – 1934) in the field of Sports Science. It is not a powerful movement, nor a fashion, but a gradual increase of citations and references to concepts and theoretical elaborations more or less originated by this Russian psychologist. Unlike other schools of thought, it is not possible to credit a research group or groups, neither a specific country, as responsible for such intellectual resurgence, for researchers from the five continents have been showing that reading and interpreting texts written more than 70 years ago still makes sense for Pedagogy in the 21st century.

The lack of knowledge about Vygotsky's thought that permeated the second half of the last century requires an explanation: what was the reason for his works to be ignored, censored, and later, misrepresented? Deceased in 1934, aged 38, despite leaving innovative and scientifically powerful works, Vygotsky had ideas that did not please the power of that time (Sève, 2008, p. 317), which made it difficult or even prevented his books and articles to be reissued. Nevertheless, his work was somehow continued by his students, namely Leontiev, Luria and Bernstein, who proposed new developments and made theoretical formulations and empirical experimentations advance, even though sometimes that happened in diverging ways.

It was necessary to wait for half a century for *The Collected Works of Lev Semonovich Vygotsky*, comprising 6 volumes, to be published in his own country. Internationalization began in an improvised manner: for example, the American edition of *Thought and Language* (1986), amputated every critical, experimental and political references in the book. This edition would later be the basis for the Spanish and Italian publications. In France, a full translation of *Thought and Language* would be published in 1985.

Whereas Anglo-Saxon authors have spent a long time unaware or indifferent to the Russian scholar, the same did not happen in French-speaking countries. For linguistic and cultural reasons, as well as for their attachment to own scientific tradition, the reception and attention paid to Vygotsky's works appeared in these countries earlier than in other places. Research groups in France and in francophone regions of Belgium, Switzerland and Canada (Bronckart, Brossard, Clot, Engeström, Friedrich, Moro, Rabardel, Rochex, Schneuwly, Sève, van der Veer, Vergnaud, to name a few) have engaged debates, promoted qualified translations and organized events, aiming to establish strong connections with Russian researchers with deep knowledge about Vygotsky's thought.

It is following this path of sharing ideas that comes up the colloquium that took place in 2017 at the University of Paris-Est/UPEC, with a theme that was a whole program: "In which ways can Vygotsky's work help us to analyse, develop and bring a better understanding of the artistic, sport and physical practices transmission processes?"

Indeed, embracing his original psychological matrix to go further, the innovative pedagogical approach to training and development of learning processes has interested not only those who study Sports Science and Physical Education, but also teachers and researchers in Performing Arts.

This colloquium brought together philosophers, sports coaches of initiation and competition, teachers from the Conservatory of Arts and Crafts, all attentive readers of Vygotsky's works with research in the field of Pedagogy and Human Movement.

The diversity of experiences and of connections with schools of pedagogical thought was the catalyst of a lively debate that revealed the richness of what has been done (unfortunately, much of these materials has not been published) and the need to advance in such fertile ground. So many decades have passed, but it is still possible to innovate in a theme that seemed to be saturated and clearly exhausted.

But how can the work of a psychologist whose writings were published from 1930 to 1938, in which the only references to physical exercises are riding a bike or typewriting, inspire physical practices? Furthermore, those are considered as activities that do not integrate the higher mental processes.

Such question comes up in a particularly delicate moment for Sports Science. A struggle for scientific hegemony in the field, which can mean increased authority and professional status and thus power to be published and internationally acknowledged, is taking place in the academic arena, with a competition for articles' metrics, attendance to congresses and access to funding. After decades of being secondary in the constellation of disciplines that contribute to sportive training, with social changes induced by the globalization of economy and by the technological boom, Pedagogy and formative processes have gained renovated importance.

Strongly marked by the optimization of performance and theoretically influenced by structuralism, training has privileged the efficacy of specific knowledge transmission and of biological intervention to improve athletic performance. A warning sign given by a stagnation of the number of participants and by the increasing lack of interest of young people in practices that are repetitive and based on the authority of adults has led teachers, coaches and researchers to look around, searching for solutions to the problems. With the decline of functionalism, constructivism, in its post-modern version, came up as theoretical support for a new pedagogy.

Movements with ideas such as *Teaching Games for Understanding/ TGfU*, *Game Sense* and *Tactical Approach* have been enthusiastically welcomed into the academy and originated an extensive and heterogeneous literature on games teaching. In several English-speaking countries, they were even adopted as theoretical foundation for the training of coaches or as teaching models for athletes.

However, the scarce theoretical investment in both *TGfU* and *Game Sense*, as well as a poor acceptance by the community of organized sports, have caused the intellectual erosion of much of constructivism, leading to an impasse situation in the second decade of the 21st century.

In parallel, the development of the Complex Systems Theory and the recovery of works based on Bioecology, especially the ones by Gibson and Bronfenbrenner, have created new attraction poles for scholars in search of epistemological support for Sports Science.

From the research in the field of motor control, notedly streamlined by Kelso and Newell, just to name the more influent authors, came up the proposals consubstantiated in *Constraint-Led Approach/CLA*, which sustains that motor learning results from the interaction of task, performer and environment. Curiously, the first inspiration for the theoretical formulation of the teaching issue lays on Bernstein's Activity Theory, which is influenced by Vygotsky.

The crossings of CLA with Dynamic Systems Theory and with Bioecology evolved to the Dynamic Ecological Systems Theory, which has been growing as epistemological basis for Sports Science, openly challenging TGfU's theoretical strength. It is against this field of dichotomous struggle, in which, on the one hand, every learning is a social construction and, on the other hand, the determinism of the constraints that involve the individual represents an undesirable reductionism, that the group of participants of the UPEC colloquium bring up epistemological doubts.

The volume herein emanates concerns and reflections that aim to set Sports Pedagogy free from theoretical limitations, which may be fascinating but make possible the absence of values and place the human being that the athlete is in a secondary position. Chapters express the contributions from the colloquium, complemented by the debates that took place then.

Beyond the patent philosophical thought that is present in Séverac and Éloi's chapter, there are empirical studies by Tomas, Ullrich, Éloi and Matthey-Jaquet *et al*, in which the fruitfulness of Vygotsky's teaching is explored, regarding the training process of athletes of different ages and dancers. In their turn, the chapters by Lemonie, Bernal, Jarrett, Wei and Wallian present a critical view on aspects of Vygotsky's works with greater relevance for Sports Science.

References

SÈVE, L. (2008). *Penser avec Marx aujourd'hui. Tome II: L'homme.* Paris, La Dispute.

PREFÁCIO

Carlos Eduardo GONÇALVES
University of Coimbra, Faculty of Sport Sciences and Physical Education, Portugal.
Serge ÉLOI
Universidade Paris-Leste, França.

A última década tem assistido a um crescente interesse pela obra de Lev Vygotsky (1896-1934) no campo das Ciências do Desporto. Não se trata de um movimento poderoso, de uma moda, mas de aumento gradual de citações, referências, remissões para conceitos e elaborações teóricas mais ou menos originadas pelo psicólogo russo. Ao contrário de outras escolas de pensamento, não é possível atribuir a um grupo ou grupos de pesquisa ou a um país específico a responsabilidade por este ressurgimento intelectual, mas pesquisadores dos 5 continentes vêm demonstrando que a leitura e interpretação de textos com mais de 70 anos continua a fazer sentido para a Pedagogia do século XXI.

O desconhecimento sobre o pensamento de Vygotsky, que atravessou a segunda metade do século anterior necessita de explicação: por que razão o seu trabalho foi ignorado, censurado, e, mais recentemente, desnaturado. Falecido em 1934, com 38 anos, apesar de ter deixado uma obra inovadora e cientificamente poderosa, as suas ideias não agradaram ao poder da época (Sève, 2008, p. 317), que dificultou e, na prática impediu, a reedição dos seus livros e artigos? Apesar disso, o seu trabalho foi de alguma forma continuado por alguns dos seus alunos, nomeadamente Leontiev,

Luria e Bernstein, que vieram a propor novos desenvolvimentos e fizeram avançar, embora por vezes de forma divergente, as formulações teóricas e a experimentação empírica.

Foi preciso esperar meio século para que as suas *Obras*, em 6 volumes, fossem publicadas no seu próprio país. A internacionalização começa, mas de modo improvisado: como exemplo, a edição americana de Pensamento e Linguagem (Thought and Language, 1986) amputa o livro de todas as referências críticas, experimentais ou políticas. Mas é esta edição que vai servir de base às posteriores edições em castelhano ou italiano. Em França, apenas em 1985 será publicada uma tradução integral de Pensamento e Linguagem.

Se os autores anglo-saxónicos permaneceram durante muito tempo desconhecedores ou indiferentes ao cientista russo, o mesmo não se passou nos países de língua francesa. Por razões de língua e cultura, bem como de filiação em tradição científica própria, a recepção e atenção prestadas à obra de Vygotsky surgiram mais cedo que em outros lugares. Grupos de pesquisa em França e em regiões francófonas da Bélgica, Suíça e Canadá (Bronckart, Brossard, Clot, Engeström, Friedrich, Moro, Rabardel, Rochex, Schneuwly, Sève, van der Veer, Vergnaud, para citar apenas alguns) alimentaram debates, fomentaram traduções de qualidade e organizaram eventos em que procuraram criar ligações fortes com investigadores russos, profundos conhecedores do pensamento de Vygotsky.

É na sequência desta partilha de ideias que surge o colóquio que teve lugar em 2017, na Universidade de Paris-Est/UPEC, com um tema que é todo um programa: "In which ways can Vygotski's work help us to analyse, develop and bring a better understanding of the artistic, sport and physical practices transmission processes?"

Porque, de facto, extravasando da sua matriz psicológica original, a inovadora abordagem pedagógica da formação e desenvolvimento dos processos de aprendizagem interessou não só os estudiosos das Ciências do Desporto e da Educação Física, mas também os professores e investigadores nas áreas das artes performativas.

O referido colóquio reuniu filósofos, treinadores desportivos de iniciação e competição, professores do Conservatório de Artes e Ofícios, todos com leitores atentos de Vygotsky e com pesquisa produzida no âmbito da Pedagogia do Movimento Humano. A diversidade de experiências e pertenças a escolas de pensamento pedagógico foi o catalisador de um vivo debate que revelou a riqueza do que foi feito (e infelizmente muito do material partilhado não foi publicado) e a necessidade de avançar em terreno que se afigura fecundo e, passados tantas décadas, ainda capaz de inovar em tema que parecia saturado e claramente exausto.

Mas o que pode trazer de inspirador para as práticas físicas o trabalho de um psicólogo que produziu a maior parte do foi publicado entre 1930--1938 do século passado e em que as únicas referências ao exercício físico são representadas por andar de bicicleta ou escrever à máquina? E que, para além do mais, são consideradas atividades que não integram os processos mentais superiores?

A pergunta surge em momento particularmente delicado para as Ciências do Desporto. A luta pela hegemonia científica no campo, que pode significar acrescida autoridade e estatuto profissional, o que confere poder de publicação e reconhecimento internacional, está a desenrolar--se na arena académica, que compete pela métrica do artigo, presenças em congressos e acesso a financiamento. Após décadas de secundarização na constelação de disciplinas que contribuem para o Treino desportivo, as alterações sociais induzidas pela globalização da economia e pela explosão tecnológica, conferiram uma renovada importância à Pedagogia e ao processo formativo.

Muito marcado pela optimização do rendimento e teoricamente influenciado pelo estruturalismo, o treino privilegiou a eficácia da transmissão de conhecimentos específicos e da intervenção biológica com vista à melhoria da performance atlética. O sinal de alarme dado pela estagnação do número de participantes e pelo crescente desinteresse dos jovens por práticas repetitivas e assentes na autoridade do adulto, levou professores, treinadores e académicos a olhar em volta para procurar soluções para os problemas. Com o ocaso do funcionalismo, era o construtivismo na sua versão pós-moderna que estava disponível como suporte teórico para uma nova pedagogia.

Movimentos de ideias como *Teaching Games for Understanding/TGfU*, *Game Sense* ou *Tactical Approach* foram acolhidos com entusiasmo na academia e estiveram na origem de uma extensa, embora heterogénea literatura sobre o ensino dos jogos. Em vários países de língua inglesa foram mesmo adoptados como fundamento pedagógico da formação de treinadores ou como modelo de ensino de atletas.

Mas o reduzido investimento teórico tanto no quadro do *TGfU* como do *Game Sense*, bem como a reduzida aceitação por parte da comunidade do desporto organizado, foram provocando a erosão intelectual dos vários construtivismos, que atingiram uma situação de impasse na segunda década do século XXI.

Paralelamente, o desenvolvimento da Teoria dos Sistemas Complexos e a recuperação dos trabalhos baseados na Bioecologia, em especial de Gibson e Bronfenbrenner, criaram novos polos de atracção para os investigadores em busca de um suporte epistemológico para as Ciências do Desporto.

A partir de pesquisa na área do controlo motor dinamizada nomeadamente por Kelso ou Newell, para citar apenas os autores mais influentes, surgiram as propostas consubstanciadas na *Constraint-Led Approach*/ CLA, que sustenta que a aprendizagem motora resulta da interacção entre tarefa, organismo e contexto. Curiosamente, a inspiração primeira para a formulação teórica do problema do ensino radica na Teoria da Actividade de Bernstein, sendo ele próprio influenciado pela Teoria da Acção de Vygotsky.

O cruzamento da CLA com a Teoria dos Sistemas Dinâmicos e com a Bioecologia evoluiu para a teoria dos Sistemas Ecológicos Dinâmicos, que tem vindo a erigir-se como referencial epistemológico nas Ciências do Desporto, desafiando abertamente a solidez teórica do TGfU. É contra este campo de luta dicotómico em que, por um lado, toda a aprendizagem é construção social e, por outro, o determinismo dos constrangimentos que envolvem o indivíduo representa um indesejável reducionismo, que o grupo de participantes no colóquio da UPEC ergue as suas dúvidas epistemológicas.

O presente volume emana de preocupações e reflexões que visam libertar a Pedagogia do Desporto de limitações teóricas, que podem ser fascinantes, mas que possibilitam a ausência de valores e a secundarização do ser humano que é o atleta.

Os vários capítulos expressam as contribuições do colóquio, complementadas pelos debates que então tiveram lugar.

Para além do pensamento filosófico patente no capítulo de Séverac e Éloi, estão presentes os estudos empíricos de Tomas, Ullrich e Éloi, em que se explora a fecundidade do ensinamento de Vygotsky no processo de treino de atletas de diferentes idades e de bailarinos. Por seu lado, os capítulos de Lemonie, Bernal, Jarrett, Wei e Wallian apresentam uma visão crítica sobre os aspectos da obra de Vygotsky com maior relevância para as Ciências do Desporto.

Referências

Sève, L. (2008). *Penser avec Marx aujourd'hui. Tome II: L'homme.* Paris, La Dispute.

Les pratiques physiques sportives et artistiques: une perspective Vygotskienne

Physical, Sporting and Artistic Practices: a Vygotskian perspective

(FRANCÊS / INGLÊS)

I. ANALYSE THÉORIQUE
THEORETICAL ANALYSIS

1.

VYGOTSKY'S PEDAGOGY AND SPORT COACHING: A NON-LINEAR RELATIONSHIP

Carlos Eduardo GONÇALVES, Portugal.
University of Coimbra, Faculty of Sport Sciences and Physical Education.

1. Learning in Sport

Vygotsky and the body: it could be considered that the development of writing is comparable to the way how we learn tennis or biking; but for him, to interiorize habits of movement has nothing in common with development. As a researcher and a practitioner in the field of sport, this statement is disturbing.

Vygotsky stresses another critical point for pedagogy when he writes that the difference between learning to typewrite and learning to write lies in the fact that the former does not allow for improvements, even if we are professional experts. In the latter case, we learn not only abilities; our language changes for a conscious and personal use of language. It is possible to find similitudes with learning in sport, viewed as more than a repetition of standardized techniques.

Furthermore, in contemporary sport pedagogy, Constructivism represents an umbrella word to cover a range of pedagogic approaches drawing on a number of authors and epistemic variants. Under this somehow plastic view, the athletes' learning is seen as a process of interpretation and adaptation where real sporting ecologies are chaotic and individual development is complex and non-linear.

Curiously, one of the references in this eclectic landscape is Vygotsky, a researcher almost unknown outside Russia till the 80s of the XX century. And apparently, Vygotsky is a constructivist only with pre-school children. Indeed, there are similitudes between Constructivism and the Vygotsky's theory:

- development needs the optimal environment in order to happen;
- learning takes place trough the re-organization of psychic functions mediated by external stimuli (in Vygotsky's case, the use of signs).

But the reception of Vygotsky in sport sciences has been slow and through second-hand sources, picking small parts of his research and forgetting to look critically at his important conceptualizations and their potential utility for sport coaching.

Although Vygotsky did not elaborate about physical exercise, his theory of imagination and the study of the role of play have the potential to provide useful insights of a holistic vision of sport settings as spaces of imagination and performance. But contemporary literature and coaching practice never seem to acknowledge sport as a performance environment where time and social comparison play a crucial role.

But Vygotsky makes us, he obliges us, to think about the problems of learning in sport with: (a) rational correctness; (b) rigorous logic; and (c) critical distance when facing personal and affective aspects.

Having these premises in mind, the purpose of this essay is to look at some of Vygotsky's concepts and theories and confront them with the reality of sport coaching, arguing that researchers and coaches must seek and recognize coherence between rational analysis and behaviours. The critical stance is important because in sport settings most of what practitioners assume as knowledge are only opinions and it still reigns a pervasive conviction that existing knowledge reflects the reality of training.

One of the major problems to deal with that "reality of training" is the absence of, not of theories, but of theorization, as reflexion on what is interpretation and what are objective facts. In sport, where the emotional and social size are always present, our brain is more likely to impose the wrong, simplistic narrative than no narrative at all, as the mind was not designed to deal with complexity and nonlinear uncertainties.

We need to theorize and to reflect about the utility of meta-theories (North, 2013), taken to mean assumptions about the nature of the social world (ontology), assumptions about the nature of knowledge (epistemology), and approaches used to gain this knowledge (methodology).

2. Hegemonic ideologies

Since the time of Vygotsky's research, sport sciences faced several hegemonic ideologies that shaped our understanding of coaching and specific learning. We look schematic at the most powerful ones.

Scientism is characterized as producing objective, value free, systematic knowledge about "real" psychological phenomenon, based on deterministic or probabilistic statistical/reductive laws/relationships between lower and higher order phenomenon.

Psychological scientism also involves the stripping of contextual influence from its research subjects. This knowledge can be used to identify and solve practical problems through a process of rationalistic social engineering.

A corollary of scientism can be reductionism, i.e., the idea that lower-level factors (biological, psychological or environmental) can account for higher-level complex social problems, simplifies the conscious, intentional, reflexive dimensions of human behaviors, group processes and social relations.

In the other side of the spectrum, interpretivism suggests that the objects of social analysis are fundamentally different to those studied through the natural sciences. Individuals and groups are self-conscious, intentional and reflexive. Their thoughts and actions are value laden and situated in the subjective lived experience. Ecology becomes a central explanatory mechanism.

Within this framework, knowing is seen as a verb related to action in practice rather than as a noun (formal knowledge). There is skepticism regarding laws and instrumental and technocratic solutions. For many is more appropriate to talk about narratives than theories, and at this point we start to question whether models could adequately capture coaching practice at all.

In the more extreme versions there is nothing more than constructions, no means of determining their epistemic value, and all knowledge is seen to be equal. This hegemonic view shapes the present situation in academic research on sport coaching.

There are authors that link Vygotsky, Paulo Freire and constructivism. It is true that both reject the banking approach: the teacher deposits the information that the learners must collect a-critically (Spaaj, Oxford & Ruth, 2016). However, unlike Vygotsky, Freire seems to believe that critique ensures the transition for development without forgetting the contents; but Freire also seems to neglect the role of the teacher. And we can always wonder about what do we really mean with democracy in sport and if there is a role for the coach as a critic. We address these questions in the next sub-chapter.

This shift from behavioural to cognitive psychology in the mid-twentieth century was accompanied by a "softening" of conceptual and methodological strategy. Researchers were now "allowed" to theorize about the less objectively, verifiable, unobservable mechanisms, processes, and concepts underlying cognition, and use a wider range of methods, including qualitative research designs and introspection. However, the whole process took place in an academic world knowing nothing about Vygotsky.

3. The role of the coach

If we accept that it is the contradiction between the actual skills of the athlete and the potential skills that he/her is able to attain in the future represents the real motor of development, then we must accept too that the mediation of adults and peers represents a key factor to a full access to the development processes. Vygotsky clearly postulates that it is not the daily random encounter with the activity that ignites development, but it is instead through a systematic, planned, top-down approach that the pupil can perform at higher levels.

Thus, it seems clear for most of scholars that we should encourage disciplinary, meta-theoretical and methodological pluralism. The debate between sides should be seen as dialectical and constructive. Here, the Vygotsky's conceptualization about dialectics in research can be useful in a field that scarcely acknowledges this intellectual resource: how to go beyond contrasting theses.

Children can imitate actions that are over their actual capacities; under adult supervision they do things that otherwise they would not do. What the child can do with the help of adults indicates the proximal development zone. Using this methodology, it is possible to assess the actual stage of maturation but also future possibilities.

The idea that coaches can draw on planning and decision-making mechanisms and repertoires at different levels – macro, meso and micro – and this attends to the social and political complexities raised through other approaches, presents some interesting suggestions but in the end is simply an extended restatement of older ideas that focus on one layer of coaching (i.e., the coach and his or her cognitive strategies). However, cognitive approaches (Schön, 1987; Vygotsky, 1980) fail to account for the sources of knowledge, and their formation and transformations in the social world.

Vygotsky sets several challenges to the current understanding of the coaches' role framing. We consider just a few.

First, the function of language; Richards and colleagues (2012) talk about declarative knowledge and the slow learning as an important tool to develop procedural learning. Hence, language has an instrumental role: everything has a name and knowing the names enhances tactical skills. But Vygotsky is not in the same page with coaches; for him, reasoning and language have different genetic roots.

Secondly, the growth and maturation issue. For coaches these are obstacles for learning and put serious problems to advance in skill level and to team cohesion. However, Vygotsky considers puberty as a time of stability, because it is a phase of higher personality gains and considers it a condition rather than the motor of development. If development is non-linear then pedagogy must be non-linear. We must understand the concept of conflict. Maturation and culture reorganize deeply the natural content of behaviour and restructures in a total new way the course of child development. In certain "critical ages" development is more destructive than constructive. And this recognition represents a hard task for coaches.

In the third place, Vygotsky does not limit individual development to the level attained in mature stages, because it would mean to refuse the dynamics of intellectual and motor development. The hegemonic paradigm in sport is based on models of development, anchored in stages according to chronological ages. For coaches, each stage has its own contents, as sport specialization is seen as a path to expertise. For coaches, the actual contradiction and a powerful source of tension is that the majority of literature puts performance and results in perspective, emphasizing the role of the coach as a facilitator and not as an expert about sport-specific contents and their sequential delivery. Thus, the concept of zone of proximal development is worth to explore.

The last topic that attracts attention is the role of imagination in sport. The development of creative thinking goes from thought to action not from action to thought and this concept is particularly important for sports and tactical learning. Vygotsky does stress its importance, but the theme remains far from a unified understanding in sport training. Modern sport constantly alludes to creativity and tactical awareness in decision-making as the key factors to success, especially in team sports. But the steps and resources needed to optimize creativity still remain an unsolved problem for coaches and researchers. At different moments Dewey (1933), Kolb (1975) and Gibbs (1988) theorize about reflective cycles as a way to improve the learners' creativity: it is an interesting avenue of research that can be linked to the work of Vygotsky.

4. Semiotics of learning

For Vygotsky, the psychic processes are genetic and at the same time resultant of social relationships. This is a controversial topic in sport sciences. Here it is important to refer Bloch (2012) and his argument about the relative ponders of genetics and learning: it is stupid to ignore both.

Vygotsky adds that the main difference between stages of development is not the transition to new functions, but most of the times we deal with an intra-function change. It is a characteristic of complex dynamic systems. He crucially points out that human activity mediates two processes: the use of instruments and signs. It is due to the mediating role of signs that higher psychic functions appear. At the same time, memorizing through signs is closely linked to the importance of language. It is possible to speculate that if actual children do not manage language proficiently, they are less prone to learn through signs, and to develop logical thinking.

5. The pace of development

Learning means the developmental process that expresses itself through the acquisition of new habits and through the capacity to solve problems. For Vygotsky learning and development are coincident. His contemporary, Piaget, believed in the impossibility of establishing causal connexions before 11 years of age. For sport it is an important argument because coaches search to teach the separation between effort and ability from early ages. But for Vygotsky (1980), the stages of Piaget are atrocious because they build a barrier between learning and intellectual development. Vygotsky writes about culture, but we can transfer his concepts to sport.

There are optimal periods for specific learning, neither too soon, nor too late. Children are able to learn languages when they are about one and a half year old, and for them it is much easier than later. Hence, learning must set challenges always higher, and must focus on the functions still in a stage of maturation.

If reading demands the fully understanding of each word, this does not mean that we have to teach that way. It is useful to draw a parallel line with the way we teach games. Because learning becomes effective in the moment it goes beyond development.

The pedagogue plants his seeds or opens paths of development that must follow their own cycles, in order to produce results. It is impossible to teach new forms of reasoning to the learners avoiding the pace of development. In order to create the proximal development zone, i.e., to create multiple processes of internal development we need a correctly built learning process.

Self-awareness develops very quickly because it is not a lonely process, but social. Children do not create meaning; they rather assimilate the meanings defined by their social use. Once again, we stress how important it is for declarative knowledge to be assimilated by the learner at the right time.

6. Formal vs. informal

A controversial feature of Vygotsky's work is his defence of formal curricula, which are viewed as essential for the global intellectual development, even if they lack any practical value. An important idea is that Vygotsky rejected the concept of development as a process determined from the interior. For him learning programmes come first and then micro-cultures. The contradiction with non-linearity as advocated by contemporary pedagogy is evident and also is the need for new research in sport settings. For Vygotsky, children acquire knowledge because adults mediate their relationships and practical links with the world. In the process of oral communication between the child and the adult, "real" and "ideal" meanings relate and interact. Once we bear in mind the complexity of the path to expertise in a given domain, it is entirely understandable that the teacher/coach must have the final word.

If Vygotsky is right when he states that the word is the end that completes the action, then verbalization in the process of training becomes a key factor to progress into higher levels of expertise.

For Vygotsky, all forms of psychic life of the child are formed in the process of communication. He also argues that an initially shared form between 2 people becomes an interiorized psychic function and that the most important factor in the process od development is the assimilation of human experience as a whole. All new knowledge reorganizes mental processes, creating new specific forms of cognitive and volitional activity. This materialist understanding of development is scarcely acknowledged in sport sciences especially by coaches.

It was William James (2017) that identified learning as development, and as a formation of conditioned reflexes. Vygotsky followed that path and we believe it is time to look closer to the acquisition of skills, their sequence, and their evolution.

7. Cognition and emotions

The separation of the intellectual side from the affective and volitional sides is one of the major weaknesses of traditional sport training. Forty years after the publication of the works of Teodorescu (2003), Mahlo (1974), or Knapp (1963), most practitioners still ignore cognition and/or tend to reject emotions. Hence reasoning is transformed in an autonomous flux of thoughts, without contact with the fullness of real life. For many coaches, good athletes do not think

Vygotsky teaches us that reasoning is not the ultimate level, because thought is not born of another thought, but from our motivation and conscience, including our preferences and needs, our affects and emotions. Without emotional commitment, and without the will to participate, sport is an empty choreography.

The main force driving development it is the contradiction between the technical capacities of the athlete and his/her motivation. It remains the problem of how to transform practical activities in mechanisms of socialization and assimilation of norms.

8. Challenges to our time

Vygotsky introduces a methodology to assess development supported in the relationship between: (a) how does the apprentice solves a problem by himself; (b) how does the apprentice solves the same problem with the help of an adult (here we have the role of the coach revisited).

The central role that is deferred to external tools in the learning process lays in their capacity to transform the internal psychological functions. For Vygotsky, development is accomplished through the internalization of signs, and the tools/artefacts used by coaches perform a crucial role in this complex semiotic system.

Take the example of an athlete who tries to catch a ball. For a researcher, it seems that he/she behaves as if he/she had solved a set of differential equations in predicting the trajectory of the ball, and it seems that at a subconscious level, something equivalent to the mathematical calculations is going on. But practitioners know that something really different is going on, and athletes rely on other resources; if the ball is already high in the air, the athlete fixes his/her gaze on the ball, starts moving and adjust his/her speed so that the angle of gaze remains constant. An athlete capable of doing so can ignore all causal variables needed to compute the trajectory of the ball. By paying attention to only one variable, the athlete will end up where the ball comes. Through a long process of learning, the athlete interprets the relevant signs necessary to succeed without computing a large number of variables (Taleb, 2012).

In sport, declarative knowledge allows the apprentice to analyse, transform, and rebuild his/her previous knowledge. The theorization of Vygotsky about the relationship between oral language and written language represents a striking example of the pedagogical value of his ideas to contemporary sport researchers and practitioners.

9. Epistemological barriers that must be overcome

The critique of pedagogical theories based on structures of knowledge or on problem-solving situations is clear and harsh. For Vygotsky, if the pupil is not confronted with alternative ways of thinking or of search for knowledge, it results impossible the formation of new zones of proximal development. At the same time, he argues that knowledge must be systematic and general, in order to carry a transforming effect, meaning that the teacher is required to be an expert in the contents and methodologies of the subject he/her teaches.

Refusing a linear conception of development, Vygotsky links learning with reflexive reasoning, contrasting with a spontaneous use of knowledge and pedagogical tools. Against constructivism, Vygotsky stresses the social and historical dimensions of work that prevent the reduction of cognitive learning to a mere construction of concepts.

Vygotsky's ideas raise interesting epistemological questions that seem at odds with contemporary sport pedagogy theories. Both constructivist and constraint-led approaches (Renshaw et al., 2016; Pill, 2017) claim that they have robust scientific foundations to explain learning in sport, but they fail to cover all the facets of the problem. The potential explanatory power of the zones of proximal development, the use of semiotic functions, the importance of declarative knowledge or the reflexive role of the coach, open promising avenues for research, but request careful consideration.

Again and again, Vygotsky (1986) reminds us that learning can not be limited to motor skills, but rather the ability to give the learner opportunities to access higher and more complex levels of knowledge. The learning process is going to have always some effects, even if the teacher/coach is not aware of them.

For contemporary researchers, the challenge is still in the path open by Vygotsky, with the need to unveil the effects and transformations caused by the learning process in *each* participant in sport activities. In the living world there are only subjects and these establish relationships of significance, not of causality. The concepts of: (a) passing from the exterior to the interior, and (b) proximal development zones, are still at "an arm's length" for researchers to explore and reorganize our understanding about the acquisition of sport expertise.

Vygotsky showed *avant la lettre* what Latour (2010) states some 70 years later: "we need to transform resources in topics (p. 37)". He always followed the logic of research, starting with the available data and not jumping to pre-defined conclusions. From this point of view his epistemology is not constructivist at all, due to a social and historic dimension that prevents to reduce cognitive development to a mere construction of concepts. The world is not made of knowledge and much less of unified knowledge. We can try to know it, but it is not the same thing.

References

Bloch, M. (2012). Anthropology and the cognitive challenge. Cambridge: University Press.

Dewey, J. (1933). How We Think: A Restatement of the Relation of Reflective Thinking to the Educative Process. Boston, MA: D.C. Heath & Co Publishers

Gibbs, G. (1988). Learning by Doing, Oxford, Oxford Polytechnic.

James, W. (2017). The will to believe. Akron, Midwest Journal Press.

Kolb, D.A. & Fry, R.E. (1975). Toward an applied theory of experiential learning. In C. Cooper (ed.), Theories of Group Processes (33-57). New York, John Wiley & Sons.

Knapp, B. (1963). The attainment of proficiency. London, Routledge & Kegan Paul PLC.

Latour, B. (2010). Cogitamus. Paris, La Découverte.

Mahlo, F. (1974). L'acte tactique en jeu. Paris, Vigot Frères.

North, J. (2013). Philosophical underpinnings of coaching practice research. Quest, 65:3, 278-299.

Pill, S. (2017). Using Appreciative Inquiry to explore Australian football coaches' experience with game sense coaching Using Appreciative Inquiry to explore Australian football coaches' experience with game sense coaching. Sport, Education and Society, 20(6), 799–818. http://doi.org/10.1080/13573322.2013.831343

Renshaw, I., Araújo, D., Button, C., Chow, J. Y., Davids, K., & Moy, B. (2016). Why the Constraints-Led Approach is not Teaching Games for Understanding: a clarification. Physical Education and Sport Pedagogy, 21(5), 459–480. http://doi.org/10.1080/17408989.2015.1095870.

Richards, P., Mascarenhas, D., & Collins, D. (2012). Developing rapid high-pressure team decision-making skills. The integration of slow deliberate reflective learning within the competitive performance environment: a case study of elite netball. Reflective Practice: International and Multidisciplinary Perspectives, 13:3, 407-424.

Schön, D. (1987). Educating the reflective practitioner. San Francisco: Jossey-Bass.

Spaaj, R., Oxford, S., & Ruth, J. (2016). Transforming communities through sport. critical pedagogy and sport for development, Sport, Education and Society, 21(4): 570-587.

Taleb, N. N. (2012). Anti-fragile. London: Penguin Books.

Teodorescu, L. (2003). Problemas de teoria e metodologia nos jogos desportivos. Lisboa, Livros Horizonte.

Vygotsky, L. (1986). Thought and Language. Cambridge, MA: MIT.

Vygotsky, L. (1980). Mind in Society. Cambridge, MA: Harvard University press

2.

LES SPORTIFS SONT-ILS LIBRES DE LEURS CHOIX ?

Pascal SÉVÉRAC, France.
Université Paris-Est, LIS (EA 4395)
Serge ÈLOI, France
Université Paris-Est, LIRTES (EA7313)

Introduction

La question des choix est au cœur des pratiques sportives. Mais que veut dire choisir lorsque le temps alloué à cette activité est réduit au plus juste ? Que veut dire choisir quand son propre choix dépend de l'activité d'autrui (partenaires ou adversaires) et qu'il aura des conséquences sur le futur du collectif ? C'est pour avancer dans cette réflexion que nous nous proposons de confronter nos points de vue : d'un côté, un philosophe qui mène des recherches sur Spinoza et Vygotsky ; de l'autre, un praticien (enseignant et entraîneur) /chercheur, vygotskien lui aussi, qui appréhende les sports collectifs comme une pratique sociale constituée d'éléments de culture dignes d'être transmis. Au cœur de la décision, et notamment celle qui doit être prise en pleine urgence, se trouve l'incertitude.

1. L'incertitude : propriétés et paradoxe.

Qu'est-ce que l'incertitude ? Peut-on vraiment la créer, et si oui, à quoi peut-elle servir ? Dans le cadre des pratiques sportives, quelle conséquence a cette incertitude sur le rapport d'opposition attaque/défense ? Voici quelques questions essentielles auxquelles il faut s'atteler si l'on veut appréhender les pratiques sportives sans dénaturer leur complexité. En définissant l'incertitude comme l'état dans lequel on se trouve lorsqu'on ne sait pas quel événement est susceptible de se produire, on peut commencer à saisir les problèmes liés à la prise de décision.

Constatons d'abord que, dans les sports collectifs, les protagonistes d'un jeu n'ont de cesse de tenter de mettre leurs adversaires dans cette situation inconfortable. Pour ce faire, ils s'essaient à rendre équiprobable l'apparition des événements qu'ils contrôlent, c'est-à-dire qu'ils s'organisent pour que leurs adversaires estiment que chaque possibilité a la même chance d'advenir. Plus la probabilité que deux événements se produisent est égale et plus l'incertitude liée à l'apparition de l'un de ces événements est élevée. Pour l'équipe qui attaque, créer de l'incertitude en manipulant l'information plonge l'équipe qui subit dans un état de doute : les joueurs en défense tentent de déchiffrer la situation imposée par leurs adversaires, et cet état de précarité les oblige à attendre, à différer le moment de la décision. Il leur faut accumuler suffisamment d'indices confirmant que c'est bien tel événement qui va se produire pour entrer en action. La propriété essentielle de la production d'incertitude, c'est donc de mettre l'adversaire en retard.

Mais cette situation nous réserve quelques surprises, car lasse de se faire manipuler, l'équipe qui défend peut à son tour user de stratagèmes pour se sortir de cette situation délicate. C'est ce que nous dénommons le « paradoxe de l'incertitude ».

Dans les sports collectifs, il y a toujours d'un côté une équipe qui prend l'initiative et de l'autre une équipe qui subit. Au volley-ball par exemple, l'équipe au service va s'évertuer, non sans quelques prises de risques, de mettre à mal la réception adverse. Lorsqu'elle y parvient, le schéma offensif (de cette équipe adverse) devient irréalisable. L'incertitude pour l'équipe en défense (celle qui vient de servir) est réduite à sa plus simple expression. Un contre collectif peut se mettre en place.

Cependant, en volley-ball, les statistiques montrent que dans six cas sur dix, le serveur ne peut pas empêcher que la réception arrive dans les mains du passeur (Éloi, 2011). Dans ces conditions, c'est l'équipe en réception qui a l'initiative dans l'échange. En choisissant un schéma offensif particulier, le passeur coordonne les appels de balle de quatre joueurs qui s'engagent dans des temps et des espaces d'attaques différents. C'est ce que l'on nomme « les alternatives spatio-temporelles d'attaques ». Les attaquants proposent, mais c'est le passeur qui dispose. L'objectif du passeur est de placer l'attaquant choisi en position de « un contre un ». En effet, il est montré que dans deux cas sur trois, l'attaquant qui n'a qu'un seul contreur en face de lui, marque le point. *A contrario*, l'attaquant qui se retrouve face à deux contreurs ne marque le point que dans un cas sur trois.

Il s'agit donc de proposer des schémas tactiques (des combinaisons d'attaques) qui sèment le doute chez les trois contreurs adverses et de bien choisir l'attaquant qui finalement devra smasher. Lorsque l'initiative reste au passeur, le contreur central adverse se retrouve sans arrêt en retard. Il subit le jeu du passeur adverse.

Cependant le contreur central peut choisir de reprendre l'initiative. Las de courir ici et là sans succès, il peut décider de faire un pari. Certes, cette prise de décision est osée. Mais entre courir après le ballon sans jamais le toucher ou prendre une option et, pour une fois, devancer le joueur qui attaque, il n'y a qu'un pas que ces joueurs feront d'autant plus volontiers qu'ils se seront sentis dépassés par les évènements précédents. C'est ainsi que les défenseurs peuvent renverser la tendance. Tel est pris qui croyait prendre. Au lieu de subir, ils prennent les devants. Ils peuvent bien évidemment faire une mauvaise option. Mais si leur choix est le bon, ils tendent leur embuscade, guettent l'attaquant, et ce sont eux qui le surprennent.

Ainsi, créer l'incertitude chez l'adversaire, c'est prendre le risque d'avoir à répondre à son tour à une réaction imprévisible, ou du moins peu prévisible, et donc prendre le risque d'être mis soi-même dans l'incertitude. D'où une dialectique de production d'incertitude réciproque entre les adversaires.

2. Comprendre les enjeux du jeu

Comment sortir du cercle de l'incertitude ? Cela est-il possible ? Comment au moins réduire cette incertitude, lorsqu'on est le maître du choix, afin de ne pas être soumis au paradoxe de l'incertitude, afin de ne pas être entraîné dans la dialectique, malgré tout risquée, de production d'incertitude ?

Le point de départ de notre réflexion sera éclairé par le dilemme de l'âne de Buridan. Reprise par Vygotsky dans son étude de la maîtrise de son propre comportement (notamment au chapitre 12 de son Histoire du développement des fonctions psychiques supérieures), cette situation met en scène un âne qui, souffrant autant de faim que de soif, se trouve à égale distance d'un seau d'eau et d'un sac d'avoine. Dans l'impossibilité de choisir, l'âne finit par mourir et de faim et de soif.

Figure 1 : La parabole de l'âne de Buridan

S'appuyant sur Spinoza, Vygotsky analyse cette situation — qu'il fait passer du cas d'école au champ de l'expérimentation —, pour conclure qu'un homme, dans des circonstances similaires (circonstances de dilemme ou de « double contrainte »), trouvera ou inventera un motif (dit « auxiliaire ») pour prendre une décision : à la différence de l'animal, l'homme se sort du dilemme par la force de sa pensée, nous dit Vygotsky. Cet homme peut par exemple, parce qu'il s'agit d'une situation radicalement indécidable, et qu'il est urgent de la dénouer, choisir de tirer au sort — ou comme nous l'avons dit de faire un pari : ce n'est peut-être pas le moyen le plus construit pour décider, mais c'est parfois la seule solution. Vygotsky s'oppose en tout cas à l'idée que l'homme, à la différence de l'animal, parvient à décider parce qu'il est doté d'un libre arbitre, c'est-à-dire d'une faculté absolument indéterminée de se déterminer soi-même : il rejette donc la solution traditionnelle au problème de l'âne de Buridan, qui est une solution spiritualiste consistant à dire que l'homme est d'une autre nature que l'animal parce qu'il est capable, par son libre arbitre, de produire ex nihilo une nouvelle situation — comme Dieu a été capable de créer le monde à partir de rien.

Plus exactement, pour contrecarrer la thèse spiritualiste du libre arbitre, Vygotsky se sert paradoxalement d'une citation d'un ouvrage de jeunesse de Spinoza (les Principes de la philosophie de Descartes), dans lequel Spinoza ne développe pas sa propre pensée, mais présente celle de Descartes (celle de ses Principes de la philosophie) : Spinoza y reprend l'affirmation cartésienne selon laquelle l'homme, à la différence de l'animal (de l'âne), peut trancher une situation de dilemme équilibré car il est une "chose pensante". Vygotsky cependant interprète cette affirmation non pas comme signifiant, à la manière cartésienne, que l'essence de l'âme est le libre arbitre, c'est-à-dire que l'esprit est doté d'une puissance de la volonté absolument indéterminée ; mais il l'interprète comme signifiant que l'esprit est une puissance de pensée au sens d'une puissance d'agir, d'une puissance de comprendre. Or, c'est justement là le sens proprement spinoziste de l'idée que l'esprit est une chose pensante. L'esprit y est entendu comme quelque chose qui, par sa puissance de pensée, a la capacité de résoudre des problèmes en produisant des idées adéquates. Ce n'est non pas la pensée comme libre arbitre, mais la pensée comme activité de conceptualisation, puissance de liaison (entre un problème et une solution) que revendique Vygotsky, qui est tout à fait conscient que Spinoza ne peut être enrôlé du côté des défenseurs d'une substance de l'âme qui agirait fondamentalement par soi sans y être déterminée par rien. Vygotsky se sert même de la référence à Spinoza pour soutenir, à propos d'une réflexion sur la mémoire, que l'esprit n'est pas libre de cette liberté d'indétermination : « Quel procédé nous recommande donc la mnémotechnique ? Chacun de nous choisit plus ou moins inconsciemment ses façons de faire. Le talent de qui se souvient consiste à saisir dans un fragment de prose des idées saillantes, de brèves phrases, de simples mots qui tirent après eux des pages entières. Nous approchons ici d'un point de la plus haute importance à partir duquel s'ouvre toute une perspective philosophique. Nous ne cherchons pas à l'explorer ici de façon tant soit peu poussée. Rappelons seulement en passant qu'un autre grand philosophe — Spinoza — voyait justement dans la mémoire la preuve que notre esprit n'est pas libre. Nous ne pouvons rien faire selon le décret de l'esprit, disait-il, si nous ne nous le rappelons pas [la formule vient du scolie de la proposition 2 de la troisième partie de l'Éthique]. Effectivement, le rôle décisif de la mémoire dans l'étude de l'intention montre à quel point toutes nos intentions sont liées à un dispositif de la mémoire qui doit par la suite les réaliser»[1] (Vygotsky, 2014, p. 436).

L'esprit n'est libre, ou ne devient libre, pour Spinoza comme pour Vygotsky, qu'en tant qu'il a la puissance de penser, ou de comprendre : «La liberté humaine consiste justement en ce qu'il pense, c'est-à-dire conçoit la situation existante» (Vygotsky, 2014, p. 470).

Le paradigme cartésien du libre arbitre est dès lors rejeté par Vygotsky à travers la figure de W. James, qu'il critique de recourir à un «fiat!» divin pour expliciter la liberté : [...] c'est quelque chose comme l'acte de création du monde qui se répète ici, bien entendu à une échelle microscopique. Ce qui revient à dire que pour expliquer l'acte volontaire, un homme de science, quelqu'un qui se tient sur le terrain de l'empirique, en vient purement et simplement au discours biblique sur la création du monde. (Vygotsky, 2014, p. 482).

Vygotsky conteste donc résolument que la solution du problème de la liberté ne puisse pas être trouvée «sur le terrain d'une étude scientifique déterministe de la volonté» (Ibid.). La solution est de concevoir la liberté à partir du déterminisme, en son sein, et ce en étant attentif à la puissance d'agir de l'esprit qui se trouve dans la situation de choisir. Selon Vygotsky, cette puissance existe déjà chez l'indigène d'Afrique du Sud dont parle

---

[1] On objectera peut-être que la mémoire est une fonction psychique soumise au déterminisme, au contraire de l'intelligence ou de l'inventivité qui, elles, supposent un dépassement du déterminisme. Comme nous allons le voir, Vygotsky répond que le psychisme est véritablement libre lorsqu'il forme une conception adéquate et fait un usage pertinent du déterminisme – non pas lorsqu'il s'en affranchit, ce qui lui est impossible.

Lévy-Bruhl, et qui, à la question du missionnaire lui demandant s'il compte envoyer son fils à l'école, répond « Je verrai ça en rêve » (Vygotsky, 2014, p. 176). Vygotsky précise bien qu'il ne s'agit certes pas là d'une pensée rationnelle, mais d'une pensée qui néanmoins a sa positivité, en tant qu'elle enveloppe « un début d'autocontrôle conscient » (Ibid.). Vygotsky va même plus loin dans le cas, toujours rapporté par Lévy-Bruhl, du cafre qui, pour mémoriser un sermon, d'abord se sert de sa seule mémoire, puis use d'un instrument, le bâton, dans lequel il fait des encoches. Vygotsky conteste alors l'interprétation de Lévy-Bruhl, pour qui cette solution marque une impuissance de l'esprit, qui se réfugie dans la mémoire plutôt que dans la réflexion : [...] nous sommes enclins à y voir justement l'inverse : un exemple de la façon dont l'intellect de l'homme l'amène à créer de nouvelles formes de mémoire. Combien de pensée faut-il pour noter un discours à l'aide d'encoches sur un morceau de bois ! Mais, cela dit en passant, la chose essentielle qui nous intéresse, c'est la différence entre l'une et l'autre mémorisation. (Vygotsky, 2014, p. 185).[2]

La première forme de mémoire, qui n'use pas d'instrument, est tout entière soumise au principe stimulus-réaction ; elle n'est que l'effet d'une cause extérieure, et la puissance de pensée du cafre ne fait alors que participer résiduellement à la causalité de cet effet. Dans la seconde forme de mémoire, en revanche, est investie une véritable activité du cafre, qui fait corps avec le bâton, qui fait cause commune avec lui, autrement dit qui fait de ce stimulus extérieur une forme d'autostimulation. Or faire cause commune avec une altérité, devenir cause adéquate de ses propres effets en demeurant cause causée, autrement dit, produire des effets qui s'expliquent par sa propre puissance, quand bien même cette puissance demeure intégralement inscrite dans le déterminisme causal, telle est la définition spinoziste de la liberté.

Il en va de même, explique Vygotsky, avec un enfant qui est, expérimentalement, mis dans les conditions proches de celles de l'âne de Buridan : il ne trouvera peut-être pas la solution tout seul — celle du tirage au

[2] Il y aurait aussi à considérer (notamment à partir du *Traité de la Réforme de l'Entendement* ainsi que de la cinquième partie de l'Éthique) comment Spinoza pense ce rapport – cette liaison inter-fonctionnelle dirait Vygotsky – entre intellect et mémoire.

sort —, mais s'il est mis sur la voie par un autre, alors est suscitée en lui une véritable activité, une activité adéquate au sens spinoziste du terme. « [...] le sujet fait preuve d'irrésolution, il hésite, pèse les motifs, tente de les mettre en balance. Parfois le choix traîne en longueur et devient extrêmement difficile. Dans ces cas-là, nous introduisons un élément complémentaire nouveau qui constitue le centre même de nos expériences : nous suggérons à l'enfant en difficulté l'idée de faire son choix en s'en remettant au sort. Pour suggérer cette idée, il y a divers moyens, à commencer par mettre tout simplement sur la table un dé à jeter, ou laisser l'enfant jouer avant l'expérience avec ce même dé pour finir par lui poser directement la question : ne veut-il pas s'en remettre au sort? ou encore, faire appel à l'imitation directe, l'enfant voyant comment un autre résout le même problème» (Vygotsky, 2014, p. 467).

À propos de l'enfant qui peu à peu prend conscience qu'il doit choisir, et qui partant investit ce moyen — le tirage au sort — de sa propre puissance de pensée, Vygotsky affirme : « sa liberté est la conscience de la nécessité» (Vygotsky, 2014, p. 471). Il use même d'une expression plus forte encore dans le cas de l'homme qui décide de faire une grève de la faim pour défendre une cause, ou de rester sur la table d'opération pour que soit opéré son bras (exemple pris par W. James) : «La liberté dont il s'agit, dans un cas comme dans l'autre, n'est bien entendu pas une liberté par rapport à la nécessité, c'est la liberté en tant que nécessité comprise. Sur ce plan, l'expression "se prendre en main" peut avoir un sens littéral, comme aussi l'expression "supporter la douleur en serrant les dents". Ce qui veut dire qu'à la base d'une telle liberté, comme à la base de la liberté par rapport au monde extérieur, il y a l'intelligence de la nécessité» (Vygotsky, 2014, p. 484).

« L'intelligence de la nécessité » : formule parfaitement spinoziste pour définir la liberté. On pourrait même préciser : la liberté, selon Spinoza, c'est la force affective que procure l'intelligence de la nécessité — définition qui conviendrait très bien à Vygotsky, en tant qu'il montre la liaison entre fonction cognitive et fonction affective.

Il retrouve là la conception spinoziste de la liberté comme compréhension des logiques qui président à une situation — ces logiques pouvant relever elles-mêmes de l'histoire de la situation : l'intelligence de la nécessité, l'intelligence de la situation telle qu'elle est déterminée peut se nourrir en effet de la connaissance de l'histoire du set ou du match joué, ou encore de l'analyse des autres matchs joués par les mêmes adversaires, ou même de l'analyse des tendances des joueurs adverses selon la configuration du jeu dans laquelle ils sont amenés à opérer.

Cette opposition entre libre arbitre et intelligence de la situation peut donc renvoyer, dans une certaine mesure, à l'opposition entre d'un côté les théories de l'action située selon lesquelles tout apparaîtrait aux acteurs ici et maintenant, tout ne se déciderait qu'in situ, où seule la situation présente hic et nunc permettait de se déterminer, de décider, et d'un autre côté ce que nous avons appelé l'intelligence de la situation, qui exige à la fois la connaissance de l'histoire, du passé de cette situation, et la saisie de ses enjeux présents. Selon cette seconde théorie, les enjeux du jeu sont toujours déterminés par la complexité de la situation, cette complexité se caractérisant par l'intrication d'une pluralité d'éléments parfois très différents, et par l'imprévisibilité de ce que le système complexe produira in fine. Dans cette perspective, la complexité ne peut que se modéliser. Il est illusoire de prétendre la résoudre. Il y a donc un intérêt majeur à modéliser un système complexe, car la possibilité d'injecter dans ce système des éléments dont on a le contrôle peut potentiellement conduire à des issues favorables.

3. L'aptitude à la pluralité simultanée.

Mais jusqu'où peut aller cette intelligence de la situation dans les circonstances de la pratique sportive, où chaque décision doit être prise dans un état de plus ou moins grande pression ? Jusqu'où peut aller, dans l'urgence d'une situation de jeu, cette modélisation de la complexité ? Qu'en est-il de nos décisions lors de situations où l'opposition des protagonistes est directe et interdépendante ?

Pour faire face à l'urgence d'une situation, dans la pratique sportive, il nous paraît nécessaire de former des joueurs aptes à la « pluralité simultanée ». Qu'entendons-nous par-là ? Prenons des exemples : au volley-ball, le stratège de l'attaque est le passeur. C'est lui qui reçoit tous les ballons destinés à être attaqués. C'est le distributeur des passes permettant les attaques smashées. Former un passeur apte à la pluralité simultanée, c'est former un passeur qui, en même temps qu'il regarde le ballon qu'il s'apprête à passer, voit — à l'aide de sa vision périphérique — le mouvement, ou l'attente, du contreur central adverse. Si, dans l'urgence de la situation, le passeur parvient à cette pluralité simultanée de perceptions, d'affections, et donne la balle toujours à l'attaquant en face duquel il n'y a qu'un seul contreur, il sera en situation de totale réussite.

Nous comprenons mieux par là ce que signifie, selon nous, décider par « intelligence de la situation », et non par « libre arbitre » : s'il existait, le libre arbitre produirait de l'arbitraire ; or un tel arbitraire, par chance, peut être un succès ; mais il peut tout aussi bien être voué à l'échec. L'intelligence de la situation, en revanche, permet de réduire l'incertitude et les risques d'échecs. Mais nous voyons que cette intelligence ne doit pas être entendue en un sens intellectualiste : comme le dirait Spinoza, l'intelligence est l'activité d'un esprit qui a lieu simultanément à l'activité d'un corps. Or cette activité du corps, selon Spinoza, se définit par son aptitude à être affecté et à affecter de plusieurs manières en même temps — dans l'urgence d'une situation sportive par exemple : c'est à cette condition que l'esprit comprendra ce qui convient le mieux de faire.

Spinoza, dans l'Éthique, définit deux critères à partir desquels on peut dire d'un corps qu'il est plus actif qu'un autre, et par conséquent à partir desquels on peut dire d'un esprit qu'il est plus actif qu'un autre (l'esprit étant défini comme «l'idée d'un corps», comme sa conscience vivante). Ces deux critères sont la multiplicité et l'autonomie (voir le scolie de la proposition 13 de la partie II de l'Éthique).

Selon le premier critère, un corps actif est un corps capable de nouer de multiples rapports avec les autres, un corps ouvert aux rencontres diverses et variées. La multiplicité est bonne, pour Spinoza, lorsqu'elle est compatible avec la simultanéité. Le corps passif est le corps enfermé en lui-même, figé dans ses expériences de telle sorte qu'il est peu affecté par les autres, et qu'il les affecte peu : le corps passif fait preuve de peu de plasticité, de peu d'adaptabilité; le corps actif est un corps hautement labile.

Or, un corps sensible, un corps plastique est un corps qui donne à l'esprit une multiplicité de choses à penser. Pour qu'un esprit comprenne quelque chose, pour qu'il devienne véritablement actif, il faut commencer par lui donner une matière à penser : il lui faut des sensations, des perceptions, des « imaginations », comme dit Spinoza, même si au départ ces idées sont confuses, floues, partielles. D'ailleurs, pour Spinoza, un esprit actif peut avoir autant d'idées inadéquates qu'un esprit passif (voir scolie de la proposition 20 d'Éthique V), cela non seulement n'est pas grave, mais — peut-on même ajouter — cela est absolument indispensable. Tout le problème est de savoir ce que fait cet esprit de cette riche matière à penser. D'où l'intervention du second critère, celui de la singularité de l'action corporelle, correspondant en l'esprit à la formation d'une compréhension distincte.

Le second critère de définition d'un corps supérieur aux autres est en effet que l'action d'un tel corps dépende le plus possible de lui seul. Comment parvenir à cette autonomie corporelle ? Comment comprendre cette faible participation des autres corps dans la production d'une action par un corps actif ? On pourrait interpréter ce second critère en imaginant la nécessité d'une certaine coupure de ce corps par rapport aux autres : le corps dont l'esprit comprend distinctement serait ainsi un « grand corps solitaire », imperméable aux influences mondaines — imperturbable, il s'enfermerait en lui-même, par exemple, durant la partie de volley-ball, se laissant le moins possible troubler par les sollicitations extérieures. Ce corps serait comme un foyer de mouvements accomplis en toute maîtrise, sans l'aide des autres. La distinction des perceptions de l'esprit viendrait justement de la distinction corporelle, qui s'obtiendrait par l'éloignement ou la mise à l'écart du corps par rapport aux autres. Il y aurait là, dans cette idée, comme un reste de cartésianisme : certes, ce n'est pas lorsque le corps est inerte ou passif que l'esprit pense bien (l'activité mentale demeure corrélative d'une activité corporelle) ; mais ce serait lorsque le corps agit en solitaire, dans une certaine forme de retrait du monde ou d'autarcie, que l'esprit pourrait s'atteler à comprendre distinctement les choses, et notamment les actions du corps lui-même. La force d'âme du joueur, sa fortitude pour user d'un mot ancien, requerraient la solitude du corps.

Or c'est justement pour déjouer une telle interprétation que le premier critère est intervenu avant le second : un corps est d'autant plus indépendant dans la productivité de ses actions qu'il n'est pas fermé aux affections des autres corps. On a là tout le paradoxe de l'activité corporelle, et toute la difficulté à articuler les deux critères de la supériorité d'un corps par rapport aux autres.

L'enjeu pour Spinoza est de penser l'autonomie du corps dans le déterminisme : mieux, il s'agit de montrer qu'un corps est d'autant plus fort qu'il fait corps avec d'autres corps. Et faire corps signifie non pas se dissoudre ou se disperser dans la multitude d'autres corps, mais devenir indépendant dans ses actions, se singulariser grâce à eux.

Reformulons le paradoxe : un corps supérieur est un corps qui agit seul avec les autres. C'est la haute plasticité du corps qui garantit sa haute indépendance.

Il n'y a pas à opposer, mais à articuler multiplicité simultanée et autonomie, déterminisme pluriel et indépendance : pour Spinoza, nous ne sommes pas actifs lorsque, produisant un effet, nous ne sommes pas déterminés par d'autres. Nous sommes actifs simplement lorsque l'explication de l'effet que nous produisons n'a pas besoin de recourir à d'autres causes, différentes de nous, pour être établie. Est actif, ou cause adéquate, pour Spinoza, celui dont l'effet peut se comprendre par lui seul. Ce qui signifie non pas que nous sommes alors une cause non causée, une cause non déterminée ou non affectée par d'autres ; mais que nous sommes actifs lorsqu'il suffit de ne prendre en compte que la causalité dont nous sommes porteurs pour rendre compte de l'effet produit. Ce qui n'est d'ailleurs possible que si nous agissons à travers une causalité commune aux causes qui nous déterminent, qui nous affectent. C'est en ce sens qu'un corps est une cause singulière, indépendante, distincte : parce qu'il fait cause commune avec la causalité d'autres corps. Et encore une fois, cette causalité commune ne signifie pas que le corps est une partie seulement de la causalité totale qui explique son action ; mais que cette causalité totale qui explique son action traverse toute entière ce corps qui est actif, ainsi que les autres corps qui l'affectent. Ce qui n'est possible qu'en vertu du premier critère, à savoir que le corps agissant de façon autonome est un corps hautement apte à être affecté. Le premier critère de la supériorité d'un corps est la condition, en vérité, du second critère : seul un corps apte à être affecté de plusieurs façons à la fois peut agir à travers les propriétés qu'il a en commun avec d'autres corps ; autrement dit, seul un corps supérieurement sensible est un corps capable d'agir seul, de produire des actions qui n'ont pas besoin du concours d'autres corps pour être comprises.

Les deux critères de la supériorité d'un corps et d'un esprit n'en font donc qu'un ; et ils s'enrichissent mutuellement. Le premier montre qu'on ne saurait comprendre la singularité d'action du corps comme exclusion pure et simple des autres corps : au contraire, un corps n'agit seul, sans le concours des autres corps, que s'il est apte à être affecté par eux de très nombreuses façons à la fois ; et réciproquement, un corps apte à être beaucoup affecté n'est pas un corps qui se disperse, s'éparpille ou se divertit dans les connexions qu'il établit avec les autres corps : c'est un corps dont la quantité d'affections simultanées lui donne la puissance de produire une action qui ne dépende que de lui seul.

Nous voyons dès lors que les idées d'activité et de passivité doivent être redéfinies : l'activité ne se définit plus par le mouvement obligé, forcé, c'est-à-dire par l'agitation ; au contraire, le corps actif peut être un corps qui attend le mouvement de l'adversaire pour se décider (tel le passeur au volley). Le joueur actif est celui qui agit en percevant la multiplicité des mouvements en jeu, en comprenant du coup leur logique, et partant en sachant quel geste convient le mieux à la nécessité de la situation. Le joueur passif, quant à lui, n'est pas nécessairement le joueur immobile, au repos : c'est le joueur qui agit, mais en étant agi par l'autre ; qui fait sans comprendre, au hasard, en étant cause seulement partielle ou inadéquate, selon les mots de Spinoza, de son propre geste – alors que le joueur actif, lui, est cause totale ou adéquate de son geste, et ce non pas parce qu'il ne serait déterminé par rien à agir, mais parce qu'il se détermine selon la logique de la situation. L'activité, en ce sens, se caractérise par une haute aptitude à la réception des informations, par une haute sensibilité aux enjeux du jeu. L'activité est l'autre nom de la liberté selon Spinoza, ainsi que pour Vygotsky qui affirme à la fin du chapitre 12 de l'Histoire du développement des fonctions psychiques supérieures : « Nous ne pouvons pas ne pas remarquer que nous en sommes arrivés à la conception même de la liberté et de la maîtrise de soi qu'a développée Spinoza dans son Éthique » (Vygotsky, 2014, p. 488).

C'est pourquoi ce n'est pas tant le joueur que la situation elle-même qui décide ; ou plutôt, c'est le joueur comme partie prenante de la situation, un joueur qui fait corps avec une nécessité, et ce d'autant plus qu'il agit dans l'urgence, sans décalage par rapport au jeu.

Conclusion

Pour conclure, nous dirons que le propre de la bonne décision, dans le moment très court où le geste devient décisif pour marquer un point, un but, un essai…, consiste à produire dans l'adversaire de l'inattendu, de la nouveauté, à tel point que cet adversaire est comme stupéfait, hébété, interdit. Est interdit en lui l'automatisme réflexe qui consiste à enchaîner tel ou tel mouvement pour agir efficacement : le contreur ne sait plus quoi faire. Les joueurs sont comme « cloués au sol », leur mouvement de pensée et d'action est comme bloqué : il est à proprement parler interdit. C'est ce phénomène psycho-physique que Spinoza appelle l'admiration, et qu'il envisage comme négation de la puissance d'agir, comme coupure de l'activité, psychique et physique. La décision en urgence efficace est donc celle qui, chez le joueur actif, ne relève pas de la mémoire, du pur automatisme mnésique, mais d'une compréhension qui dépasse l'enchaînement ordinaire, automatique, des mouvements, et qui du coup, chez le joueur passif, empêche à son tour tout recours à un enchaînement mnésique de mouvements. Et si nous disons que les théories de l'action située ne suffisent pas à rendre compte de cette activité de production de nouveau propre à l'intelligence de la situation, c'est qu'il faut bien du travail en amont — travail de formation des joueurs et de préparation du jeu — pour parvenir à des décisions efficaces dans un contexte d'urgence.

Bibliographie

Spinoza, (1988). Éthique. Traduction Bernard Pautrat. Paris, Seuil.

Clot, Y. (2003). Vygotsky, la conscience comme liaison. Préface à la 1re édition de *Conscience, inconscient, émotions*, Lev S. Vygotsky, Paris, La Dispute.

Clot, Y. (2017). L'affect et sa signification. Postface à la 2e édition de *Conscience, inconscient, émotions*, Lev S. Vygotsky, Paris, La Dispute.

Éloi, S. (2011). Analyse technologique du rôle de libéro en volley-ball : une influence paradoxale sur le jeu. *EJRIEPS*, (23), 46–75.

Sévérac, P. (2005). *Le devenir actif chez Spinoza*. Paris, Honoré Champion.

Spinoza (1964). *Principes de la philosophie de Descartes* dans Œuvres I, traduction Charles Appuhn. Paris, GF-Flammarion.

Vygotsky, L. S. (2014). *Histoire du développement des fonctions psychiques supérieures*. Traduction de Françoise Sève, édition préparée par Michel Brossard et Lucien Sève. Paris, La Dispute.

II. DE LA THÉORIE À LA PRATIQUE
FROM THEORY TO PRACTICE

1.

CONSTRUIRE UN OUTIL D'OBSERVATION DU JEU DE RUGBY À 7 PAR DES ÉTUDIANTS FUTURS INTERVENANTS ÉDUCATIFS : UNE ACTIVITÉ INSTRUMENTALE MÉDIATISÉE

Gilles UHLRICH, France
Université Paris Sud, Paris Saclay, CIAMS (ED566)

Résumé

Les recherches convoquant les travaux de Vygotsky évoquent le développement des sujets non comme un processus qui se fonde sur des étapes à franchir selon une logique obéissant à des lois naturelles mais par des crises et des sauts qualitatifs. Ces états sont difficiles à appréhender et à contrôler par l'intervenant éducatif parce qu'ils sont très en lien avec les milieux matériels et sociaux mis en place. Ils sont aussi inférés à l'histoire et au vécu des sujets. Vygotsky (2014) exprime l'idée que c'est par la mise en œuvre d'activités instrumentales médiatisées que le développement des sujets est stimulé. Ces activités médiées par des outils contribuent à la construction d'instruments psychologiques propres à chaque sujet. Dans cette logique, nous montrerons ici comment la mobilisation d'un outil considéré comme un artefact matériel (Éloi & Uhlrich, 2011), le logiciel Sportscode de construction d'observation du jeu, intégré dans un dispositif de formation à l'observation d'étudiants en formation à l'intervention éducative en sport provoque chez eux du développement à partir des conflits qu'il génère.

Introduction

Le système scolaire français semble être depuis quelques temps au centre de profondes mutations qui interrogent spécialistes et chercheurs (Van Zanten, 2000). L'école fonctionne depuis longtemps en empruntant largement à certains concepts Piagétiens sans en apprécier les limites souvent évoquées par l'auteur lui-même. Par exemple, les stades de développement distingués par Piaget, principalement sur la petite enfance, semblent organiser l'ensemble du système scolaire français par ses différents niveaux d'école (maternelle, primaire, collège, lycée) selon un principe de progression quasi naturel et linéaire. Pourtant, certaines propositions en termes d'éducation empruntent à une autre perspective et tendent à prendre de l'importance. Parler de perspective socio constructiviste plutôt que constructiviste et envisager l'apprentissage d'un élève comme une condition du développement plutôt que l'inverse n'est plus saugrenu. Ces idées empruntent largement aux travaux de Vygotsky même si là encore, il convient d'être très prudent quant à une utilisation abusive de ces concepts. Sans entrer dans une description détaillée des soubassements des théories piagétiennes et vygotskiennes, et en soulignant le rôle majeur des travaux de l'un puis de l'autre dans la réflexion sur l'apprentissage et le développement, nous distinguons quand même deux positions. Il semble que chez Piaget si les structures cognitives individuelles sont bien sollicitées par le rapport du sujet avec son environnement, les outils de pensée reposent sur une construction en grande partie autonome, et fonctionnellement endogène. Le développement d'un individu est alors conditionné par sa structure interne que semble être le berceau de la construction et de la stabilisation d'invariants opératoires ou de schèmes. Cette structure interne stable conditionnerait le rapport de l'individu avec son environnement. Or, chez Vygotsky, le développement cognitif proprement humain est d'abord conditionné par son rapport à l'extérieur. C'est bien par la dynamique de l'interaction entre un milieu social culturellement riche et les fonctions psychologiques de niveau supérieur d'un individu que se construit le développement. Cette dynamique est alimentée par l'utilisation de signes et d'instruments de pensée qui partant de l'extérieur vont être intériorisés par les individus en développement.

En retenant cette perspective, Il semble alors judicieux pour un formateur de penser la proposition d'instruments dans l'activité d'un sujet. Mais il convient surtout d'envisager son activité d'utilisation en ce qu'elle permet le développement du signe qui alimente alors un instrument psychologique. C'est ce positionnement théorique que nous allons interroger à l'occasion de la mise en œuvre d'un dispositif de formation à l'observation du jeu de rugby à 7 par des étudiants destinés à devenir des professionnels de l'intervention éducative en sport.

1. Vygotsky et l'éducation.

Vygotsky interroge la question de l'éducation non pas comme un phénomène naturel de développement d'un individu que l'on va remplir de connaissance mais la définit comme « le développement artificiel de l'enfant » (2014, p. 572). Il ajoute que l'éducation « est la maitrise artificielle des processus naturels du développement » et ne « fait qu'exercer son influence sur tel ou tel processus de développement » (2014, p. 573). Dans cette dynamique, Vygotsky remet en cause la théorie des « dons naturels » ou bien encore du développement d'un individu qui obéirait à des passages logiques par des stades qui limiterait l'activité des apprenants tout au long de leur évolution dans le temps.

Considérant cette orientation, Vygotsky précise ce qu'il entend par développement. « Dans le processus de développement, l'enfant est équipé et rééquipé d'outils les plus variés ; entre l'enfant de niveau plus âgé et le plus jeune, ce qui fait la différence, c'est encore le niveau et le caractère de son outillage, de son instrumentation, c'est-à-dire le niveau de maitrise de son propre comportement. » (2014, p. 573) La plus ou moins grande capacité à faire usage de ses fonctions naturelles et l'appropriation d'outils psychologiques sont les déterminants essentiels de tout le type de développement de l'enfant. La conception du développement de l'enfant de Vygotsky est alors « une conception historico-culturelle qui s'attache à penser comment l'appropriation et l'usage d'outils et techniques culturels, de nature sémiotique et/ou instrumentales confère au développement ses formes ses contenus et ses contradictions au travers d'activités, souvent de nature asymétrique, partagées avec autrui » (Rochex, 2003, p. 5). C'est en s'appuyant sur ces idées que nous menons nos travaux de recherche en évoquant plus précisément la notion d'activité instrumentale médiatisée selon le principe de double stimulation. Nous cherchons à comprendre comment en « adjoignant aux stimuli naturels des stimuli artificiels bien choisis » (Sève, 2014, p. 54), les étudiants produisent une activité instrumentale qui peut être significative d'un développement culturel. Nous évoquons alors le concept d'activité instrumentale médiatisée.

2. Déterminer une activité instrumentale médiatisée.

Selon Sève l'activité instrumentale médiatisée « est l'interposition d'un instrument médiateur - outil, signe - entre le sujet et son objet, qui n'en accroit pas seulement l'efficacité mais en change qualitativement la structure, devenue triangulaire » (Vygotsky, 2014, p. 54). Nous nous inscrivons résolument dans cette perspective en analysant le fonctionnement de cette structure triangulaire dans laquelle nous considérons le fonctionnement de l'instrument comme artefactuel. Nous allons maintenant préciser ce que nous entendons par activité instrumentale médiatisée.

2.1 Activité, actions, opérations.

En s'appuyant sur les concepts de la théorie de l'activité développés par Vygotsky (1978) et Léontiev (1981), nous considérons l'activité comme toute action humaine médiée par des artefacts porteurs d'une dimension historique et culturelle qui rattachent la pensée de l'individu à la société dans laquelle il vit. Il convient dans ce cadre d'envisager non seulement l'individu mais aussi la nature collective de cette activité. L'activité se réalise alors dans un environnement social. Léontiev détermine l'activité comme l'ensemble des actions humaines se déroulant dans un contexte donné reposant sur des motifs d'agir particuliers, des actions réalisées selon un but fixé par le sujet et des opérations considérées alors comme les moyens mobilisés pour agir. Dans cette organisation en système, l'instrument mobilisé par le sujet répond à ces fonctions d'incitation, d'orientation autant que de réalisation. Ainsi, l'individu peut articuler dans toute activité sens et efficience.

2.2 L'instrument dans une logique de genèse instrumentale (Rabardel, 1995)

Pour déterminer le concept d'instrument, nous nous sommes inspirés des travaux de Rabardel (1995) qui posent les bases d'une théorie instrumentale en distinguant l'outil technique et l'instrument. Il caractérise alors le processus de genèse instrumentale. Un sujet qui s'empare d'un outil, quel qu'il soit, engage un double mouvement d'instrumentation et d'instrumentalisation. L'outil, par sa mobilisation, devient un artefact en ce sens qu'il provoque un incident dans l'activité du sujet. L'instrumentation correspond à l'exploration des potentialités de l'outil proposé que nous considérons alors comme un moment de « prise en main » (Uhlrich & Éloi, 2016). Ce premier mouvement amène le sujet à donner du sens et une orientation à l'activité qu'il réalise. L'artefact devient instrument. Le second mouvement correspond à l'instrumentalisation. Le sujet fait évoluer ses modes d'utilisation pour le « mettre à sa main ». Il détermine alors son activité à partir de nouvelles actions nécessitant d'autres opérations précises et identifiables. Pour le chercheur, ces deux mouvements sont à caractériser en considérant qu'ils s'expriment dès le début de la mobilisation de l'outil mais qu'il existe certainement des moments charnières à repérer. En s'appuyant sur la dynamique de genèse instrumentale, nous introduisons dans l'activité de nos étudiants des outils technologiques considérés alors comme des artefacts. L'artefact est un incident volontairement introduit dans l'activité de l'apprenant afin de faire évoluer son expérience. Nous cherchons alors à comprendre l'effet de cet artefact sur l'activité des formés et plus particulièrement leur évolution dans la conceptualisation qu'ils font de leur propre pratique. Nous nous plaçons ainsi dans une double posture qui interroge l'activité instrumentée. D'une part, « À chaque artefact correspondent des possibilités de transformations des objets de l'activité, qui ont été anticipées, délibérément recherchées et qui sont susceptibles de s'actualiser dans l'usage » (Rabardel,

1995, p. 60). D'autre part, ignorer les modifications auxquelles conduit l'introduction d'un artefact dans les interactions conduit l'intervenant éducatif à prendre le risque de ne participer qu'à une reproduction de l'identique (Rochex, 2003). L'artefact a pour vocation de produire un effet propice. Il est finalisé car il vise à apporter une solution avantageuse à un problème donné. Il est évolutif et peut se perfectionner dans le temps. Mais il est aussi imprévisible car sa mise à l'épreuve ne présage pas des usages futurs qui pourront en être fait (détournement, catachrèse). Notre travail consiste donc à distinguer des moments particuliers qui correspondent à des moments de doutes, d'interrogation de controverses chez les formés en postulant que le développement d'un individu ne se fait pas de manière linéaire mais par des moments de crise et du coup de « saut pédagogiques ». Nous rejoignons alors la position de Vygotsky décrite par Sève quant à l'éducation : « À l'encontre des illusions de l'éducation sans effort, il faut organiser les sauts dont nul élève ne peut faire l'économie pour accéder à des niveaux de développement supérieurs » (Sève, 2014, p. 56). Ces sauts s'organisent en proposant des dispositifs qui impliquent une nécessaire médiatisation.

2.3 Autour du concept de médiatisation.

Étymologiquement, médiate est opposé à immédiat. La médiatisation implique alors d'agir indirectement, l'activité du sujet n'est en rapport avec autre chose que par un intermédiaire de juridiction médiate, de connaissance médiate, abstraite ou intellectuelle, par opposition à une connaissance immédiate. La médiatisation correspond donc à une médiation technique. Médiatiser consiste à offrir des supports aux activités des sujets qui vont assister sa conceptualisation : schémas, grilles, aides à la réalisation. Ainsi, dans chaque action de médiatisation existe du conceptuel. Dès lors, les opérations de médiatisation qui concernent la scénarisation de contenus doivent envisager la médiation de la relation qui s›instaure entre l›émetteur et le destinataire. Si donc la médiatisation peut se concevoir comme une forme de médiation, elle ne le sera concrètement que si elle est conduite de manière professionnelle, dans la connaissance et la maîtrise des spécificités des outils employés et de leurs usagers. Sève (2014, p. 63) considère la médiatisation au cœur de la psychologie vygotskienne. Par-delà le cours d'activité « naturel » opéré par le sujet se développe par la médiatisation de l'instrument une signification de l'action vectrice d'une pensée conceptuelle.

Fort de ce positionnement théorique interprété des travaux de Vygotsky, nous allons présenter succinctement ce sur quoi nous portons notre attention depuis plus de 10 ans (Uhlrich, 2005 ; Éloi & Uhlrich, 2011 ; Uhlrich, Éloi & Bouthier, 2011 ; Uhlrich & Éloi 2016). Nous analysons l'impact de l'introduction d'un artefact matériel dans la formation de futurs intervenants éducatifs en sport et particulièrement leur capacité à observer et interpréter le jeu de rugby qui se déroule sous leurs yeux.

3. Étude de l'activité instrumentale médiatisée dans un dispositif de formation à l'observation du jeu de rugby à 7.

Nous fonctionnons professionnellement dans une situation particulière puisque nous intervenons auprès d'étudiants dans une institution de formation de futurs intervenants éducatifs. Ainsi, non seulement, selon un premier niveau, il convient de former les étudiants à des nouveaux concepts qui leur permettent à la fois de décrire des pratiques physiques et sportives avec précision mais il s'agit aussi, selon un second niveau, d'interpréter le comportement des autres (les joueurs) à des fins de leur proposer des situations qui vont permettre leur propre transformation. Le futur intervenant éducatif d'être capable de « dire sur le faire » des autres. Il est alors nécessaire pour nous d'envisager le développement de ces étudiants en nous appuyant sur les perspectives vygotskiennes évoquées plus haut. Nous avons-nous mêmes à mettre en place des situations d'apprentissage qui ne consiste pas à reproduire des recettes mais qui permettent le la mobilisation de signes à des fins de développement d'instruments psychologiques par les étudiants. Enfin, il existe un troisième niveau que nous intéresse professionnellement, c'est que les dispositifs mis en place sont à interroger selon une logique scientifique. Dans le cadre d'une démarche technologique, des travaux de recherche sur ces mêmes situations d'apprentissage posent la question de leur efficacité et de l'identification du « mouvement » des sujets nous permettant ainsi de distinguer « du développement » (Uhlrich, Éloi & Bouthier,

2011). Nous interrogeons donc l'usage des artefacts dans le développement de l'activité humaine. Nous questionnons l'apprentissage requis pour maîtriser ces objets techniques selon un processus de genèse instrumentale. C'est pourquoi nous installons les étudiants dans une « activité instrumentale médiatisée ».

3.1 La prise en main du logiciel, la période d'instrumentation

Nous proposons à des étudiants futurs intervenant éducatifs en sport inscrit dans un cursus universitaire STAPS (Sciences et Techniques des Activités Physiques et Sportives) de mobiliser un outil informatique de description des actions de jeu en rugby à 7. Ils mobilisent le logiciel Sportscode qui est considéré comme un artefact matériel (Éloi & Uhlrich, 2014). L'objectif initial de la formation est de faire fonctionner à minima cet outil technique. Les étudiants ont à prendre en main le logiciel de description du jeu qui leur permet tout au long du déroulement d'un match de distinguer des actions selon un guide précis (annexe 1). Notre première intention est que les étudiants concernés s'approprient des indicateurs qui leur permettent de distinguer les actions de rugby les unes des autres afin de mieux identifier le jeu qui se déroule sous leurs yeux. Cette activité a donc pour fonction de permettre aux étudiants d'illuminer ce qui se déroule de manière éphémère et complexe afin qu'ils puissent le qualifier. Cette activité culturelle leur permet de construire du signe, particulièrement lorsqu'ils ont à distinguer les moments d'équilibre et de déséquilibre pour qualifier l'évolution d'un rapport de force entre deux équipes qui s'affrontent. Le logiciel d'observation est ainsi fait qu'il oriente le regard du formé sur la prise en compte systématique de ce rapport d'opposition en rugby en considérant l'action des attaquants au regard des réactions des défenseurs qui leur font face.

Durant la première période de mobilisation du logiciel, les sujets effectuent une « prise en main » de l'artefact. Les étudiants testent des « routines de saisies » qui donnent des résultats plus ou moins probants. Ils sont installés dans une situation de simulation sous la forme de binômes, ce qui engage inévitablement une médiation. Le travail d'observation se déroule en salle face à un match projeté sur un écran. Cette configuration permet de repérer les moments de tâtonnement et d'incertitude qui conduisent à suspendre la retransmission. Les étudiants occupent alternativement deux rôles :

- Le rôle du secrétaire qui saisit les données : il saisit à l'aide du logiciel les informations qui lui sont communiquées à voix haute par son collègue. Il ne regarde que l'écran de l'ordinateur.
- Le rôle du commentateur (aboyeur) : il décrit les actions de jeu qu'il repère au fur et à mesure du déroulement du match et les communique à son camarade. Il ne regarde que le jeu (écran de télévision ou match en direct depuis le bord du terrain)

Ce travail en collaboration amène les étudiants à mobiliser l'instrument selon des tâches distinctes qui ne manquent pas de provoquer de la controverse. En effet, au fur et à mesure du travail d'observation, aucun des protagonistes ne peut se cantonner strictement à son rôle. Nous observons à partir d'images enregistrées que l'aboyeur ne peut s'empêcher de vérifier l'exactitude de la saisie à laquelle procède son partenaire. De son côté, le secrétaire contrôle que l'aboyeur caractérise convenablement les actions de jeu à saisir en regardant l'écran de la vidéo qui filme le match. Il s'installe dès lors des échanges qui amènent à de la controverse sur la qualification des phases de jeu. L'outil vidéo permet alors d'effectuer un retour en arrière et de soumettre au débat ces moments caractéristiques nécessitants une clarification des phases de jeu observées. Les échanges portent sur les indicateurs pris sur les joueurs qui permettent la qualification de la phase de jeu. Puis, pour se mettre d'accord, les étudiants reviennent sur la définition isolée de la modélisation du jeu qui alimente un guide de description. Ils se positionnent en mettant en relation des attitudes de joueurs, des trajectoires de courses d'attaquants ou de défenseurs ou encore des gestes de l'arbitre. Le moment de la controverse est particulièrement fructueux pour mettre à jour les conceptions qui sous-tendent leur observation du jeu de rugby. Au fur et à mesure des échanges se construit alors un langage commun sur la description du jeu. Ils développent une nouvelle interprétation du jeu. Les signes sur le jeu deviennent des signes pour eux-mêmes alimentant de fait leur instrument psychologique.

3.2 La période d'instrumentalisation.

La période d'instrumentalisation constitue un prolongement de la période d'instrumentation. Ici, le sujet se construit un référentiel des utilisations adéquates ou inefficaces de l'outil. Il met l'instrument « à sa main ». Dans notre cas, ce deuxième temps se réalise en phase de finalisation du module de formation à l'observation. La phase d'instrumentalisation correspond à la nécessité suggérée par le formateur de faire évoluer l'outil dans la perspective de son utilisation en direct lors d'un tournoi international universitaire de rugby à 7 (le central Seven). Le fait de devoir mobiliser l'outil en situation de match réel, amène les étudiants à se concentrer sur son caractère ergonomique pour le rendre le plus adapté à une saisie rapide et efficiente. En effet, ils ne pourront plus faire d'arrêt sur image voire des retours en arrière pour qualifier les actions qui se dérouleront sous leurs yeux. Ils auront à mobiliser leurs instruments psychologiques au feu de la réalité. Ils ne seront plus dans une activité simulée. En effet, les observations réalisées seront à communiquer aux entraîneurs des équipes concernées dès la fin du match ce qui implique un rendu fidèle du « scénario de match ». Au fur et à mesure du travail de réorganisation ergonomique de la saisie, ils ont la liberté, offerte par le logiciel, de modifier la disposition des icônes Ils sont également amenés à ajouter les icones qui leur manquent. Le processus de genèse instrumentale est ici poussé à un autre niveau. Les étudiants capables de provoquer des évolutions dans le dispositif princeps en respectant les conceptions initiales montrent qu'ils ont compris la logique de la modélisation sous-jacente proposée qui a en partie contribuée à la construction de l'artefact matériel. Ils se décentrent alors d'une simple exécution de tâches imposées par l'instrument pour le remettre lui-même en question. On retrouve ici ce que Brossard (2018) considère comme une inversion d'interprétation du fonctionnement humain par l'utilisation de médiateurs ou de moyens artificiels. « Au lieu d'être dépendants des lois naturelles, les individus s'assignent désormais eux-mêmes des buts et sont en mesure de produire et de transformer en permanence non seulement leur milieu extérieur, mais aussi leur propre mode de fonctionnement. L'activité devient un moment d'une histoire humaine et non pas la simple résultante de processus naturels », (Brossard, 2018, p. 19). Cette assignation d'un nouveau but dans leur activité ainsi que la liberté ou le dépassement de fonction qui sont accordées aux étudiants les amène à d'une part personnaliser l'instrument qu'ils mobilisent et d'autre part les conduits à de nouvelles interrogations sur le déroulement du jeu dans cette perspective de description du rapport d'opposition entre l'attaque et la défense. Là encore, nous repérons ces évolutions à partir des questions qu'ils se posent et des propositions qu'ils font en vue de la modification du logiciel. L'obstacle qu'ils tentent à nouveau de surmonter provoque du développement dans l'observation qu'ils font du jeu de rugby à 7.

Conclusion

Le recours à l'artéfact matériel s'avère donc particulièrement pertinent dans cette phase de formation initiale. Il s'agit pour l'étudiant de transformer l'identification d'une situation de jeu par un clic sur une touche sur l'ordinateur. Il y a transformation de l'étudiant parce qu'une phase de jeu réalisée par d'autres est identifiée, puis interprétée pour devenir une occurrence dans une grille d'observation. Et c'est bien tout le problème de l'identification des évolutions de l'étudiant qui est au cœur de cette formation à l'observation. Dans cette dynamique, en quoi la mobilisation d'artefacts permet-elle ce mouvement ? C'est nous semble-t-il le mode d'utilisation de l'artefact qui permet de contribuer à cette évolution. En effet, loin d'enfermer l'observateur dans un fonctionnement stéréotypé, la mise à l'épreuve de l'artefact le contraint à faire des allers et retour entre le souvenir de ce qui vient de se dérouler sous ses yeux et les possibilités de caractérisations qui lui sont offertes. Tout l'intérêt est de tirer parti d'éventuelles dissonances et de se ménager la possibilité de faire évoluer l'artefact. Cette capacité à créer du sens à propos du jeu observé alimente une nouvelle signification. Cette signification qui alimente la conception du formé est bien entendu très en lien avec la subjectivité de chaque acteur et il n'est pas envisageable pour nous de généraliser ces évolutions. Mais, à partir de cet exemple, la question peut réellement se poser de savoir comment l'activité instrumentale médiatisée a comme conséquence de favoriser chez le formé, la construction d'une conceptualisation en acte (Vergnaud, 1996) permettant d'utiliser avec efficience l'artefact matériel. Nous faisons l'hypothèse que la mobilisation de l'artefact matériel conduit à la construction « vicariante » d'un artefact cognitif (Éloi & Uhlrich, 2011) favorable à la construction d'un véritable instrument de pensée.

Bibliographie

Brossard, M. (2018). Vygotsky aujourd'hui. *In EPS et culturalisme : jeux, arts, sports et développement humain.* Contrepied hors-série n° 20-21, centre EPS et société.

Éloi, S. & Uhlrich, G. (2011). La démarche technologique en STAPS : analyse conceptuelle et mise en perspective pour les sports collectifs. *eJRIEPS, 23.* 20 – 45

Éloi, S. & Uhlrich, G. (2014) : Utilisation d'artefacts dans le domaine des pratiques physiques, sportives et artistiques (PPSA). *TrasnFormations, Recherches en éducation et formation des adultes, 12, 117 – 137.*

Leontiev, A. N. (1981). The problem of activity in psychology. *In* J.V.Wertsch (ed.), *The concept of activity in Soviet psychology.* Armonk, NY : M. E. Sharpe.

Rabardel, P. (1995). *Les hommes et les technologies, approche cognitive des instruments contemporains.* Paris : Armand Colin.

Rochex, Y. (2003). La théorie Vygotskienne n'est pas un temple mais un chantier. *In Vygotsky et l'éducation.* Ss la dir. de A. Kozulin et al. Ed. Retz, pp; 4 – 6.

Sève, L. (2014). Présentation. In Brossard et Sève. *Histoire du développement des fonctions psychiques supérieures.* Paris : La Dispute.

Uhlrich, G. (2005). *Rôle des artefacts matériels et cognitifs dans le développement des compétences de l'intervenant éducatif et rugby.* Thèse non publiée. Université Bordeaux 2, V. Segalen.

Uhlrich G., Éloi S. & Bouthier D. (2011). « La technologie dans le contexte des STAPS : de la conception d'outils à la conceptualisation… et réciproquement », *eJRIEPS 23*, p. 4-19.

Uhlrich, G & Éloi, S. (2016). Formation à l'observation de futurs intervenants éducatifs en rugby : quelles conséquences pour leur conception du jeu ? *Revue des sciences de l'éducation, 42/2,* 123 -147.

Van Zanten, A. & al. (2000). *Les transformations de l'école.* Ed. La Découverte, 2000, 415 p

VERGNAUD, G. (1996). « Au fond de l'action, la conceptualisation ». In J.-M. Barbier, *Savoirs théoriques et savoirs d'action.* Paris : PUF. p. 275-292.

VYGOTSKY, L. (1978 / 1930). *Mind in society: The development of higher psychological processes.* Cambridge, MA: Harvard University Press.

VYGOTSKY, L. (2014). *Histoire du développement des fonctions psychiques supérieures.* Paris : La Dispute.

Annexe 1 : guide d'utilisation du logiciel sportscode

INDEX DU PACà7 *: Chaque action caractérisée ci-dessous associe la qualité technique et énergétique de la réalisation et la pertinence du choix tactique de l'attaque.*				
Contexte	Score	Essai Transformation Pénalités		
Phase Statique	CE/CR			**CE/CR +** : récupération du ballon **CE/CR -** : récupération par l'adversaire et déséquilibre **CE/CR Neutre** : récupération par l'adversaire avec équilibre
	Pénalité			**Pénalité + :** création d'un déséquilibre ou gain de terrain important. **Pénalité - :** choix non adapté mettant l'équipe sous pression de la défense adverse ou perte de balle (touche non trouvée…) **Pénalité Neutre :** création d'aucun déséquilibre, gain de terrain négligeable.
	Touche			**Touche +** : gain du ballon et utilisation avec possibilité de créer un déséquilibre immédiat. **Touche -** : perte du ballon. **Touche Neutre** : gain du ballon avec obligation d'une circulation à l'équilibre.
	Mêlée			**Mêlée +** : gain du ballon et utilisation avec possibilité de créer un déséquilibre immédiat. **Mêlée -** : perte du ballon **Mêlée Neutre** : gain du ballon avec obligation d'une circulation à l'équilibre.
	Devant la Défense	Jeu à la main	Contournant	*Passe(s) longue(s) sur la largeur afin de déborder le dispositif défensif (intervalle entre la touche et le dernier défenseur)* **Déployé Contournant +** : création d›un déséquilibre sur l›extérieur, débordement. **Déployé Contournant -** : jeu en débordement et perte du ballon. **Déployé Contournant Neutre** : circulation du ballon sur la largeur sans déséquilibre
			Pénétrant	*Initiatives du relayeur ou passe(s) sur la largeur avec franchissement de la défense dans un intervalle.* **Déployé Pénétrant +** : création d›un déséquilibre autre que sur l›extérieur, franchissement. **Déployé Pénétrant -** : attaque de l'intervalle et perte du ballon. **Déployé Pénétrant Neutre** : attaque d'un intervalle et création d'aucun déséquilibre.
		Jeu au pied	Dégagement	*Jeu au pied qui soulage l'équipe de la pression par gain de terrain.* **Jeu au pied de dégagement +**: gain de terrain important avec inversion de la pression **Jeu au pied de dégagement -** : gain de terrain négligeable, nouvelle pression sur son équipe **Jeu au pied de dégagement Neutre** : gain de terrain important, nouvelle pression sur son équipe
			Offensif	*Jeu au pied avec intention de récupérer le ballon à la chute.* **Jeu au pied offensif +** : réception du ballon par son équipe. **Jeu au pied offensif -** : réception du ballon par l'adversaire et mise en difficulté de son équipe. **Jeu au pied offensif Neutre** : réception du ballon par l'équipe adverse sans création de déséquilibre

Phase de plein mouvement	**Au contact de la Défense**	Blocage Long	*Ruck ou maul long, la défense est en place à la sortie du ballon.* **Blocage long +** : conservation du ballon, progression et création d'un déséquilibre exploitable. **Blocage long -** : perte du ballon **Blocage long Neutre** : conservation du ballon sans création d'un déséquilibre.
		Blocage Court	*Ruck ou maul court, le déséquilibre est conservé à la sortie du ballon.* **Blocage court +** : conservation du ballon, progression et création d'un déséquilibre exploitable. **Blocage court -** : perte du ballon. **Blocage court Neutre** : conservation du ballon sans création d'un déséquilibre
		Pivot Axial	*Passe profonde dans l'axe afin de prolonger le mouvement en cours ou le transformer.* **Pivot Axial +** : Par la passe, éloignement du ballon des défenseurs avec création d'un déséquilibre **Pivot Axial -** : Par la passe perte du ballon **Pivot Axial Neutre** : Par la passe, éloignement du ballon des défenseurs sans création de déséquilibre
	Dans la Défense	Duel 1/1	*Le rideau est franchi, duel homme à homme contre le libéro.* **Duel 1/1 +** : adversaire éliminé individuellement, gain de terrain significatif. **Duel 1/1 -** : perte du ballon Duel 1/1 neutre : adversaire non éliminé individuellement, conservation du ballon
		Manœuvre Collective	*Le rideau franchit, 2 attaquants ou plus contre le libéro.* **Manœuvre Collective +** : adversaire éliminé par une manœuvre, gain de terrain significatif. **Manœuvre Collective -** : perte du ballon. Manœuvre collective neutre : adversaire non éliminé par une manœuvre, conservation du ballon.
	Contre-attaque		*Récupération du ballon sur la ligne de front ou derrière.* **Contre-Attaque +** : création ou utilisation d›un déséquilibre avec gain de terrain significatif. **Contre-Attaque -** : Perte de ballon et/ou perte de terrain significative. **Contre-Attaque Neutre** : Pas de création de déséquilibre et pas de gain de terrain.

2.

APPRENDRE À FAIRE DES CHOIX EN VOLLEY-BALL DANS UNE SITUATION DE 2 CONTRE (1+1). APPORT DE LA THÉORIE INSTRUMENTALE DE VYGOTSKY

Serge ÈLOI, France
Université Paris-Est, LIRTES (EA7313)

Introduction

Les pratiques physiques sportives et artistiques se manifestent dans différents secteurs : celui de l'enseignement (scolaire, universitaire), celui de l'entraînement (fédérations, clubs), celui de l'animation (centres de loisirs, colonies de vacances), et même celui de rencontres auto-organisées pour lesquelles les pratiquants se retrouvent de gré à gré sans qu'aucune structure identifiée ne coordonne les pratiques. Quels que soient les secteurs, la question de la transmission, plus ou moins rationalisée, des savoirs liés à ces pratiques reste une préoccupation permanente (Éloi et Uhlrich, 2011). Nous voulons explorer ici une situation maintenant bien décrite (Éloi et Uhlrich, 2013 ; Éloi & Uhlrich, 2014 ; Éloi, 2017). Celle du 2 contre (1+1) en volley-ball. Nous nous proposons de préciser les étapes du processus de genèse instrumentale (Rabardel, 1995) préalablement décrit dans les textes cités précédemment en le nourrissant de la théorie instrumentale de Vygotsky. Nous nous focaliserons plus particulièrement sur le concept de signe tel qu'il a été conceptualisé par Vygotsky dans différents ouvrages (1978 ; 1934/1997 ; 1935/1997 ; 2012 ; 1931/2014) pour comprendre comment, dans cette situation particulière, il joue un rôle prépondérant. Cette étude prend appui sur des expérimentations réalisées lors de l'enseignement du volley-ball dans le cadre de la formation initiale d'étudiants en 2e année universitaire qui se destinent à devenir des enseignants d'éducation physique.

1. La situation de 2 contre (1+1)

L'objectif de ce cours de volley-ball de 2e année de Licence vise à mobiliser autant les ressources motrices des étudiants que de susciter leur réflexion sur l'enseignement de cette discipline sportive. Ce cours a donc une double valence « Pratique du volley-ball - Réflexion didactique sur le volley-ball ». Les caractéristiques des groupes d'étudiants qui se succèdent tous les ans ne changent pas fondamentalement. Les mêmes observations peuvent être renouvelées. Les mêmes obstacles peuvent être identifiés. Il faut préciser que ces étudiants ne sont pas spécialistes de volley-ball. Au cours de cette pratique, l'enseignant peut observer un stéréotype qui se présente systématiquement y compris dans une situation à effectif réduit tel que le 2 contre 2. On peut décrire ce stéréotype ainsi : au cours d'un échange, lorsqu'un étudiant reçoit la balle, il utilise invariablement et indépendamment de la structure de l'opposition (placements et déplacements du partenaire et des deux adversaires) un des deux choix suivants.

- Le choix « Collectif » : on peut le repérer parce que ces étudiants font invariablement une passe à leur partenaire.
- Le choix « Individualiste » : on peut l'identifier parce que ces étudiants renvoient toujours directement la balle chez l'adversaire.

Or, l'efficacité de la réponse trouve sa justification dans l'adaptation de sa propre action au rapport d'opposition du moment. Ainsi, ni l'un ni l'autre de ces choix n'est a priori le meilleur. Tantôt, il faut faire une passe, tantôt il faut renvoyer la balle directement. Dans la pratique des sports collectifs, rien n'est écrit à l'avance. Le rapport de force étant fluctuant, il faut « lire » la situation pour jouer à bon escient.

Nous nous intéressons ici aux problèmes des choix tactiques. Comment libérer les étudiants de ce stéréotype décisionnel ? Peut-on transmettre la capacité de choisir ? Peut-on définir ce qu'est un bon choix ? On notera que ces questions dépassent amplement la seule formation des futurs enseignants d'EPS. Elles rejoignent une problématique culturelle plus générale : celle de la prise de décisions.

2. La genèse instrumentale

C'est pour tenter de remédier à ce problème de stéréotypes que nous avons introduit la situation de « 2 contre (1+1) » au volley-ball (Éloi et Uhlrich, 2013). La situation a recours à un artefact c'est-à-dire un incident que l'on peut caractériser « comme l'utilisation d'un objet matériel ou non, volontairement introduit par l'intervenant dans l'activité du sujet visant à la modification du cours normal de sa pratique dans le but de provoquer une compréhension nouvelle de son activité » (Éloi et Uhlrich, 2011, p. 30). Ici, il s'agit d'un artefact réglementaire. Nous parlons d'artefact réglementaire parce qu'il s'agit d'une règle nouvelle qui va être introduite dans la situation de jeu. La règle officielle va donc subir une « transformation transitoire » et c'est par la médiation de cette nouvelle règle que l'intervenant éducatif va chercher à provoquer un changement dans l'activité des sujets.

Prolongeant les travaux de Rabardel (1995), nous pensons que dans le cadre de l'enseignement ou de l'entraînement sportif, l'introduction d'un artefact déclenche un processus de genèse instrumentale et que ce processus se réalise dans une succession de périodes d'instrumentation et d'instrumentalisation cycliques. Ces cycles peuvent alors se reproduire autant que nécessaire au cours du développement du sujet. C'est ce que nous avons montré avec cette situation du « 2 contre (1+1) » au volley-ball (Éloi & Uhlrich, 2013).

2.1. L'instrumentation

L'instrumentation correspond à une période durant laquelle le sujet « prend en main » l'artefact (Éloi & Uhlrich, 2013). Il en teste les usages possibles, les effets, les limites. « Nous utiliserons le terme d'instrumentation… pour désigner les aspects du processus de genèse instrumentale orientés vers le sujet lui-même » (Rabardel, 1995, p. 137). Le sujet doit trouver les ressources en lui pour utiliser a minima l'outil proposé. « L'instrumentation, c'est donc ce processus par lequel les contraintes et les potentialités d'un artefact vont conditionner durablement l'action d'un sujet pour résoudre un problème donné » (Trouche, 2005, p. 274).

2.2. L'instrumentalisation

À la suite de cette phase et de façon plus ou moins imbriquée va succéder une autre phase dite d'instrumentalisation. Elle correspond à « la mise à sa main » (Éloi et Uhlrich, 2013) de l'artefact par le sujet. Ici, le sujet va en quelque sorte reprendre le dessus sur l'artefact pour l'adapter à son usage personnel. « Nous réservons celui (le terme) d'instrumentalisation pour les processus dirigés vers l'artefact » (Rabardel, 1995, p. 137). Cette « reprise en main » peut aller jusqu'à la modification de l'artefact. Ici, l'activité du sujet est tournée vers l'artefact.

2.3. Le processus d'appropriation : un double mouvement

C'est donc ce double mouvement qui pour nous, caractérise la genèse instrumentale. Notons que Félix et Vérillon (2017) évoquent deux axes de développement : « Dès lors, on voit se dessiner pour les instruments deux axes distincts, quoique plus ou moins solidaires, de développement potentiel : un axe de développement opératoire centripète, dit d'instrumentation (développement schématique, représentationnel…) au cours duquel les utilisateurs tentent de "prendre en main" (Éloi & Uhlrich, 2013 ; 2014) l'artefact et un axe de développement artefactuel centrifuge, dit d'instrumentalisation (développement des fonctionnalités de l'artefact) au cours duquel les utilisateurs s'efforcent de le "mettre à leur main" (ibidem) dans une perspective continuée de l'artefact » (Félix et Vérillon, 2017, p. 19)

Il s'agit maintenant de présenter l'artefact réglementaire et la façon dont il opère.

2.4. Divergences scientifiques

Nous voulons souligner ici un point de discussion avec la thèse initiale de Rabardel qui suggère que « la découverte progressive des propriétés (intrinsèques) de l'artefact par les sujets s'accompagne de l'accommodation de leurs schèmes, mais aussi de changements de signification de l'instrument résultant de l'association de l'artefact à de nouveaux schèmes » (Rabardel, 1995, p. 116). Les éclairages que nous allons développer s'éloignent des théories de l'école Piagétienne et du recours au schème. Nos travaux trouvent une voie de développement que nous jugeons plus féconde en nous appuyant sur les textes de Vygotsky et notamment dans le caractère dialectique de sa théorie instrumentale. Cette thèse n'est donc pas celle de Rabardel. Pour lui, instrumentation et instrumentalisation peuvent se présenter dans n'importe quel ordre, voire l'une sans l'autre. Elles ne constituent pas des phases bien identifiées. Nous considérons pour notre part qu'une fois le processus de genèse instrumentale enclenché, les phases vont se succéder en alternance. Nous pensons que c'est ici que l'éclairage de Vygotsky peut nous ouvrir de nouvelles perspectives scientifiques. Il n'en reste pas moins que l'intuition de Rabardel d'une genèse instrumentale structurée par des moments d'instrumentation et d'instrumentalisation ouvre des horizons heuristiques des plus enthousiasmants.

3. L'artefact réglementaire du 2 contre (1+1)

L'artefact réglementaire est introduit par l'intervenant éducatif lorsque les stéréotypes (collectif vs individualiste) sont flagrants dans une situation de 2 contre 2.

Comment sortir les étudiants de leurs stéréotypes décisionnels ?

Cette situation nous a été inspirée par les jeux vidéo. L'artefact réglementaire est présenté comme une fable ce qui ne manque pas d'interpeller le chercheur sur les émotions suscitées par la mise en place de cette situation (Prot, 2017). Cette métaphore est construite sur l'idée que l'on n'est jamais éliminé du jeu. Les protagonistes disposent donc d'un stock illimité de vies. Le principe du jeu est en fait assez simple. Le joueur qui renvoie la balle chez l'adversaire est provisoirement « mort ». Pour recouvrer sa « vie », il doit aller toucher l'un des deux plots qui délimitent l'arrière de son terrain (cf. figure 1). Une fois le plot touché, ce joueur peut revenir dans l'échange avec les mêmes prérogatives. Bien évidemment, si un joueur est pris à jouer le ballon alors qu'il est encore « mort », l'échange s'arrête et le point est accordé aux adversaires. Symboliquement, c'est celui qui tente de « tuer » ses adversaires qui paye de sa « vie » cette initiative, telle l'abeille qui pique, perd son dard et en meurt. Cette disposition provoque subséquemment un emboîtement de configurations plus ou moins fugaces de « 2 contre 1 + 1 » (le « + 1 » représentant le joueur parti toucher le plot). C'est alors que les effets de cette mesure conduisent à transformer les objets de l'activité des sujets, c'est-à-dire ce sur quoi elle porte, et ces objets vont varier en cours d'apprentissage.

Les tentatives réalisées dans le but de gagner l'échange sont maintenant subordonnées au respect d'une disposition nouvelle (la nouvelle règle) qui va tout d'abord désorienter les pratiquants. L'activité des joueurs est alors redirigée massivement vers le respect de ce nouvel élément réglementaire au détriment de l'efficacité du renvoi. Ce détour peut paraître paradoxal et fastidieux puisque l'objectif annoncé de l'enseignant est de rendre les étudiants capables de s'adapter aux adversaires. En fait, on perd du temps pour mieux en gagner. C'est un passage obligé pour relancer la motricité « sclérosée » des étudiants. L'introduction de l'artefact réglementaire s'avère être le point de départ d'un processus de causes et d'effets en cascade qui va conduire à rendre indispensable la prise en compte des placements et déplacements des adversaires. Reconstituer les voies du développement nécessite de saisir les changements initiés par l'artefact depuis son introduction sans omettre aucune des étapes sous peine d'étudier « la réaction complexe dans sa forme morte, comme une chose déjà faite, après que son processus de développement est achevé » (Vygotsky, 1931/2014, p. 229).

3 .1. Le 2 vs (1+1) : une expérimentation multidimensionnelle

L'expérimentation menée au cours d'un cycle d'enseignement où la situation est renouvelée sur une séquence de 10 à 15 minutes lors de chacune des dix séquences nécessite une analyse multidimensionnelle.

Il faut en effet renseigner quatre dimensions :

– Celle des points de vue : intervenant éducatif - pratiquant.
– Celle des phases : instrumentation - instrumentalisation.
– Celle des statuts : attaquants – défenseurs
– Celle de la place du signe : externe -interne ; le sujet - autrui

3.2. Les points de vue

Dans notre situation, c'est l'intervenant éducatif qui décide de l'introduction de l'artefact réglementaire. Il choisit le moment de cette introduction au regard du comportement de ses apprenants (élèves, étudiants, joueurs). Cependant, l'introduction d'un artefact dans le processus enseignement-apprentissage n'est qu'une proposition mise en place par l'intervenant éducatif qui poursuit ses objectifs. Cela n'augure en rien de l'utilisation qui sera faite de cet artefact par les apprenants.

3.3. Instrumentation – Instrumentalisation

L'enjeu de cette dimension consiste à repérer les deux phases. Comment garantir que ce que l'on observe relève de l'instrumentation ou de l'instrumentalisation ? Qu'est-ce qui permet le passage de l'une à l'autre ?

3.4. À l'attaque – En défense

La particularité des sports collectifs d'opposition directe (basket-ball, football, handball, rugby, volley-ball, hockey…), c'est que les protagonistes peuvent basculer du statut d'attaquant à celui de défenseur dans l'instant. Cette spécificité engage à envisager que la genèse instrumentale se déroulera pour l'une comme pour l'autre de ces prérogatives.

3.5. Où est le signe ? Quel est son rôle ?

Vygotsky énonce une règle générale : « dans la structure supérieure, ce qui est le tout déterminant fonctionnel ou le foyer de tout le processus, c'est le signe et son mode d'utilisation » (Vygotsky, 1931/2014, p. 246). Nous serons amenés à identifier le signe utilisé, mais aussi à discerner sa place tout au long du processus analysé. Quel signe est utilisé et à quelles fins ? Comment est-il émis ? Qui le reçoit ?

4. Le processus de genèse instrumentale et ses effets sur le jeu.

Nous devons procéder maintenant à la description la plus fine de l'enchaînement des phases qui sont liées à cette situation. Tout commence lorsque l'enseignant introduit l'artefact réglementaire et en expose le principe.

4.1. Instrumentation défensive : aller toucher le plot

L'enseignant propose un exercice sous la forme d'une situation de 2 contre 2, mais avec une règle différente qui stipule qu'après avoir attaqué (renvoyé le ballon chez l'adversaire), « on est mort ». Il est impossible de rejouer dans l'échange sans avoir « recouvré sa vie ».

Dans cette première phase d'instrumentation défensive, les étudiants doivent réaliser un travail de « prise en main » de cette nouvelle règle. Elle constitue tout d'abord une astreinte, un obstacle inédit. Ce caractère d'obstacle peut être objectivé par les observations récurrentes de joueurs qui oublient d'aller toucher un plot ou au contraire, qui vont toucher un plot alors qu'ils viennent de faire une passe à leur partenaire (et non un renvoi chez l'adversaire). Le pratiquant oublie parce qu'à ce moment de sa progression dans l'exercice, rien ne lui rappelle la nouvelle règle alors qu'il est engagé dans l'action. Il est d'ailleurs trop impliqué dans l'action pour s'ouvrir à autre chose. C'est alors que le caractère collectif de la tâche va participer du développement de chacun. En effet, les points de vue sont différents entre celui qui doit intervenir sur la balle et qui est « sous pression », et son partenaire qui constate qu'il reste le seul valide sur le terrain (puisqu'immédiatement, son partenaire « meurt »). C'est donc le partenaire qui va rappeler à l'ordre celui qui vient de renvoyer la balle chez l'adversaire en lui criant : « Va toucher ! » ou « Le plot ! ». La situation particulière du 2 contre (1+1) contribue à réveiller les solidarités endormies dans le jeu conventionnel du 2 contre 2. Il devient alors possible de surmonter l'obstacle. Le partenaire pense pour l'autre et l'avertit quand il prend conscience, au fil des échanges qui se succèdent, qu'il va se retrouver seul si son coéquipier ne va pas rapidement toucher le plot.

Regardons ce qui évolue dans cette phase : au début de l'exercice, pas un mot. Puis on entend petit à petit les joueurs interpeller leurs partenaires : « va toucher !» ou « le plot ! » L'alternance des rôles - celui qui intervient sur le ballon / le partenaire - est liée aux aléas du jeu. Elle permet aux protagonistes de comprendre au travers de la position du coéquipier ce qu'il doit faire lui-même quand il se retrouve à sa place. Comme le souligne Vygotsky, « c'est par l'intermédiaire des autres que nous devenons nous-mêmes » (Vygotsky, 1931/2014, p. 285).

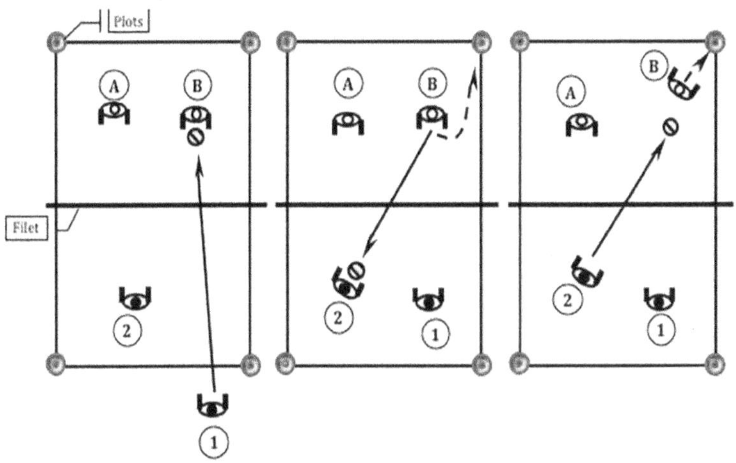

Figure 1 : Situation typique de jeu en 2 contre (1+1) au volley-ball
Les 3 terrains correspondent à 3 moments successifs du déroulement du même échange.
Terrain de gauche - le joueur **1** sert, le joueur **B** réceptionne.
Terrain du centre - **B** renvoie vers **2** et doit se retourner pour aller toucher le plot derrière lui.
Terrain de droite - **2** renvoie directement vers **B** qui doit aller toucher le plot. Fin de l'échange.

4.2. Instrumentation offensive : renvoyer directement sur l'adversaire mort

Peu à peu, les avertissements s'estompent. Les joueurs intériorisent qu'ils doivent aller toucher un plot. Mais les stéréotypes restent en place (collectif vs individualiste). Se pose alors la question de la résolution stratégique du problème. L'enseignant impulse la verbalisation de cette solution, mais certains étudiants la mettent déjà en place. La résolution stratégique du problème est verbalisée collectivement. On regroupe les participants et l'on pose la question : « comment faire pour être sûr de gagner l'échange ? » Il faut peu de temps pour que les étudiants élaborent la réponse : « On doit viser directement vers l'adversaire "mort" ». Mais le dire, ce n'est pas le faire. En effet, un tel objectif requiert de prendre en compte la trajectoire du ballon qui se dirige vers soi, de prendre l'information sur les adversaires et de renvoyer le ballon avec une certaine précision vers un point particulier du terrain.

Dans cette phase d'instrumentation, les étudiants doivent « prendre en main » un nouvel artefact, cognitif celui-là : la solution stratégico-tactique. Elle est applicable dans tous les cas ou presque. Il n'est plus nécessaire de se poser la question de savoir s'il faut faire une passe ou s'il faut renvoyer. Le renvoi direct est toujours la bonne solution parce qu'ici, il permet de prendre de vitesse les adversaires. Reste à s'en souvenir et à déterminer dans quelle direction le faire. Et pour cela, il faut cesser de joueur en aveugle.

<u>Regardons ce qui évolue dans cette phase</u> : dans un premier temps, les renvois directs augmentent, même si la direction semble secondaire. Puis, au fur et à mesure, la précision s'affine. D'abord le bon côté du terrain, celui de l'adversaire « mort ». Puis on cherche à le viser. C'est même un jeu très amusant que de lui faire tomber la balle sur le dos alors qu'il se baisse pour toucher le plot et qu'il est à deux doigts de recouvrer sa vie. La prise en main effective de l'artefact réglementaire peut s'observer concrètement sur les deux plans. Sur le plan défensif, par des allers-retours incessants vers les plots et sur le plan offensif, par une augmentation significative des renvois directs vers l'adversaire « mort ». La « pompe » de la situation est amorcée et les instrumentalisations défensives et offensives qui vont suivre ne nécessitent plus l'intervention de l'enseignant. Le nouveau stimulus n'est

donc que l'effet de causes enclenchées auparavant par l'artefact réglementaire (la nouvelle règle) et par l'artefact cognitif (la solution stratégico-tactique du problème).

4.3. Instrumentalisation défensive : compenser l'absence de son partenaire « mort »

Au fil des confrontations, les renvois sur le partenaire « mort » sont de plus en plus fréquents. Les pertes de points (pour l'équipe en défense) se reproduisent souvent dans les mêmes conditions. En effet, il faut pallier l'absence du partenaire parti toucher le plot. Les attaques systématisées des adversaires vers l'espace laissé provisoirement libre par le partenaire plongent le défenseur qui reste seul dans un dilemme.

- Soit, il reste de son côté et laisse un espace béant offert aux adversaires.
- Soit, il s'engage vers le milieu de son terrain pour tenter de protéger à la fois son côté et le côté abandonné par son partenaire.

Regardons ce qui évolue dans cette phase : c'est la seconde solution qui est petit à petit retenue par tous les étudiants. On assiste alors à une systématisation de cette couverture défensive, cette compensation qui nécessite pour le défenseur resté seul, un déplacement vers l'axe du terrain. Cette adaptation défensive nécessite simultanément, chez les attaquants, un renvoi de plus en plus précis, car la bande de terrain inaccessible au défenseur adverse se réduit drastiquement. Il est remarquable de signaler que l'intervenant éducatif n'a pas à solliciter cette compensation.

4.4. Instrumentalisation offensive : prendre l'information voire, jouer à contre-pied

Une fois encore, c'est à travers le collectif et notamment par l'intermédiaire des comportements défensifs que vont être sollicitées les adaptations offensives. Les étudiants sont placés devant un problème. Plus ils appliquent la consigne stratégico-tactique élaborée collectivement qui consiste à renvoyer sur l'adversaire « mort » et plus le ballon leur revient instantanément. C'est que dans le même temps, le défenseur adverse qui est resté seul a pris le parti de protéger le côté du terrain délaissé par son partenaire « mort ». Certains se positionnent directement sur la moitié délaissée par le coéquipier parti touché le plot. D'autres peuvent même aller au-delà de l'axe médian de leur camp. Cette couverture de l'espace laissé libre n'a qu'un objectif : anticiper l'attaque des adversaires et se placer idéalement sur la trajectoire du ballon destinée initialement à « achever » leur partenaire. Ainsi donc, la pertinence de la solution stratégico-tactique adoptée trouve ses limites. Le constat de cette perte de fiabilité est d'autant plus facile à faire que des deux côtés du terrain, on « compense » de la même manière. Il faut donc trouver une solution à cette nouvelle situation. Ici, c'est au second degré que l'artefact cognitif (la solution stratégico-tactique) continue de jouer son rôle. En effet, ce sont les comportements qu'il engendre (la compensation) et non plus l'artefact en tant que tel (le renvoi direct sur l'adversaire « mort ») qui nécessitent une nouvelle adaptation des protagonistes.

Regardons ce qui évolue dans cette phase : l'artefact cognitif, c'est-à-dire, le plan stratégico-tactique adopté collectivement est maintenant appliqué par tous quand cela est possible. Mais les joueurs sont pris de plus en plus fréquemment à leur propre piège puisque tout le monde connaît cette solution stratégico-tactique et peut donc l'anticiper, y compris lorsque c'est l'adversaire qui la met en œuvre. Ce constat conduit dans un premier temps à affiner les renvois. La meilleure solution consiste alors à « voir » quel est le côté où l'adversaire est parti toucher le plot et de renvoyer le ballon de ce côté et le plus près de la limite latérale du terrain adverse. L'augmentation des ballons qui tombent de ce côté ou juste en dehors du terrain est un bon révélateur de ces tentatives. Cependant, nous avons pu remarquer que chez certains étudiants singulièrement clairvoyants, une nouvelle solution voit le jour. Pour ceux-là, il s'agit de s'assurer que l'adversaire va bien réagir « normalement ». Ils s'emploient donc à le conforter dans son jugement initial, à savoir que c'est bien la solution du renvoi vers le partenaire « mort » qu'ils vont utiliser. Ces joueurs particulièrement futés vont s'employer à leurrer leurs adversaires. Tout dans leur comportement (déplacement, position du corps, position des mains, regard…) est fait pour conforter leur adversaire dans sa croyance initiale. Celui-ci doit rester persuadé que le renvoi tentera bien d'atteindre son partenaire « mort ». Un jeu de mime précède alors la touche de la balle puis, au dernier moment, le joueur qui agit sur le ballon change brusquement d'orientation et dévoile sa véritable intention en renvoyant le ballon à contre-pied du déplacement de son adversaire.

La boucle est bouclée : l'enseignant à la suite d'un détour qui peut paraître fastidieux a atteint ses fins. En changeant momentanément la règle du jeu, il a mis en place les conditions qui ont permis aux étudiants d'ouvrir les yeux, de regarder à travers le filet, de scruter au-delà de leur propre camp pour prendre en compte le jeu de leurs adversaires. L'artefact réglementaire a créé une véritable mise en scène de l'opposition en même temps qu'il a dessiné les voies d'une conception dialectique pour générer de tels apprentissages. Deleplace indique que « le processus recherché est de faire "découvrir" logiquement, dans l'opposition vécue, la relation au partenaire comme une conséquence de la relation à l'adversaire, la trame de fond du comportement adéquat pouvant s'énoncer dans l'alternative :

- ou bien je peux franchir moi-même une portion de l'obstacle (voire tout ce qui reste d'obstacle à franchir) et je dois le franchir, tout de suite, avec toute mon énergie et toute ma détermination.
- ou bien je ne peux pas, ou je ne peux plus, franchir moi-même l'obstacle adverse et je dois le faire franchir à un autre ou à certains autres de mes partenaires sans plus attendre, en mettant toute mon énergie et toute ma détermination à les y aider au maximum » (Deleplace, 1979, p. 101). Se pose maintenant la vraie question qui consiste à décider si le renvoi direct est possible ou s'il faut faire une passe à son partenaire. L'artefact réglementaire se comporte ici comme le démarreur du processus qui nécessite ensuite l'élaboration d'un artefact cognitif (la solution stratégico-tactique) dont la mise en application provoque à son tour des adaptations relativement autonomes (c'est-à-dire, sans qu'elles soient suscitées par l'intervenant éducatif). Cet artefact est construit sous la direction de l'intervenant éducatif. Mais comment les sujets intègrent-ils ses nouveautés ? Comment deviennent-ils capables de se sortir de leurs stéréotypes initiaux ? Le détour par le concept de signe peut nous procurer quelques explications.

5. Le signe selon Vygotsky

Pour percevoir ce qu'est le signe chez Vygotsky, il faut l'envisager comme faisant partie d'un système : celui de la signification. « Si l'activité fondamentale et la plus générale des grands hémisphères chez les animaux et chez l'homme est la signalisation, l'activité fondamentale et la plus générale de l'homme, qui le distingue en premier chef de l'animal du point de vue psychologique, c'est la signification, c'est-à-dire la création et l'utilisation de signes. […] La signification est la création et l'utilisation de signe, c'est-à-dire de signaux artificiels » (Vygotsky, 1931/2014, p.192). C'est donc pour Vygotsky, une spécificité des êtres humains que de disposer d'un processus par lequel il se signale leurs propres contraintes (à eux-mêmes comme aux autres) pour mieux s'émanciper des aléas de la vie. Sève souligne le mode de pensée dialectique mis en œuvre ici : « Ce qui fait de la démarche de Vygotsky une démarche dialectique n'est donc pas simplement son souci constant et universel de l'essence historique du psychisme humain, c'est de toujours s'attacher à comprendre cette histoire comme un tissu de contradictions et de la traiter comme telle » (Sève, 2018, p. 56). On ne peut donc faire l'économie de traiter ces contradictions si l'on veut comprendre le processus de développement mis en œuvre dans notre situation. Pour Vygotsky, tous les moyens artificiels introduits par l'homme dans les situations usuelles et qui remplissent la fonction de stimulation d'autrui ou d'autostimulation sont des signes. « Selon notre définition, est un signe tout stimulus conventionnel artificiellement créé par l'homme, qui est un moyen de maîtriser le comportement – celui d'autrui ou le sien propre » (Vygotsky, 2014, p. 190). Ainsi donc, et contrairement à l'animal, l'humain est en capacité de s'autostimuler, de s'auto-signaler, d'inventer ses propres moyens d'agir, mais aussi, d'agir sur les autres. « S'ils agissent comme les autres, ces stimuli proviennent d'une source entièrement différente. Ils ne sont plus donnés par la nature, mais produits par l'invention humaine, ce qui change tout : la stimulation se convertit en autostimulation […] » (Sève, 2008, p. 325).

Comment tirer parti de cette capacité humaine lorsque l'on est intervenant éducatif ?

Voilà le défi tout à fait passionnant que nous tentons de relever dans le cadre de nos enseignements des pratiques physiques sportives et artistiques.

C'est dans cette perspective que nous allons reprendre la situation de 2 contre (1 + 1) en nous attachant à repérer l'évolution des signes usités par l'enseignant ou les étudiants tout au long du processus de genèse instrumentale.

6. Métamorphose et migration des signes

L'ambition de se paragraphe est de suivre l'itinéraire des signes tout au long de l'évolution de la situation de (2 contre 1+1) en repérant qui les introduit, comment ils évoluent, qui les utilise et à quelles fins ? Tantôt, ces signes sont ostensibles, tantôt ils semblent invisibles. Cela est dû à la spécificité des fonctions psychologiques supérieures. Vygotsky propose une loi générale : « au cours du développement culturel de l'enfant toute fonction entre en scène deux fois, sur deux plans – une première fois sociale, ensuite psychologique, une première fois entre les individus à titre de catégorie interpsychologique, puis au dedans de l'enfant » (Vygotsky, 1931/2014, p. 547).

Un premier cheminement du signe de l'extérieur vers l'intérieur peut donc être repéré au travers de la fonction de signification. « Pour nous, dire d'un processus qu'il est extérieur revient à dire qu'il est social. Toute fonction psychologique supérieure a été extérieure - ce qui signifie qu'elle a été sociale ; avant d'être une fonction, elle a été une relation sociale entre deux personnes. Les moyens d'agir sur soi ont été initialement moyen d'agir sur les autres, et des autres sur la personne » (Vygotsky, 1929/2014, p. 545).

Un autre cheminement du signe peut aussi être suivi. C'est celui de sa transformation à l'intérieur. « Nous appelons la reconstruction interne d'une opération externe, internalisation » (Vygotsky, 1978, p. 56). Le travail qu'il faudrait mener consisterait à identifier les étapes du processus d'internalisation. « L'internalisation des formes de comportement culturel implique la reconstruction d'activité psychologique sur la base des opérations de signe » (Vygotsky, 1978, p. 57). En effet, comprendre le processus de développement dans son ensemble nécessite d'identifier chaque étape du processus, car « l'internalisation des activités socialement enracinées et historiquement développées est la caractéristique discriminante de la psychologie humaine, la base du saut qualitatif entre la psychologie animale et la psychologie humaine (Vygotsky, 1978, p. 57). Vygotsky fait référence à Janet dans cette analyse puisqu'il le cite ainsi dans la note 7 de « Histoire du développement des fonctions psychiques supérieures » (1931/2014, p. 280). « [...] toutes les lois psychologiques ont deux aspects : un aspect extérieur portant sur les autres hommes, un aspect intérieur portant sur nous », cette seconde forme, « postérieure à la première », consistant à s'« appliquer à soi-même » le comportement des autres entre eux ou envers nous-mêmes » (Janet, 1929, p. 521).

7. Différenciation signe – outil

Les activités médiatisées ont ceci de commun qu'elles empruntent des chemins détournés. C'est le cas pour le signe comme pour l'outil. Vygotsky attire notre attention sur l'importance de différencier outil et signe même si « l'analogie fondamentale entre le signe et l'outil repose sur la fonction de médiation qui caractérise chacun d'eux » (Vygotsky, 1978, p. 54). Pourtant, ces deux entités sont très différentes et les confondre nous condamne à ne pas comprendre les fonctions psychiques supérieures. Pour Vygotsky, « une différence essentielle entre signe et outil, base d'une divergence réelle entre les deux lignes, est constituée des différentes manières d'orienter le comportement humain. La fonction de l'outil est d'agir comme le conducteur de l'influence humaine sur l'objet de l'activité ; il est orienté vers l'extérieur ; il doit conduire à des changements dans les objets. C'est un moyen par lequel l'activité humaine externe vise à maîtriser et à triompher de la nature » (Vygotsky, 1978, p. 55). L'outil permet à l'humain de transformer le monde dans lequel il vit. Son utilisation conduit à l'observation de faits ostensibles qu'il permet de produire. « Le signe, en revanche, ne change rien dans l'objet de l'opération psychologique. C'est un moyen de l'activité interne visant à la maîtrise de soi ; le signe est orienté vers l'intérieur » (Vygotsky, 1978, p. 55). Le signe est dédié à notre propre contrôle. Le comportement humain auquel il conduit n'est que la conséquence d'une activité psychologique qui elle, n'est pas visible. Pour Vygotsky, « Ces activités sont si différentes les unes des autres que la nature des moyens qu'elles utilisent ne peuvent pas être les mêmes dans les deux cas » (Vygotsky, 1978,

p. 55). Il nous faut donc discerner, dans le processus de développement mis en œuvre dans le 2 contre (1+1), ce qui relève de l'outil et ce qui relève du signe. Où sont les signes ? Qu'est-ce qui les engendre ? Qui sont les utilisateurs du signe ? Comment sont-ils construits ? Comment s'imposent-ils ?

7.1. Lors de la phase d'instrumentation défensive de l'artefact réglementaire

Lorsque l'enseignant introduit l'artefact réglementaire, il l'utilise comme un outil didactique qui a pour ambition de changer l'univers dans lequel évoluent ses étudiants. Sa mission est de transformer les apprenants. Il va donc utiliser différents outils de développement. L'artefact réglementaire n'est donc pas un signe, mais un outil. Tout comme le maçon utilise une truelle, le menuisier un rabot, l'enseignant d'éducation physique utilise des situations d'apprentissage, c'est dire qu'il place ses apprenants dans un contexte qui a pour vocation de les inciter à agir différemment. Dans notre cas, il s'agit d'une situation d'opposition présentée sous la forme d'une fable et pour laquelle l'enseignant a procédé à quelques aménagements réglementaires. Notre artefact réglementaire est un outil qui va transformer la relation aux adversaires d'une part et la relation au partenaire d'autre part. C'est cette situation qui va provoquer l'apparition des signes que nous allons décrire.

Dans cette situation, il s'agit donc d'aller toucher un plot. Or, le fait d'aller toucher un plot est un signe pour les différents acteurs de la situation.

- Tout d'abord, pour le joueur qui vient d'attaquer et qui est « mort ». Toucher le plot est le signe qu'il peut revenir à la vie, revenir dans le jeu.
- C'est aussi un signe pour l'enseignant qui peut alors acter que les étudiants entrent dans la situation et commencent à « prendre en main » l'artefact réglementaire.

Mais, aller toucher le plot ne va pas de soi. Au tout début, la plupart des protagonistes oublient.

- Curieusement, sans que l'enseignant en fasse la demande, se produit un évènement notable. C'est le joueur qui va se retrouver seul à pouvoir jouer qui va faire signe à son partenaire d'aller toucher le plot en lui criant : « va toucher ! Va toucher ! » ou « Le plot, le plot ! ». C'est donc dans un premier temps le partenaire de l'attaquant « mort » qui lui rappelle qu'il doit aller toucher le plot. En effet, l'activité de l'attaquant « déborde » ses capacités de traitement. Il n'est pas en mesure d'assumer dans le même temps, son intervention sur le ballon et le respect de la nouvelle règle du jeu. Dans la note 17, Vygotsky (1931/2014, p. 546) relève à nouveau une citation de Pierre Janet : « Au début, le mot et l'acte étaient inséparables, le mot n'était que le début de l'action, le cri que le chef poussait en commençant un acte pour en rendre l'exécution plus facile. Mais déjà dans le commandement le mot s'est séparé de l'acte, puisque le mot existait chez l'un, le chef, et que l'acte existait chez un autre individu, chez celui qui obéissait » (Janet, 1926, p. 220). C'est la même situation que l'on retrouve ici où alternativement, les deux partenaires prennent le rôle du « chef ».
- Ce rôle de « chef » est redoublé ici du fait de la particularité des situations d'opposition sportives. Le manquement à la règle est une faute qui peut être signalée par le partenaire, mais aussi par les adversaires. Pour chacun des protagonistes, il s'agit donc petit à petit de vérifier que l'équipe adverse respecte bien la nouvelle règle. Il se peut que les quatre joueurs ne voient pas que l'un d'entre eux a oublié d'aller toucher le plot. Au début, il s'agit réellement d'un oubli de bonne foi. Ils n'en sont pas encore à tricher. Pour tricher, il faut maîtriser la règle, ce qui pourra apparaître plus tard. L'intervenant éducatif doit donc focaliser l'attention des pratiquants vers un arbitrage sans concession.
- En effet, ces carences d'arbitrage sont un signe pour l'enseignant qui les repère et qui constate que « la prise en main » de l'artefact réglementaire n'est pas encore achevée.

C'est plus tard que le repérage méthodique par les protagonistes de cet oubli (aller toucher le plot) se révélera être à son tour, un indicateur fiable.

– *A contrario*, le signalement systématique par les adversaires de ce manquement à la règle constitue le signe pour l'enseignant que la phase d'instrumentation relative à l'introduction de l'artefact réglementaire est en phase d'achèvement. C'est également le signe qu'il est temps d'introduire l'artefact cognitif lié à la résolution stratégico-tactique du problème posé par l'artefact réglementaire. On le voit donc ici, les signes se construisent collectivement et ont une vie avant d'être internalisés.

7.2. Lors de la phase d'instrumentation offensive de l'artefact cognitif

À partir du moment où l'enseignant constate une certaine systématisation du respect de la règle (il y a de moins en moins de manquements à la règle et ils sont systématiquement signalés par le partenaire ou par les adversaires), il va introduire l'artefact cognitif. Ici encore, cette situation de regroupement des pratiquants qui a pour fin d'énoncer une solution stratégico-tactique au problème est un outil. Il ne s'agit pas là d'une situation de jeu, mais d'une situation de réflexion collective. Cette situation est provoquée par l'enseignant qui invite les étudiants à procéder à l'analyse de la situation, à en débattre et à adopter la solution idoine, c'est-à-dire la solution stratégico-tactique qui consiste à renvoyer directement le ballon vers l'adversaire « mort ». Mais ce renvoi direct est encore difficile à exécuter. Il faut à nouveau, pour les étudiants, entrer dans une phase d'instrumentation du nouvel artefact. Au début, ils persistent dans leurs stéréotypes. Le plus souvent, on observe une passe vers le partenaire. Puis, sous l'impulsion des partenaires et de l'enseignant qui doit réguler sans relâche les phases de jeu qu'il observe, apparaissent timidement des renvois directs dans le camp adverse. On notera que l'intervenant éducatif joue un rôle déterminant dans l'activation du processus. C'est son opiniâtreté qui permet de maintenir les étudiants sous tension en rappelant sans cesse, *in situ*, que la solution est de renvoyer vers l'adversaire mort. Il produit le signe de ce que l'étudiant doit réaliser sous la forme d'une analyse qui fait suite à une situation de « flagrant délit ». Il s'agit alors de repérer les cas où le renvoi direct était facilement réalisable, de stopper le jeu (y compris durant l'échange) et de questionner le joueur concerné. Te rappelles-tu ce que tu viens de faire ? Est-ce que cela correspond à ce que tu aurais dû faire ? Qu'aurais-tu pu faire d'autre ? Bien souvent, il faut du temps à l'étudiant concerné pour se remémorer l'échange et pour prendre conscience de l'occasion manquée. Le témoignage des autres protagonistes est parfois utile. Ce rappel de l'échange constitue aussi un signe pour eux. Bien qu'au début de cette nouvelle phase, la précision ne soit pas toujours au rendez-vous, l'enseignant doit encourager ces tentatives en focalisant l'attention des joueurs sur la destination de leurs renvois. En conséquence, la nécessité de rendre adéquates la prise d'informations et la réalisation matérielle engage le pratiquant à développer non pas une seule forme gestuelle « canonique », mais une motricité qui s'adaptera à chaque nouvelle situation. Car renvoyer sur l'adversaire qui est resté en jeu est risqué. On s'expose à un retour aussi instantané que fatal. *A contrario*, renvoyer sur la bonne cible, c'est-à-dire l'adversaire « mort », est l'assurance d'un succès immédiat qui amène à une grande jubilation surtout si le ballon lui tombe dessus au moment où il touche le plot. C'est donc ici l'adversaire « mort » qui s'en va toucher le plot qui devient le stimulus permettant de maîtriser son comportement. Pourtant, contradictoirement, le signe le plus fort est certainement celui qui se matérialise dans l'adversaire qui renvoie le ballon. En effet, c'est parce que l'on se trompe de destinataire (l'adversaire « en vie » à la place de l'adversaire « mort ») que le ballon revient aussi vite qu'il est parti. Ici encore, un signe qu'un autre que soi peut transmettre (ici les opposants) et qui, dans ce cas précis, engage au fur et à mesure, à plus de précision. Encore un signe donné par l'adversaire qu'il ne faut pas sous-estimer. La jubilation des uns provoque la frustration des autres et ces différents sentiments renvoient le signe de ce qu'il faut faire et ne pas faire. Le jeu est prétexte à accorder aux signes le statut de véritable stimulus permettant de mobiliser des ressources insoupçonnées par le sujet lui-même, ressources qui le conduisent finalement à mettre en œuvre les moyens d'une action efficace. Les protagonistes sont pris dans le tourbillon des enjeux qui stimule leur imagination et au-delà, leur engagement dans l'action. « Le pouvoir d'agir est hétérogène. On peut dire qu'il augmente ou diminue en fonction de l'alternance fonctionnelle entre le sens et l'efficience de l'action où se joue le dynamisme de l'activité… » (Clot et Simonet, 2015, p. 40).

7.3. Lors de la phase d'instrumentalisation défensive : la compensation

Maintenant, la situation se développe de façon autonome, l'enseignant n'a pas à intervenir. L'absence du partenaire devient le signe que quelque chose de dangereux est susceptible de se produire et qu'un espace est à combler. La potentialité d'un retour du ballon dans la zone délaissée par le partenaire qui est parti toucher le plot pose un dilemme au joueur resté seul. Doit-il se contenter de protéger son côté du terrain en attendant le retour de son binôme ou doit-il protéger l'ensemble du terrain ? Ce dilemme se résout d'autant plus facilement que les velléités des adversaires s'affirment. Plus les retours directs du ballon dans la zone du partenaire sont fréquents et plus cette compensation « spontanée » se systématise. C'est une conjonction de signes qui fonctionne ici : d'une part, le retrait du partenaire (parti toucher le plot) ; d'autre part, la menace de plus en plus pressante d'un retour immédiat du ballon dans sa zone.

7.4. Lors de la phase d'instrumentalisation offensive : jouer à contre-pied

Comme pris dans un engrenage, les étudiants avancent dans la situation qui offre au fur et à mesure toutes ses potentialités. Dorénavant, les stéréotypes s'effacent au profit d'une nécessaire lecture de la situation. Plus les étudiants sont en capacité de renvoyer sur leur adversaire « mort » et plus la compensation « spontanée » s'automatise. C'est l'attaque du partenaire qui est maintenant le signe de la compensation. On constate même que certains anticipent radicalement le renvoi direct de leur adversaire en se positionnant en lieu et place de celui-ci. Ils espèrent ainsi surprendre leur adversaire, lui qui pourtant applique à la lettre la solution stratégico-tactique convenue. Car les choses ne peuvent en rester là. Ainsi, chez certains étudiants particulièrement clairvoyants, le constat de l'anticipation surprenante de l'adversaire devient le signe qu'il convient de jouer autrement. À leur tour, ils vont donner à voir à leur adversaire le signe de ce qu'ils attendent, à savoir, un déplacement, une orientation du corps, une fixation du regard qui engage à croire que c'est bien sur l'adversaire parti au plot qu'ils vont renvoyer le ballon. Tout dans leur comportement incite à protéger la zone momentanément délaissée. L'« anticipateur » est alors pris au piège. Gonflé de certitude, il se précipite dans l'espace provisoirement délaissé par son partenaire (parti toucher le plot) au point d'en être emporté par son élan. Le piège tendu peut se refermer. L'adversaire guette cette précipitation et soudain, au dernier moment, change son option de jeu pour renvoyer le ballon à l'opposé, c'est-à-dire dans la zone maintenant laissée libre par le « compensateur ». Ce type d'action est la plus belle preuve que les protagonistes du jeu ont laissé leur stéréotype au vestiaire et qu'ils jouent maintenant en regardant au-delà du filet. Dans cette dernière étape de la situation, c'est le mouvement de compensation du joueur resté seul qui devient le signe de la pertinence du contre-pied.

8. Apport de la théorie instrumentale

Le processus de développement que nous avons mis en œuvre dans notre expérimentation du 2 contre (1+1) peut s'expliquer au travers du prisme de la théorie instrumentale de Vygotsky. Cela requiert en premier lieu de faire la distinction entre outils et signes. Les deux outils mis en œuvre par l'intervenant éducatif sont l'artefact réglementaire (la règle spécifique de cette situation) et l'artefact cognitif (la résolution stratégique du problème posé par cette nouvelle règle). Les signes sont nombreux et ont différents destinataires : le partenaire, les adversaires, l'intervenant éducatif. Mais en quoi les signes et les outils ont-ils une fonction différente dans le processus de développement ? Vygotsky est très clair à ce propos dans sa thèse 13 de la méthode instrumentale en psychologie. « La différence essentielle de l'outil psychologique (le signe) avec l'outil technique réside dans l'orientation de son action vers le psychisme, vers le comportement, alors que l'outil technique, qui lui aussi s'insère comme moyen terme entre activité de l'homme et objet extérieur, est orienté vers l'obtention de tel ou tel changement dans l'objet même ; l'outil psychologique ne modifie en rien l'objet ; il est un moyen d'influence sur soi-même (ou sur autrui) - sur le psychisme, sur le comportement, et non pas un moyen d'action sur l'objet. Dans l'acte instrumental se manifeste par conséquent une activité en rapport non avec la chose, mais avec soi-même »

(Vygotsky, 1930/2014, p. 571). L'essence de la méthode instrumentale réside en la capacité des humains à s'autostimuler ou stimuler les autres en usant de signes. La conséquence d'une telle possibilité « est qu'en un même stimulus sont simultanément présents des stimuli de deux ordres, ceux à la fois de l'objet et de l'outil, donc chacun joue qualitativement et fonctionnellement un rôle différent » (Vygotsky, 1930/2014, p. 570). Le signe constitue donc le facteur déterminant de l'acte instrumental en ce qu'il devient une opération intellectuelle. Mais pour qu'un signe remplisse son rôle, il doit montrer sa capacité d'influence sur le psychisme et sur le comportement. À de nombreuses reprises, tout au long de ce texte, nous avons pointé les différents signes qui se succèdent dans la situation du 2 contre (1+1) : le plot, le signalement du partenaire « Va toucher ! Le plot ! », l'adversaire momentanément « mort » ; et pour l'enseignant, le repérage par les étudiants des oublis de leur adversaire, le renvoi systématique sur l'adversaire mort… Tous ces signes sont en capacité d'influencer le psychisme et par voie de conséquence, le comportement des protagonistes : se rappeler qu'il faut aller toucher le plot, savoir vers quelle partie du terrain renvoyer le ballon, savoir qu'il faut le renvoyer aussi vite que possible (en renvoi direct). « La méthode instrumentale est un mode d'investigation du comportement et de son développement qui s'appuie sur la mise au jour des outils psychologiques utilisés dans le comportement et de la structure des actes instrumentaux qu'ils engendrent » (Vygotsky, 1930/2014, p. 574). C'est à cet exercice que nous avons voulu participer dans le cadre de cette contribution.

Bibliographie

Clot, Y. & Simonet, P. (2015). Pouvoirs d'agir et marges de manœuvre. *Le travail humain* 2015/1, (Vol. 78).

Deleplace, R. (1979). *Rugby de mouvement rugby total.* Paris : Ed. EPS

Éloi, S. (2017). Genèse instrumentale et activité médiatisante : introduction d'un artefact réglementaire en volley-ball ? Dans S. Éloi et G. Uhlrich (s/d), *De l'usage des artefacts dans les métiers de l'intervention* (p.119-138). Toulouse : Octares

ÉLOI, S. & UHLRICH, G. (2011). La démarche technologique en STAPS : analyse conceptuelle et mise en perspective pour les sports collectifs. *eJRIEPS*, 23, 20-45.

ÉLOI, S. & UHLRICH, G. (2013). La mobilisation d'un artefact réglementaire dans le cadre de la formation d'étudiants en STAPS. Une illustration en volley-ball. *Recherche et formation*, 73, 73-88.

ÉLOI, S. & UHLRICH, G. (2014). Utilisation d'artefacts dans le domaine des pratiques physiques, sportives et artistiques (PPSA). *Transformation*, 12, 117-135.

FÉLIX, M-C. & VÉRILLON, P. (2017). Pilotage à distance de l'activité par les dispositifs : dilemmes professionnels, pouvoir d'agir et renormalisation du milieu de travail. Dans S. Éloi et G. Uhlrich (s/d), *De l'usage des artefacts dans les métiers de l'intervention* (p.139-149). Toulouse : Octares

JANET, P. (1926). *De l'angoisse à l'extase*, Alcan, Paris, Tome I.

JANET, P. (1929). *L'évolution psychologique de la personnalité*, Chanine, Paris.

PROT, B. (2017). Le plaisir du contre-pied - Deux interprétations de l'usage d'un artefact pour développer des gestes techniques. Dans S. Éloi et G. Uhlrich (s/d), *De l'usage des artefacts dans les métiers de l'intervention* (p.139-149). Toulouse : Octares

RABARDEL, P. (1995). *Les hommes et les technologies. Approche cognitive des instruments contemporains*. Paris : Armand Colin.

TROUCHE, L. (2005). Des artefacts aux instruments, une approche pour guider et intégrer les usages des outils de calcul dans l'enseignement des mathématiques ». Université d'été « *Le calcul sous toutes ses formes* », Saint-Flour, France

SÈVE, L. (2008). *Penser avec Marx aujourd'hui*. « L'Homme », tome 2. Paris : La Dispute.

SÈVE, L. (2018). Vygotsky : une démarche dialectique en psychologie. Dans J-Y. Rochex, C. Joigneaux et J. Netter (dir.) *Histoire, culture, développement : questions théoriques, recherches empiriques*, Actes du 6e séminaire international Vygotsky, pp. 51-65. Équipe CIRCEFT-ESCOL, Université Paris 8 Saint-Denis et CRTD - CNAM Paris.

TROUCHE, L. (2005). Des artefacts aux instruments, une approche pour guider et intégrer les usages des outils de calcul dans l'enseignement des mathématiques, Université d'été « *Le calcul sous toutes ses formes* », Saint-Flour, France.

VYGOTSKY, LS. (1978). *Mind in Society: The Development of Higher Psychological Processes*. Michael Cole et al., eds. Cambridge: Harvard University.

VYGOTSKY, LS. (1934/1997). *Pensée et langage*. Traduction de F. Sève. Paris : La dispute.

VYGOTSKY, LS. (1935/1997). Le problème de l'enseignement et du développement mental à l'âge scolaire. Dans B. Schneuwly & J-P Bronckart (Ed), *Vygotsky aujourd'hui*, pp. 95-117, Lausanne : Delachaux et Niestlé.

VYGOTSKY, LS. (2012). *Vygotsky, une théorie du développement et de l'éducation.* Recueil de textes et commentaires. Sous la direction de Frédéric Yvon et Yuri Zinchenko. Moscou MGU.

VYGOTSKY, LS. (1929/2014). Sur la conception historico- culturelle du psychisme humain. Dans F. Sève (Trad), M. Brossard et L. Sève (Ed) *Histoire du développement des fonctions psychiques supérieures*, pp. 543-564 Paris : La dispute.

VYGOTSKY, LS. (1930/2014). La méthode instrumentale en psychologie. Dans F. Sève (Trad), M. Brossard et L. Sève (Ed) *Histoire du développement des fonctions psychiques supérieures*, pp. 567-574 Paris : La dispute.

VYGOTSKY, LS. (1931/2014). *Histoire du développement des fonctions psychiques supérieures*. Traduction de F. Sève. Édition préparée par M. Brossard et L. Sève. Paris : La dispute.

3.

LES CONTRADICTIONS COMME FORCE MOTRICE DE LA ZONE PROXIMALE DE DÉVELOPPEMENT : APPRENTISSAGE, ENSEIGNEMENT ET DÉVELOPPEMENT DE L'ACTIVITÉ

Yannick LÉMONIE, France
CNAM, CRTD, (EA. 4132)

Introduction

Si le travail de Vygotsky a eu une influence importance dans le domaine de l'Éducation Physique (EP) à travers la création de curriculums ancrée dans des perspectives constructivistes (Rovegno & Dolly, 2006) ou dans le cadre de la promotion de démarches d'apprentissages coopératifs (Dyson & Casey, 2012), son travail théorique a pourtant reçu très peu d'attention empirique dans le champ de l'EP (Barker, Quennerstedt & Annerstedt, 2015). Peut-on y voir une difficulté à travailler avec Vygotsky dans le champ de l'EP?

Travailler avec et à partir de Vygotsky confronte le chercheur à une multitude d'obstacles s'il souhaite se saisir de la profondeur théorique des concepts. Parmi ces obstacles, Kozulin (2016) identifie trois problèmes majeurs associés à la publication et à la traduction des textes de Vygotsky. Le premier problème concerne le fait que Vygotsky n'a pas pu ou n'a pas souhaité publier de son vivant. Ainsi, il est impossible de savoir si la majorité du travail publié après sa mort l'a été dans la forme souhaitée par son auteur. Il est ainsi difficile pour celui qui souhaite travailler avec Vygotsky de démêler « qui a écrit Vygotsky et ce qu'a écrit réellement Vygotsky » (Yasnitsky & Van der Ver, 2016, p.73).

Ici découle un second problème lié à la diffusion du travail de Vygotsky : les traducteurs ont cherché à ajuster les textes de Vygotsky à ce qu'ils considèrent comme « *acceptable* » relativement à l'audience envisagée pour ces textes. Bien souvent dans ce cadre, les éditeurs ont cherché à adapter le texte de manière à le faire rentrer dans des cadres préexistants (cognitivistes ou socio-constructivistes) que Vygotsky lui-même aurait rejetés (Jornet, 2018 ; Setstensko, 2008). Ainsi, il est sans doute possible d'affirmer que le travail de Vygotsky ne peut pleinement exprimer tout son potentiel sans une compréhension élargie du contexte ontologique/épistémologique qui a donné naissance aux concepts largement diffusés dans la littérature (médiation, zone proximale de développement).

Le troisième problème plus profond se réfère aux difficultés liées à la traduction des textes. Cole (2009), éditeur de la version anglaise de « *Mind in Society* » évoque ainsi la simplification du terme russe *Obuchenie*. La traduction de l'essai publié en 1935, après la mort de Vygotsky intitulée « Enseignement/apprentissage (obuchenie) et développement chez l'enfant d'âge scolaire » a-t-il été traduit par « Interaction entre apprentissage et développement » dans le chapitre 6 de *Mind in Society*. Or, en langue russe, le terme *Obuchenie* se réfère à un processus à deux faces : une face tournée vers l'apprentissage, et un autre tourné vers l'organisation de l'environnement par l'adulte. Plus adéquatement, le terme *Obuchénie* se réfère à un processus complexe d'enseignement-apprentissage. Schneuwly (1995) précise d'ailleurs que cette simplification du terme *Obuchénie* par celui d'apprentissage se retrouve dans les éditions françaises, allemandes, espagnoles et anglaises. De cette simplification dans la traduction, résultent des implications profondes dans la manière d'appréhender et de travailler avec Vygotsky. Comme le note Cole, si la position de Vygotsky relativement aux liens entre apprentissage et développement est connue et s'oppose tant aux conceptions de Thorndike et de Piaget : « Notre concept de développement implique le rejet de l'opinion souvent répandue selon laquelle le développement cognitif résulte de l'accumulation progressive de changements distincts. Nous croyons que le développement de l'enfant est un processus complexe caractérisé par la périodicité, l'inégalité dans le développement des différentes fonctions, la métamorphose ou la transformation qualitative d'une forme en une autre, l'entrelacement des facteurs externes et internes et les processus adaptatifs qui permettent de surmonter les obstacles que l'enfant rencontre» (Vygotsky, 1978, p. 73).

Il reste que la relation entre apprentissage, développement et enseignement reste largement inexpliquée. Comme le note Cole (2009, p.294), «Ce qui reste inexpliqué dans cette définition explicite du développement, c'est la nature des relations complexes entre l'enseignement, l'apprentissage et le développement qui ont lieu dans le contexte de l'éducation formelle» (Cole, 2009, p. 294).

À rebours d'une acception usuelle du concept de Zone Proximale de Développement (ZDP), nous chercherons dans cette contribution à réintégrer l'enseignement dans l'analyse des apprentissages et du développement dans les pratiques d'EP. En nous appuyant sur des résultats issus d'une recherche sur l'enseignement-apprentissage de la danse en éducation physique, nous montrerons que les apprentissages et le développement de l'activité des danseurs s'appuient sur les contradictions entre l'activité d'enseignement et l'activité d'apprentissage. Engagés nous-mêmes dans des recherches visant à améliorer ou transformer les activités d'enseignement, nous discuterons alors de la nécessité d'analyser les contradictions inévitables entre activité d'enseignement et activité d'apprentissage de manière à concevoir une zone proximale de développement pour les enseignants.

Nous chercherons ainsi à répondre à trois questions dans cette contribution :

- Comment mobiliser le concept de ZDP pour investiguer les apprentissages en EP?
- Quelles évidences pour argumenter que ce sont les contradictions entre activité d'enseignement et activité d'apprentissage qui sont le moteur des apprentissages et du développement de l'activité des danseurs en EP?
- Comment pouvons-nous étendre le concept de ZDP pour stimuler le développement professionnel des enseignants qui collaborent avec nous dans le cadre de nos recherches?

Pour répondre à ces questions, nous nous appuierons sur une étude menée en EP sur une unité d'enseignement de la danse. Ces données proviennent d'un projet plus large qui cherchait à rendre compte de l'usage par les enseignants des prescriptions officielles à un moment de réécriture des programmes nationaux d'EP pour le collège. L'enseignant possède une expérience de 10 années dans l'enseignement de l'éducation physique, mais il enseigne la danse pour la première fois de sa carrière au cours de notre étude. Trois élèves ont été choisis pour participer à des autoconfrontations selon une procédure mobilisant deux critères :

- l'accord explicite des élèves à participer à l'étude et à des entretiens avec les chercheurs ;
- leur pratique extra-curriculaire d'une pratique physique artistique.

Dans les extraits présentés, nous nous centrerons sur un groupe d'élèves composé de deux élèves n'ayant pas de pratiques artistiques en dehors de l'école et de deux élèves pratiquant de manière intensive à l'extérieure de l'école : Mathilde qui pratique la danse et Lucie qui pratique le patinage artistique.

1. Le concept de Zone Proximale de Développement et son usage pour investiguer l'apprentissage en EP

1.1 Trois dimensions du concept de ZDP

Dans les recherches en EP, le concept de ZDP est très largement utilisé pour argumenter les démarches d'enseignement qui valorisent la coopération entre des élèves de niveaux différents (D'arripe-Longueville & al., 2002). Plus largement, dans les recherches en éducation, le concept de ZDP a été mobilisé dans « toute situation dans laquelle, tout en participant à une activité, des personnes sont en train d'acquérir la maîtrise d'une pratique ou de comprendre un sujet » (Wells, 1999, p. 333).

Nous voudrions dans ce qui suit situer trois dimensions du concept de ZDP.

1.1.1 La ZDP est une émergence

Assez communément, la définition qui sert de référence à de tels travaux est la suivante : « La distance entre le niveau de développement réel déterminé par la résolution indépendante de problèmes et le niveau de développement potentiel déterminé par la résolution de problèmes sous la direction ou en collaboration avec des pairs plus compétents. » (Vygotsky, 1978, p.86).

De manière complémentaire, il est possible d'ajouter que « avec la collaboration, la direction ou toute autre forme d'aide, l'enfant est toujours capable d'en faire plus et de résoudre des tâches plus difficiles qu'il ne peut accomplir seul. » (Vygotsky, 1987, p. 209).

Cette définition semble du point de vue de Roth & Radford (2010) avoir orienté une lecture très simplifiée du concept dans la mesure où l'interprétation qui en a été faite par les auteurs tend à opposer des individualités. L'une de ces individualités est l'enseignant ou un élève plus capable, l'autre étant l'élève en train d'apprendre. Selon Roth et Radford (2010), cette interprétation oriente sur une lecture substantialiste de l'apprentissage vue comme assimilation de connaissances, et sur le collectif conçu comme ensemble d'individus interagissant sans problèmes. Pour Barker, Quennestedt & Annestedt (2015), suivant Roth & Radford (2010), il est improductif de penser la ZDP en termes de position fixe. Au contraire, la ZDP émerge de l'interaction entre des participants qui deviennent à la fois enseignants et apprenants. Autrement dit, il est illusoire de penser que la mise en situation d'élèves présentant une asymétrie de connaissances garantit l'émergence d'une ZDP : « Les apprenants tentent, mais n'y parviennent pas, de créer une communication collective et donc une ZPD. Le novice dans la situation ne parvient pas à exprimer ce qu'il doit apprendre ou comment il doit apprendre et ne devient donc pas un expert en ce qui concerne son propre apprentissage » (Barker, Quennerstedt, & Annerstedt, 2015)

1.1.2 L'imitation un concept central pour comprendre la ZDP

Pour avancer davantage dans le concept de ZDP, il est nécessaire de revenir au concept d'imitation sur la base duquel Vygotsky **élabore celui de ZDP** (Chaiklin, 2003). L'imitation n'est pas conçue chez Vygotsky comme une copie des actions. Au contraire, Vygotsky, donne une autre signification à l'imitation qui implique pour lui la compréhension des relations structurelles du problème à résoudre. Vygotsky utilise le terme d'imitation en se référant aux situations dans lesquelles un enfant est capable de s'engager dans une interaction avec un autre plus compétent pour une tâche qu'il ne serait pas capable d'accomplir seul. L'exemple qu'il donne de l'apprentissage des échecs est éclairant : « Si je ne suis pas capable de jouer aux échecs, je ne pourrai pas jouer un match même si un maître me montre comment. Si je connais l'arithmétique, mais que je rencontre des difficultés avec la solution d'un problème complexe, une démonstration conduira immédiatement à ma propre résolution du problème. D'autre part, si je ne connais pas les mathématiques supérieures, une démonstration de la résolution d'une équation différentielle ne fera pas avancer ma propre pensée dans cette direction par un seul pas. Pour imiter, il doit y avoir une possibilité de passer de ce que je peux faire à ce que je ne peux pas faire» (Vygotsky, 1934/1987, p. 209).

En d'autres termes, il n'est possible d'imiter que dans la mesure où l'imitation s'accompagne d'une compréhension. Pour Chaiklin (2003), l'imitation est rendue possible (a) dans la mesure où les fonctions psychologiques sont encore insuffisantes pour soutenir une performance individuelle ; (b) sont suffisamment développées pour que ; (c) que l'élève soit en mesure de savoir comment utiliser les actions collaboratives d'un pair plus expérimenté. En cela, le concept d'imitation est central pour comprendre celui de ZDP.

1.1.3 Une ou deux ZDP?

Reprenant l'exemple célèbre de Vygotsky de l'enfant qui dessine, Clot (2008) propose de distinguer deux zones potentielles de développement. Rappelons cet exemple de Vygotsky: le chercheur propose à un enfant de dessiner. Au bout d'un certain temps, cette activité de l'élève montre des signes de saturation. Le chercheur demande alors à cet enfant de montrer à un camarade comment dessiner. L'enfant reprend alors le dessin avec un intérêt renouvelé. Le sens de l'activité a changé et a été relancé par le chercheur. Dessiner consiste d'abord à produire une œuvre, elle acquiert ensuite un statut instrumental dans la démonstration à un pair. En s'appuyant sur la distinction réalisée par Leontiev (1978) entre activité, action et opération, Clot souligne combien le sens, c'est-à-dire le rapport des buts des actions au motif de l'activité évolue. Clot, (1999, p.173) soutient « la thèse d'une dynamique de l'action soumise à deux exigences psychologiques différentes : le sens et l'efficience. Chacune de ces tensions psychiques se résout en traversant des zones de développement potentiel distinctes, même si elles ont en commun d'étayer d'un sujet par l'activité d'un autre ou de plusieurs autres ». Allant plus loin, il ne peut y avoir pour Clot de développement de nouveaux motifs sans développement des moyens d'action et inversement.

Nous retiendrons de cette relecture de Vygotsky au prisme des travaux de Leontiev (1978) et de Clot (1999) qu'il n'existerait pas une, mais deux zones potentielles de développement et que le développement de l'activité s'inscrit dans l'alternance d'un développement du sens et d'un développement de l'efficience.

1.2 ZDP, Imitation, développement du sens dans l'activité des élèves au sein d'un cycle de danse

1.2.1 L'organisation du cycle de danse

Restituons tout d'abord l'organisation générale des leçons telles qu'elles sont mises en œuvre par l'enseignant. Lors des leçons n° 1 et n° 2 du cycle, l'enseignant a mobilisé des photos issues d'univers différents de la danse en demandant de choisir trois photos pour créer une chorégraphie collective sur la base des postures identifiées. Lors des leçons n° 3 et n° 4, il propose de partir de gestes sportifs relevant de l'expérience personnelle des élèves (dans leur pratique extrascolaire ou dans le cadre de leur pratique en EP) de manière à pouvoir composer une seconde phrase dansée qui sera introduite dans la chorégraphie finale à réaliser par les élèves.

1.2.2 L'imitation au cœur des apprentissages des élèves

Durant le cycle danse, les élèves ont eu le choix de constituer leur groupe. Les deux élèves pratiquant une activité artistique en dehors de l'école (Mathilde et Lucie) se sont mises ensemble et ont constitué leur groupe avec deux élèves filles non spécialistes. Cette hétérogénéité leur permet de choisir des mouvements pour la production de la chorégraphie collective finale. Les deux élèves plus expertes choisissent les éléments à incorporer dans la chorégraphie finale au regard de deux buts contradictoires :

- choisir un mouvement qui exprime un certain degré de maîtrise technique de manière à démontrer leur expertise devant la classe en fin de cycle ;
- adapter lc degré de difficulté des mouvements choisis aux capacités des élèves les plus en difficulté du groupe :

> Mathilde : Je choisis les images (support de la tâche de l'enseignant en leçon 3) de manière à ce que ça colle bien avec la chorégraphie que nous voulons faire à la fin du cycle.
> Mathilde : Je choisis les images pour pouvoir les adapter le niveau de difficulté au groupe. Par exemple, on n'a pas choisi d'aller au sol parce que c'est trop difficile pour nous de se relever d'une manière esthétique.

Après avoir choisi les mouvements, le groupe répète face au miroir de la salle de danse, outil qu'elles sont les seules à utiliser. L'enseignant n'y a pas fait référence durant l'ensemble du cycle. Pourtant, c'est un outil qui leur permet de produire collectivement la chorégraphie en ajustant collectivement le niveau de difficulté. Au cours du cycle, les élèves collaborent et mobilisent un processus d'imitation pour apprendre. C'est l'observation de leur production dans le miroir qui renseigne les élèves les plus expertes sur la pertinence du choix des mouvements dansés, autant que sur les conseils nécessaires à ce que les élèves moins expertes s'approprient les mouvements.

1.2.3 Un développement du sens dans l'activité des danseuses

Lors de la leçon 3, un épisode interpelle les chercheurs engagés dans la recherche. Lorsque l'enseignant demande aux élèves de choisir parmi des gestes sportifs pour composer une séquence dansée, Mathilde et Lucie interpellent l'enseignant :

L'enseignant revient vers le groupe et mime une manchette. Les filles font la moue.
Mathilde : « Mais la danse c'est un sport comme un autre ! »
Enseignant : Mais oui si tu veux c'est qu'on va partir d'autre chose que de la danse pour venir vers la danse, mais bien entendu la danse c'est un sport »
Mathilde : Mais donc on doit prendre autre chose
Enseignant : Bien oui parce que l'idée c'est d'utiliser tout ce qu'on sait faire. Par exemple c'est quoi ça (mime un shoot au basket)
Lucie : Basket.
Enseignant : (mime une manchette)
Lucie : Volley
Enseignant : Donc vous voyez, des choses simples. Moi je montre ça parce que c'est ma culture, mais après vous pouvez choisir autre chose.

L'enseignant s'éloigne et revient parce que l'élève E2 l'appelle.

Lucie : On peut prendre du patinage monsieur ?
Enseignant : Ben pourquoi pas. Patinage de vitesse où je ne sais pas quoi ? Tu vois pour marquer la position. Mais vous pouvez bien sûr.

Rappelons-le, Lucie est l'élève qui pratique le patinage artistique. Lorsque l'enseignant lui répond sur cet épisode, il évoque (de manière non--consciente dira-t-il lors de l'entretien d'autoconfrontation) le patinage de vitesse qui est une pratique sportive et non une pratique artistique. Quelle différence entre ces deux formes de pratiques ? Qu'est-ce qui permet de différencier un mouvement sportif d'un mouvement dansé ? Quand s'effectue le passage ? Ces questions sont délicates. Elles font l'objet de débat encore à l'heure actuelle dans le milieu de la danse (Guarino, 2015). Cette controverse, autant que la négociation qu'entament les élèves avec les règles formulées par l'enseignant montre à l'évidence que la tâche ne fait pas sens au regard de l'objet de l'activité des élèves. Quel est-il ?

L'objet de l'activité des élèves consiste à démontrer leur compétence face aux autres élèves de la classe. La pratique de la dance n'est pas anodine de ce point de vue. Elle engage les élèves dans une mise en scène d'eux--mêmes face au groupe classe. C'est d'ailleurs certainement plus le cas en danse qu'en gymnastique où les mouvements sont codifiés. En ce sens, la question de la qualité de leur mouvement apparaît comme quelque chose d'essentiel pour ces élèves. En ce sens, le challenge d'inventer une chorégraphie à partir des images ou de gestes apparaît sans doute trop difficile dans le laps de temps dédié au cycle (7 leçons de 1h). À cet égard, choisir une chorégraphie à démontrer devant la classe et l'adapter aux exigences demandées par l'enseignant apparaît moins difficile.

Lucie : Inventer une chorégraphie complète est trop difficile en si peu de temps. C'est pour ça que j'ai choisi d'apprendre la chorégraphie de Beyoncé sur YouTube au début du cycle.
Lucie : Je choisis les mouvements de manière à faire une chorégraphie que j'aime.

Par ailleurs, si les outils fournis par l'enseignant (fiches avec des verbes d'action pour les déplacements)

Mathilde : Après nous bougeons dans un petit espace, mais pas trop.
Chercheur : C'est un critère pour toi ?
Mathilde : Oui, parce que dans la dance que je fais en dehors de la classe nous utilisons beaucoup l'espace de la scène. C'est un critère important dans la danse de salon.
Chercheur : Mais la chorégraphie de Beyoncé se fait face à une caméra non ? Il n'y a pas trop d'utilisation de la scène.
Mathilde : Oui, c'est pourquoi nous ne bougeons pas trop.

Au travers de cette analyse, il ressort que si la question de la qualité du mouvement ou le message porté par la chorégraphie est évacué des propositions de l'enseignant, c'est paradoxalement l'activité des élèves qui font resurgir ces dimensions essentielles. Un autre élément intéressant c'est que l'objet de l'activité déployée par le groupe s'inscrit dans un horizon temporel plus large que celui de la leçon : les apprentissages ne prennent sens que dans la perspective de démontrer leurs compétences dans une chorégraphie empruntée en partie à Beyoncé et connue de leurs camarades de classe. Conséquemment, il est possible de dire que les élèves apprennent malgré la tâche proposée par l'enseignant et non avec. L'efficacité de leurs actions ne peut se juger qu'à l'aune de l'objet poursuivi. Pour paraphraser Clot (2008), l'efficacité n'est pas seulement l'atteinte de buts poursuivis, fixés par l'enseignant (réaliser une séquence dansée avec des gestes empruntés aux pratiques sportives), c'est la découverte par ces élèves de buts nouveaux (intégrer ces éléments à une chorégraphie envisagée au début du cycle). Il s'agit pour les élèves d'aller au-delà de ce que demande les enseignants pour réaliser ce motif, mais également que leur production puisse être en phase avec ce qu'elle envisage comme critères de qualité d'une chorégraphie reconnue par leurs camarades.

> **Lucie :** L'enseignant souhaite que nous choisissions des gestes simples, mais nous souhaitons choisir des gestes plus « techniques » (dans le sens de, plus difficile à réaliser)
> **Mathilde :** Nous avons choisi la chorégraphie de Beyoncé parce que c'est certain que tout le monde la connaît.

C'est finalement ce qu'on appelle dans le langage courant, le souci et la réalisation du travail bien fait, celui dans lequel on peut se reconnaître individuellement et collectivement. Allons plus loin : c'est parce qu'elles arrivent à faire avec ce que leur demande l'enseignant que se joue l'alternance fonctionnelle entre sens et efficience de leurs actions. On le voit, loin d'empêcher la réalisation de leur dessein, c'est parce qu'elles s'arrangent avec la tâche que la répétition nécessaire à l'automatisation de leurs gestes prend sens. Se joue donc bien ici l'alternance fonctionnelle entre sens et efficience décrite par Clot (1995).

Comme le notent Griffin & Cole (1984, p. 62) «*La sagesse adulte ne fournit pas de téléologie pour le développement de l'enfant. L'organisation sociale et les activités dirigeantes créent un fossé au sein de l'enfant qui peut développer une nouvelle analyse créative... Une zone proche du développement est un dialogue entre l'enfant et son avenir ; ce n'est pas un dialogue entre l'enfant et le passé d'un adulte.*». En ce sens, la ZDP ouvre inévitablement sur un processus créatif. À l'opposé donc d'une conception traditionnelle de la ZDP qui oriente vers une conceptualisation d'une zone de transmission de connaissances d'un sujet plus expérimenté vers un autre, les résultats tendent à montrer que ce qui s'apprend n'est pas de l'ordre du connu, du déjà-là. Il ne s'agit pas pour les élèves de reproduire la chorégraphie de Beyoncé, mais au contraire d'incorporer ce que leur demande de faire l'enseignant dans ce qu'elle souhaite faire de la chorégraphie de Beyoncé.

1.2.4 Une première modélisation de la ZDP ouverte par les élèves

À ce stade de l'analyse, il est possible de modéliser la zone proximale de développement

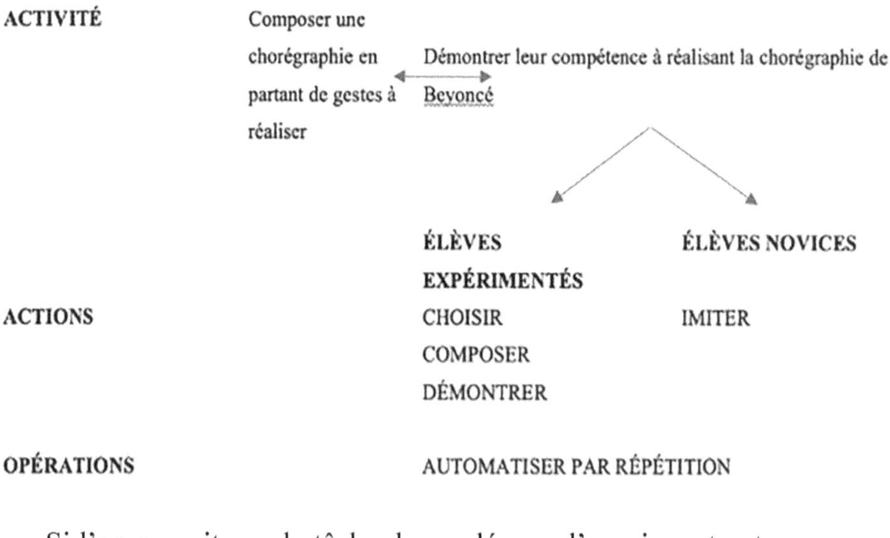

Si l'on perçoit que la tâche demandée par l'enseignant entre en conflit avec le motif de l'activité des élèves, il est nécessaire de poursuivre

l'analyse pour identifier les contradictions entre activité d'enseignement et activité d'apprentissage des élèves. C'est sous ce prisme que nous pourrons répondre à la question des relations entre enseignement, apprentissage et développement.

2. Les contradictions entre activité d'enseignement et activité d'apprentissage comme moteur de la ZDP

Dans les développements qui suivent, nous réintégrons l'activité de l'enseignant dans l'analyse de manière à identifier les contradictions entre activité d'enseignement et activité d'apprentissage.

2.1 L'activité de l'enseignant

Le fait de permettre à tous les élèves de réaliser une chorégraphie collective organise l'enseignant, à la fois dans l'accompagnement qu'il fait des élèves comme au niveau de la constitution des groupes.

Chercheur : *Sur la base de quels principes tu élabores tes groupes ?*
Enseignant : Un : pas de mixité. Ce n'est pas ce qui me soucie le plus sur ce niveau 1. Sur un niveau 2 oui, j'insisterai davantage là-dessus. Sur le premier niveau, c'est plus sur ce que j'avais pu voir de leur capacité d'expression, de reproduction, j'essaye de mélanger un peu les niveaux, tout en gardant un niveau affectif un petit peu optimal pour qu'ils se sentent à l'aise.
Chercheur : *Pourquoi tu mélanges les niveaux ?*
Enseignant : Pour permettre d'avoir un meilleur rendu collectif. C'est intéressant d'avoir deux élèves dans un groupe de 4 qui vont peut-être un peu plus mener les autres et les amener à se développer. Donc ça, c'est un des premiers points.
Chercheur : *Et du coup et ce qu'il va y avoir forcement de la coopération ?*
Enseignant : Non pas forcement. Parce qu'il va y avoir le corps vu par les autres, ce n'est pas simple, c'est pour ça que je...

Chercheur : Parce que là, si on regarde ces programmes, on voit « *participe activement à l'élaboration* » (dans les programmes de 2008), on pourrait dire sauf si je me trompe que tu mets en coopération les élèves pour qu'il y ait un rendu correct de la prestation
Enseignant : Oui
Chercheur : Mais elle ne détermine pas forcement le fait que les élèves participent activement, tous au sein du groupe à l'élaboration. C'est-à-dire qu'on peut penser que s'il y a des niveaux qui sont différents, ceux qui vont être plus à l'aise vont davantage élaborer pour les autres.
Enseignant : Tout à fait, c'est d'ailleurs ce qui se passe un petit peu.

Ici, on le voit, l'enseignant est particulièrement lucide sur le fait que sa détermination des groupes va entraver la participation active de tous les élèves du groupe à une élaboration collective destinée à être vue et jugée par l'ensemble du groupe. Pourtant, ce ne sont pas les attendus du cycle, mais bel et bien la compétence définie dans le programme, à savoir la *production* d'un projet artistique, qui détermine son enseignement. La question de l'appropriation par les élèves des éléments simples de composition et d'interprétation est de fait pensé comme ressource au service de la production des élèves. Autrement dit, elle est davantage pensée comme un moyen au service de cette production attendue que comme une acquisition qui implique que les élèves apprennent à mettre en relation avec les émotions ou les effets qu'ils veulent produire sur le spectateur. Dès lors, l'enseignant fournit aux élèves via des supports écrits la multiplicité des procédés leur permettant de créer une prestation certes originale, mais qui ne s'inscrit pas de fait dans le cadre d'un *projet artistique*, c'est-à-dire porteur d'un message à transmettre. En situation d'observation, nous avons été frappés par la faible utilisation de ces fiches par les élèves (un seul groupe de quatre élèves a consulté les fiches en 4 leçons !).

Par ailleurs, la question de l'expression, de la qualité du mouvement ne rentre pas directement en ligne de compte du fait de la complexité qu'elle introduit dans l'enseignement. Dès lors, l'objet de l'enseignant consiste à répondre aux attentes du programme à travers la compétence attendue ou la compétence visée sans s'interroger sur le sens artistique qui relève pour l'enseignant d'un niveau d'exigence plus élevé:

Enseignant : Oui, mais moi je leur ai proposé (des solutions) pour les élèves qui étaient en difficulté, qui ne savait pas comment on se déplaçait, je leur ai proposé des verbes pour se déplacer. D'autres, je n'ai pas besoin. Mais j'ai, j'aurai très bien pu pour voir ce qu'ils allaient faire ne rien leur dire. Ce n'est pas de la créativité totale, mais entre une pause 1 et une pause 2 il faut qu'ils se débrouillent du coup, **il faut qu'ils soient créatif**s, mais pour moi ce n'était pas forcement le but. **Moi, le but c'était surtout qu'ils comprennent et c'est le but pour ce premier niveau, c'est que danser ça peut être tout**. Tu vois on part de photos, c'est-à-dire de reproduction, on part de gestes sportifs et qu'à partir du moment où on a un projet ensemble de déplacement esthétique, en vue d'être montré à d'autre et qu'il y a une expression de leur sentiment, de leur sensibilité, c'est de la danse et **qu'il n'y a pas de terme technique à mettre derrière la danse**.
Chercheur : D'accord, mais la question de la qualité du mouvement, de l'expression du message
Enseignant : Ce n'est pas mon but à ce premier niveau.

Dans cet extrait, deux aspects ressortent plus particulièrement :

- la difficulté à identifier ce qui relève légitimement d'un mouvement dansé qui est évacué de la réflexion un peu plus loin dans l'entretien par un but qu'il se donne : «je veux leur faire comprendre que tout mouvement destiné à être montré est de la danse» ;
- les injonctions contradictoires (il faut qu'ils [les élèves] soient créatifs) qui montrent bien que l'objet de l'activité d'apprentissage à construire n'est pas réellement identifié.

Dans ce cadre, il existe bel et bien une contradiction entre l'objet de l'activité de l'enseignant qui est de permettre aux élèves de réaliser une chorégraphie collective pour répondre aux exigences des programmes et l'objet de l'activité d'apprentissage des élèves qui est de réaliser une chorégraphie de qualité pour démontrer leurs compétences vis-vis de leurs camarades de classe.

2.2 Modélisation des contradictions entre activités d'enseignement et activité d'apprentissage

En appui sur la modélisation des systèmes d'activité proposée par Engeström (2001), nous nous proposons ici de modéliser les contradictions entre les systèmes d'activité d'enseignement et d'apprentissage (figure 2).

Deux types de contradictions apparaissent :

- une contradiction interne au système d'activité entre l'objet de l'activité : que les élèves élaborent une chorégraphie originale et le fait de fournir des solutions toutes faites pour les élèves en difficulté ;
- une contradiction d'objet entre les élèves et l'enseignant.

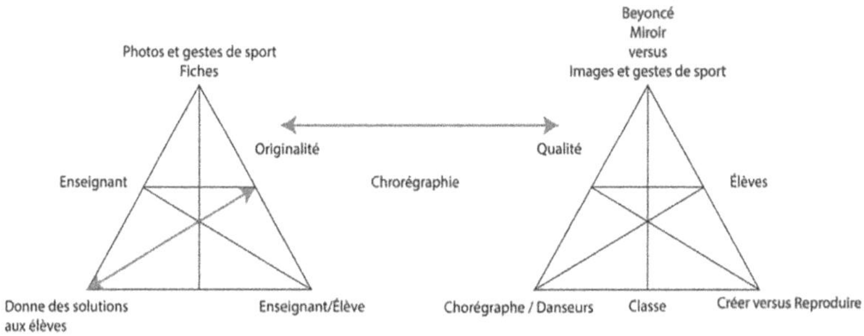

Figure 1 *: Les contradictions entre activité d'enseignement et activité d'apprentissage*

3. Extension du concept de ZDP au sein de recherches collaboratives développementales

Quelle leçon tirer de cette étude de cas pour des recherches visant à transformer l'activité des professionnels qui participent à ces recherches ?

Nous avons vu que la ZDP émerge chez les élèves du fait d'un conflit entre ce qu'elles souhaitent faire et ce que l'enseignant leur demande de faire. Ce conflit est perçu de manière consciente par les élèves. Ce conflit émerge dans l'épisode où les élèves négocient les règles de la tâche formulée par l'enseignant. Pourtant, l'enseignant ne perçoit pas du tout la contradiction entre son activité et celle poursuivie par les élèves.

Ici, il y a lieu de bien distinguer contradictions, dilemmes et conflits (Engeström & Sannino, 2011). Dans le cadre de la théorie historico-culturelle de l'activité, les conflits ou les dilemmes sont considérés comme les manifestations des contradictions sous-jacentes. Les conflits sont considérés comme des formes de résistance, de désagrément ou de critique. Pour De Dreu & Van de Vliert (1997, p. 1), « *il y a conflit lorsqu'une personne ou un groupe se sent lésé par une autre personne ou un autre groupe, par exemple en raison d'une divergence d'intérêts perçue ou d'un comportement incompatible d'une autre personne ou d'un autre groupe* ». Pour Engeström & Sannino (2011), les manifestations discursives des conflits peuvent s'entrevoir à travers des désaccords entre les participants.

Dans ce cadre, le désaccord entre les élèves et l'enseignant qui émerge en leçon 3 nous semble bien pouvoir être l'expression d'une contradiction entre activité d'enseignement et activité d'apprentissage des élèves. Ce point nous semble particulièrement important pour pouvoir étendre la notion de zone proximale de développement. Pour Eyme (2017, p. 503), « les contradictions diffèrent des conflits ou des problèmes qui n'en sont que des symptômes, et dont la résolution répond aux exigences de la situation, mais sans être prometteuse de transformations ». En cela, transformer le travail des enseignants engagés au sein de recherche collaborative passe par la confrontation de ceux-ci aux contradictions entre système d'activité d'enseignement et système d'activité d'apprentissage. Formulé autrement, il s'agit au sein de ces recherches de transformer les contradictions en objet de conflit pour permettre aux enseignants de recréer leurs systèmes d'activité d'enseignement. Il s'agit ainsi d'étendre la notion de ZDP aux recherches collaboratives que nous menons. Dans ce cadre, nous pourrions souligner à quel point les contradictions inscrites dans l'activité conjointe d'enseignement-apprentissage constituent un outil au service de l'ouverture d'une telle zone de développement potentiel.

Conclusion

La notion de ZDP telle qu'elle est usuellement mobilisée dans la littérature relative aux activités physiques et sportives renvoie à une interprétation à la fois commune et réductrice. Particulièrement mobilisée dans l'acquisition d'habiletés discrètes ou d'actions, elle ne se réfère pas à la construction ou à la production par les élèves de leur propre activité. Les élèves engagés dans la pratique de la danse en EPS présentés dans cette séquence sont bel et bien engagés dans la production de leur propre activité au service de la démonstration de leur compétence vis-à-vis des autres élèves. Elles élaborent cette activité malgré les contraintes que l'enseignant leur fixe, ou plutôt, en dialogue avec ces contraintes. Elles ne sont pas les simples reproductrices d'une forme culturelle, elles en sont les créatrices.

Il y a donc lieu d'élargir l'usage de la notion de ZDP pour permettre de comprendre cette activité de création culturelle par les élèves en EP. Dans le même temps, cet élargissement doit permettre d'entrevoir le rôle créateur des contradictions dans l'émergence de cette ZDP. De manière complémentaire, il nous semble que cette orientation ouvre des pistes pour la transformation du travail enseignant s'appuyant sur le dépassement des contradictions entre les systèmes d'activité d'enseignement et d'activité d'apprentissage. Il y a donc lieu de prendre au sérieux le concept de ZDP dans toute méthode visant la transformation du travail enseignant.

Bibliographie

Barker, D., Quennerstedt, M. & Annerstedt, C. (2015) Inter-student interactions and student learning in health and physical education: a post-Vygotskian analysis. *Physical Education and Sport Pedagogy*, 20:4, 409-426, DOI: 10.1080/17408989.2013.868875

Chaiklin, S. (2003). The zone of proximal development in Vygotsky's analysis of learning and instruction. In A. Kozulin, B. Gindis, V. Ageyev, S. Miller (Eds.), *Vygotsky's educational theory and practice in cultural context.* Cambridge : Cambridge University Press.

CLOT, Y. (1995). *Le travail sans l'homme?* Paris : La dispute.

CLOT, Y. (1999). *La fonction psychologique du travail*. Paris : PUF.

CLOT, Y. (2008). *Travail et pouvoir d'agir.* Paris: PUF.

COLE, M. (2009). The perils of translation. A first step in reconsidering Vygotsky's Theory of Development in Relation to Formal Education. *Mind, Culture and Activity,* 16(4), 291-295

D'ARRIPE-LONGUEVILLE, F., GERNIGON, C., M., HUET, L., CADOPI, M. & WINNIKAMEN, F. (2002). Peer Tutoring in a Physical Education Setting: Influence of Tutor Skill Level on Novice Learners' Motivation and Performance. *Journal of Teaching in Physical Education*, 22 (1): 105–123.

DE DREU, C.K.W. and VAN DE VLIERT, E. (1997). Introduction: using conflict in organizations. In C.K.W. De Dreu & E. Van de Vliert, (Eds), *Using Conflict in Organizations*. Sage: London.

DYSON, B. & CASEY, A. (2012). *Cooperative learning in physical education: a research-based approach.* London: Routledge

ENGESTRÖM, Y. (2001). Expansive Learning at Work: Toward an Activity Theory reconceptualization. *Journal of Education and Work*, 14(1), 133-156.

ENGESTRÖM, Y. & SANNINO, A. (2011). Discursive manifestations of contradictions in organizational change efforts: a methodological framework. Journal of Organizational Change Management, 24(3), 368-387.

EYME, J. (2017). Engeström ou la troisième génération de la « théorie de l'activité ». In J.-M. Barbier & M. Durand (Eds.), *Encyclopédie d'analyses des activités* (pp. 495-505). Paris : PUF.

GRIFFIN, P. & COLE, M. (1984). Current activity for the future: The zo-ped. In B. Rogoff & J.Wertsh (Eds), *Children's learning in the 'zone of proximal development'* (pp.45-64). San Francisco: Jossey-Bass.

GUARINO, L. (2015). Is Dance a Sport? A twenty-First century debate. *Journal of Dance Education,* 15, 77-80.

JORNET, A. (2018). Vygotsky and Marx: toward a Marxist Psychology. *Mind, Culture and Activity*. Doi: 10.1080/10749039.2018.1480635

KOZULIN, A. (2016). Foreword: How to reconstruct deconstructions. In A. Yasnitsky & R. Van der Veer (Eds), *Revisionist revolution in Vygotsky studies: The state of the art.* London: Routledge.

LEONTIEV, A. (1978). *Activity, Consciousness, and Personality*. Englewood Cliffs, N.J.: Prentice-Hall.

ROTH, W.-M. & RADFORD, L. (2010). Re/thinking the Zone Proximal of Development (Symmetricaly). *Mind, Culture & Activity*, 17(4), 299-307.

ROVEGNO, I. & DOLLY, J.P. (2006). Constructivist perspectives on learning. In D.Kirk, M. O'Sullivan & D. Macdonald (eds), *Handbook of Research in Physical Education* (pp.242-261). Thousand Oaks, CA; London: Sage.

SCHNEUWLY, B. (1995). De l'importance de l'enseignement pour le développement. Vygotsky et l'école. Psychologie et Éducation, 21— 25-37.

STETSENKO, A. (2008). From relational ontology to transformative activist stance on development and learning: expanding Vygotsky's (CHAT) project. *Cultural Studies of Science Education*, 3, 471-491.

VYGOTSKY, L.S. (1978). *Mind in society*. Cambridge, MA: Harvard University Press.

YASNITSKY, A., & VAN DER VEER, R. (2016). *Revisionist revolution in Vygotsky studies: The state of the art*. East Sussex, UK: Routledge.

III. MISE EN PRATIQUE
METTRE EN PRATIQUE

1.

REALITE AUGMENTEE (RA), ACTIVITE DE CONCEPTION ET DEBAT D'IDEES: CO-CONSTRUIRE PAR LES ARTEFACTS LES SAVOIRS TACTIQUES DU JEU COLLECTIF EN EPS A L'ECOLE PRIMAIRE TAIWANAISE

Ching-Wei CHANG, Taiwan
École Normale Supérieure de Taiwan (NTNU, ROC)
Nathalie WALLIAN, France
Université de La Réunion, ICARE (EA 7389)

Introduction

En éducation physique et sportive (EPS) à Taiwan, le travail du didacticien des jeux collectifs est en pleine mutation et subit la double influence de l'occident et de l'orient. En effet, les approches vygotskiennes commencent à pénétrer les domaines de la recherche et de la formation des enseignants en rencontrant les préoccupations du terrain : le regard du chercheur et du praticien tend à se détourner des approches centrées sur l'acquisition de techniques corporelles au profit d'une réflexion approfondie sur les manières dont le pratiquant co-construit ses compétences ainsi que sur les savoirs correspondants. En s'ouvrant aux approches japonaises contemporaines inspirées de Satô (2012) – qui fait mention des travaux de Vygotsky –, l'influence du concept de « *communauté collaborative d'apprentissage* » prend en contexte un sens fort et replace la notion de savoir au cœur de la dimension sociale partagée. Enfin, les nouvelles technologies intègrent aisément les pratiques enseignantes car elles font pleinement partie de la culture des élèves taïwanais. C›est ainsi que le contexte taïwanais est un contexte favorable au croisement des approches vygotskiennes en prenant en charge de façon signifiante les nouvelles technologies comme moyen de susciter chez les élèves des pratiques réflexives. En favorisant chez eux une activité de conception qui autorise le développement de la réflexivité et *in fine* de l'autonomie dans la prise de décision, Taiwan engage une mutation culturelle majeure, loin des préceptes confucéens fondés sur la répétition et la correction des erreurs par la mémorisation, modèle prévalent dans l'apprentissage du Chinois traditionnel.

L'objet de cet article consiste à investiguer le lien entre nouvelles technologies (NT) et appropriation de savoirs tactiques en jeux collectifs du point de vue de la genèse d'une activité de conception du joueur et de l'usage des artéfacts pour cet apprentissage. L'idée soutenue consiste à considérer les conditions d'usage des NT dans une perspective « augmentée ». Le choix de l'enseignement des jeux collectifs (basketball et handball) à l'école primaire pour une étude de cas se justifie d'une part par la richesse offerte par ces activités collectives aux élèves en termes d'alternatives décisionnelles et d'autre part par la nécessité de proposer aux enseignants du premier degré généralistes des outils pratiques efficaces d'intervention éducative.

La première partie de cette étude consistera à positionner les notions de «réalité virtuelle/augmentée» dans le contexte d'enseignement de l'EPS. Puis la pensée Vygotskienne et Satoienne sera reliée avec la notion de « situation incarnée » [situative embodiement] (Barab & al., 2007) en apprentissage moteur. En second lieu, les modalités d'introduction des NT dans l'enseignement réciproque entre pairs permettront d'envisager des conditions d'usage de la réalité augmentée (RA) en EPS. Enfin, en situation de jeu complexe, l'usage de la RA sera questionné au regard des effets d'artéfacts pour les élèves. Des perspectives seront formulées pour les perspectives d'études à venir sur les approches didactiques de l'EPS en RA.

1. Activité de conception, réalité virtuelle/augmentée et situation incarnée

Vygotsky affirme que la conscience est associée à l'usage d'outils et d'artéfacts qui opère la médiation au monde, distinguant de la sorte l'espèce humaine de l'espèce animale. L'*augmentation* de la réalité tient au fait que les technologies de RA permettent sous conditions d'améliorer et d'enrichir le réel en portant une attention particulière au contexte. L'usage des artéfacts introduit la dimension matérielle de la réalité sur un mode culturellement et historiquement situé, la réalité étant constamment médiée et réinterprétée par les pratiques : l'enjeu de la RA est de changer de perspective, d'améliorer la compréhension et la construction de significations en augmentant la réalité par des outils d'information éducatifs additionnels (Bowker & Starr, 2000) : les nouvelles technologies sont supposées amener un changement qualitatif dans le rapport au réel observé. Ainsi en EPS, elles intéressent tout particulièrement le domaine des conduites motrices qui par essence sont immatérielles, instables, situées et éphémères : la question est de savoir comme le joueur agit de façon réflexive et déploie une action réfléchissante.

En stimulant la cognition incarnée, la RA aide à construire des significations à partir de la réalité intime [inner reality], aspects contextuels, culturels et sociaux inclus : Barab & al. (2007) parlent à ce sujet d'»incorporation située» [situated embodiement] dans laquelle « l'apprenant entre dans la situation aux plans narratif et perceptif, a un projet, endosse une participation légitime et s'engage dans des actions qui ont des conséquences ». Squire (2010) considère que dans ces conditions, ... « le curriculum fondé sur les technologies (RA) active les identités estudiantines comme des résolveurs de problèmes plutôt que comme des consommateurs d'information conformes ». Selon Cook (2010), les RA « agissent comme des capteurs sensoriels, facilitant des visualisation spécifiques données à représenter aux apprenants de façon située ».

À l›école primaire taïwanaise, la question de la généalogie de la conscience prend une importance cruciale dans un contexte d›enseignement traditionnel centré sur la mémorisation, la répétition et la correction des erreurs. En introduisant la pensée réflexive en EPS, le système éducatif opère un changement de paradigme qui engage chez l›élève un changement de posture auquel le contexte culturel ne l›a pas familiarisé. Ce changement est radical mais vital car l›environnement naturel taïwanais est fortement incertain (ex : typhons, tremblements de terre, tsunamis, animaux dangereux...) et exige des citoyens une très forte adaptabilité, loin des normes et procédures de sécurité éprouvées en cours. L›école primaire en est impactée jusque dans la formation des enseignants et voit l›EPS s›emparer avec force du paradigme réflexif inspiré de Vygotsky mais également de Satô (佐藤学, 2012, 2015) et Okano (岡野昇, 2015). L'influence de ce dernier, originaire du Japon et fermement opposé aux évolutions du système néolibéral, défend l'idée d'un apprentissage collaboratif fondé sur trois principes : une philosophie des affaires publiques, une démocratie dans l'accès aux savoirs et l'excellence construite pour tous. En permettant à l'apprenant de déployer une pensée réflexive, il lui permet d'accéder à une forme d'autonomie critique et à terme autorise l'émancipation. La question est de savoir comment en EPS le processus de socialisation par un partage des savoirs est favorisé par une réflexivité augmentée.

1.1 Jeux collectifs, réflexivité et conscience ; un processus dialogique

En jeux collectifs, l'activité d'apprentissage s'inscrit dans un contexte situé au sein d'un collectif qui opère un processus de co-construction. Dans le rapport dialogique qu'il noue au monde, à autrui et à soi, l'individu opère des transformations constantes : en fonction des effets produits par ses actions, il engage récursivement une restructuration de ses intentions et de ses stratégies. En jeux collectifs, le joueur engage une relation à ses partenaires et adversaires dans un cadre réglementaire contraint. À la manière dont il noue le dialogue en s'inscrivant dans le jeu, il (ré)oriente ses actions et ses intentions : si par exemple il se fait intercepter la balle sur une passe, il choisira soit un autre partenaire, soit évitera de l'envoyer en présence de tel défenseur, soit s'abstiendra de la partager en tentant de tirer etc. Ainsi, le jeu se co-construit au fil des actions plus ou moins efficaces en relation avec des partenaires qui eux aussi partagent des modalités d'interaction signifiantes.

Mais le travail de conceptualisation de l'action est un travail complexe, immergé et difficile à interpréter pour l'enseignant. En cherchant à susciter la réflexivité dans l'action, l'intervenant amènera le joueur à « revenir sur lui-même » en mobilisant des opérations de pensée active et autoréflexive : la posture du joueur s'en trouvera modifiée avant même qu'il acquiert des techniques corporelles élaborées. Bronckart (2002, p. 27) affirme à cet effet qu'« Être conscient, c'est pouvoir accéder à sa propre pensée et agir sur elle ». Le « retour en miroir sur soi », au sens Lacanien du terme (Lacan, 1946), n'est possible que dans la rencontre avec cet autre qui produit de la différence et de l'altérité. Ainsi, le joueur se co-construit dans le dialogue avec les autres joueurs, partenaires et adversaires, dans et par le rapport dialectique de collaboration-opposition, en situation d'affrontement ludique : c'est sous le regard de l'autre, dans l'échange avec autrui - qu'il soit verbal et/ou non verbal - que s'élabore la posture de joueur prenant des décisions et celle d'élève apprenant des savoirs d'action (Avenier & Schmitt, 2007). En « adressant » une passe à un partenaire plus ou moins adroit, distancié et/ou « marqué », le porteur de balle va rendre sa passe « attrapable » et valider - ou non - la qualité de celle-ci en fonction des effets de l'action. Ainsi, le travail de conceptualisation de l'action est orienté par l'élaboration d'une réflexivité orientée qui interprète en contexte et de façon récursive la valeur pragmatique de l'action.

Au sens vygotskien, toute action présente un double caractère (Bronckart, ibid, p. 39) : d'une part une dimension *historico-sociale* qui inscrit l'expérience humaine dans un hic et nunc et également une dimension *méta--réflexive* qui dédouble l'expérience sous une posture conscientisée en actes. Ce caractère autoréflexif du mécanisme de la conscience est articulé avec les expériences capitalisées, actionnables en contexte, qui par la mémoire opère une remobilisation des savoirs, loin d'une sédimentation telle que provoquée par une répétition orientée vers la détection des erreurs et la réduction des écarts. Dans l›activité motrice se pose alors la question de la trace : comment envisager une « reprise » de l›action alors même que celle-ci est éphémère, immatérielle et instable ?

1.2 Traces d'activité, débats d'idées et interprétation

En EPS, la question de la « trace de l'activité motrice » pose de sérieuses difficultés, surtout avec de jeunes élèves pour qui la mise en mots de l'action est une réelle épreuve. Or il s'avère que le travail de conceptualisation de l'action exige une mise en mots et une « explicitation » qui mobilise tant des concepts (p. ex. montée de balle, démarquage, rapport de force) que la formulation des règles de l'action efficace (ex: pour passer, il faut...) et l'usage d'un vocabulaire approprié (ex: une « faute » n'est pas une « effraction » pour un arbitre; le signe « marcher » dans le non verbal d'un arbitre signifie « balle à l'adversaire »). Du coup se pose la question de pouvoir proposer à l'élève une *trace d'activité* qui autorise la reprise de son expérience d'un point de vue externaliste, certes, mais en croisant des points de vue (p. ex. porteur, partenaire, adversaire, arbitre, spectateur) à distance de l'action (différé immédiat ou reporté au cours suivant).

En autorisant l'usage de tablettes en cours d'EPS, la teneur même du statut de joueur s'en trouve changée : à tout instant il lui est possible d'opérer un « retour en arrière » sur le cours de l'action. En considérant que l'action motrice, une fois enregistrée et numérisée - c'est-à-dire bornée et stabilisée - est comparable à un texte (Hjelmslev, 1985, p. 85 ; Wallian, 2015), il devient alors possible de lui appliquer l'analyse textuelle, soit l'analyse de contenu et l'analyse du discours. « Le langage signifie quand, au lieu de copier la pensée, il se laisse défaire et refaire par elle. Il porte son sens comme la trace d'un pas signifie le mouvement et l'effort d'un corps » (Merleau-Ponty, 1960, p. 56). Aussi, la situation de « débat d'idées » (Gréhaigne, Godbout et Bouthier, 2001) apparaît en jeux collectifs propice à l'analyse de l'activité : l'analyse discursive autorise sous conditions l'accès à ce qui fait sens pour l'élève et au processus de co-construction d'un sens partagé. Cette situation consiste, après une phase de jeu en situation réduite (4X4 en Basketball), à donner un temps d'échanges aux joueurs autour de 1) ce qui s'est passé, et 2) ce qu'il y a à faire pour gagner. Les récits descriptifs et narratifs des événements ainsi que l'argumentation autour des événements marquants du jeu permettent d'extraire les règles de l'action efficace pour cet état du rapport de forces entre les équipes. Il apparaît alors que l'activité d'interprétation - ou activité sémiotique - opère 1) une mise en mots de l'action et des intentions qui la sous-tendent, 2) une confrontation argumentée de points de vue et 3) un arbitrage consenti à propos de ce qu'il y a à faire ensemble.

La question de la nature de la trace, support des interprétations, ainsi que de ses modalités de recueil, se pose alors. Comment engager une approche conceptualisante à partir d'éléments prélevés dans le jeu et présentés pour interprétation réflexive en autoscopie ? Nous allons définir les notions de réalité virtuelle/augmentée (RV/RA).

1.3 Autoscopie, réalité virtuelle et réalité augmentée

La distinction entre « réalité virtuelle » et « réalité augmentée » est opérée par Milgram & al. (1994) qui les positionne selon un continuum virtuel : dans l'intervalle entre ces deux réalités (RA et RV) se situent les réalités mixtes (RM) composées de l'environnement réel de la RA, de la VA et de la réalité virtuelle (RV).

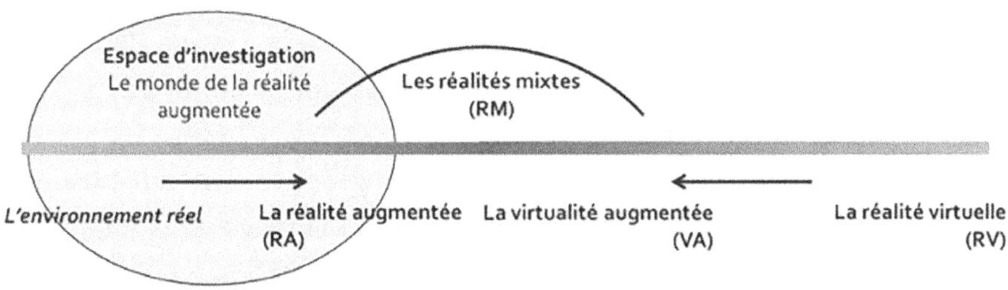

Figure 1. Continuum des environnements connectés réel/virtuel (d'après Milgram & al., 1994)

L'espace correspondant à l'investigation dans le monde de la réalité augmentée est celui dans lequel se situe cette étude : l'approche des jeux collectifs avec usage de tablettes numériques pour garder trace de l'activité en autoscopie en est l'application correspondante. En immergeant le joueur dans un espace RA, le dispositif l'autorise à remplacer et simuler à un certain degré le monde physique éprouvé afin de lui permettre de suspendre l'effort physique au profit de la réflexion sur et dans l'action. Ce temps de suspension est propice à l'élaboration d'une réflexivité sur et pour le jeu, en simultané comme en léger différé.

2. Enseignement réciproque entre pairs, RA et artéfacts en jeux collectifs

La technologie RA peut, sous conditions, autoriser ce que Vygotsky désigne par « médiation au monde » : elle représente un contact avec une réalité et permet le déploiement de la réflexivité en « économisant » l'effort au sens large (énergétique, émotionnel, informationnel...) par la suspension de l'action. Le déploiement de la réflexivité par l'élève engage d'une part, un décentrage pour une réflexivité plus consciente parce qu'intentionnée et d'autre part, un dégagement de l'emprise - toujours oblitérante - de l'urgence de l'action. En opérant une médiation au monde expériencé, la RA favorise l'interaction et l'abstraction réfléchissante (Fitzgerald & al., 2012). Ainsi par exemple, en formulant le constat à propos de l'issue du jeu et des déterminants stratégiques de l'action collective ; en argumentant à propos de ce qu'il y a à faire pour gagner en contexte ; en discutant des positionnements mutuels pour l'occupation stratégique de l'espace, le joueur apprend à mettre en relation le rapport de force avec autrui, la gestion de fenêtres temporelles au regard de la prise de décision et l'optimisation des ressources en fonction des contraintes du jeu.

La RA affecte la manière dont l'élève interagit avec le monde physique et représente une aide dans la construction des interprétations à partir de la réalité expériencée. Le joueur « entre dans une situation au plan narratif et perceptuel ; il a un projet, doit argumenter son rôle et s'engage dans des actions qui ont des conséquences » (Barab & al., 2007).

2.1 Vers une modélisation par étapes des artéfacts selon le processus réflexif

Plusieurs étapes de construction des usages de l'AR dans l'action ont émergé à Taiwan grâce au dispositif mis en place pour la collecte de traces d'activités en autoscopie.

Dans un premier temps, les joueurs ont pris pour focale des éléments techniques simples comme par exemple le tir à l'arrêt au panier de Basketball. Dans ces conditions, le joueur observateur produit un artéfact qui part de la motricité d'un pair en situation authentique d'apprentissage pour autoriser la reprise en différé.

Figure 2. RA produisant un artéfact de niveau 1 : la *quête réciproque* d'indicateurs sur la trace

Dans ces conditions, le dispositif s'inscrit en continuité avec le «style réciproque» (Mosston, ???) qui envisage, dans une grille préétablie d'items descriptifs, l'analyse du joueur «par comparaison d'écarts et par hiérarchisation». L'artéfact sert ainsi de point de comparaison entre la trace et la référence traduite en indicateurs observables dans une fiche d'observation. Cette étape est appropriée pour les habiletés motrices basiques et techniquement stabilisées.

La seconde étape de construction concerne la lecture orientée des traces moyennant l'identification sur l'image des indicateurs comportementaux décisifs et pertinents. Dans ce cas, l'interprétation est déjà prise en charge par des marqueurs qui ciblent pour le lecteur les points d'attention et lui permettent de les comparer avec la prestation du joueur observé.

Figure 3. RA produisant un artéfact de niveau 2 :
la *quête orientée* d'indicateurs sur la trace

Dans cette situation, le dispositif part de traces destinées à être explicités, décrites, commentées, comparées et argumentées. Le joueur apprend à interpréter l'activité d'un pair en la comparant avec la production attendue, telle que présentée en RA. Les indices pertinents d'interprétation permettent d'orienter la lecture comparée et de détecter le différentiel dans les traces collectées. Là encore, ce sont des éléments de motricité élémentaire qui sont pris en charge par l'artéfact et l'interprétation est relativement réduite et désambiguïsée.

La troisième étape s'intéresse à la quête élargie des indicateurs pertinents pour l'action.

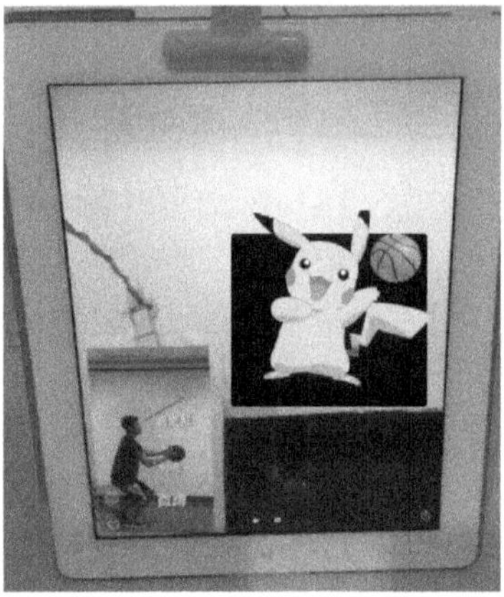

Le jeu d'opposition peut intégrer un attaquant surnuméraire, le Joker, qui va entrer dans le jeu à des moments précis en déséquilibrant les rapports de force qui vont se rééquilibrer ultérieurement. En précisant les attentes avec des « puces » animées qui remplacent le jeu de joker, l'artéfact met le joueur en situation simulée de déséquilibre pour lequel il va devoir s'adapter. La « puce » qui perturbe le jeu oblige le joueur à se décentrer de son espace proche au profit d'une prise en compte élargie des éléments déterminants du jeu et de la prise de décision.

Figure 4. RA produisant un artéfact de niveau 3 :
la *quête élargie* d'indicateurs sur la trace

Ainsi, l'enseignement peut :

1°) pourvoir différentes tâches d'apprentissage ajustées à des besoins particuliers
2°) engager des tâches communes avec des difficultés
3°) proposer un cycle d'apprentissage présentant des cheminements variés.

La quatrième étape concerne la prise en charge de la traçabilité du cheminement engagé par le joueur au cœur de l'artéfact.

Ainsi, en intégrant traçabilité dans la quête des indices de trace par le joueur, le dispositif permet d'identifier les manières de procéder pour accéder à des niveaux de complexité supérieur. En effet, en stockant en mémoire les étapes singulières du cheminement, l'artéfact permet à la fois de relever le rythme de progression, les moments de latence, les étapes signifiantes de progrès décisif ainsi que la trajectoire globale de progression.

Figure 5. RA produisant un artéfact de niveau 4 :
la *quête traçable* d'indicateurs sur la trace

La traçabilité de la navigation dans le dispositif permet donc de restituer en temps réel, et pour le joueur et pour l'enseignant, l'historicité de la démarche dynamique de construction selon différentes échelles temporelles ; dans la micro-situation d'apprentissage, à l'échelle d'un cycle complet d'apprentissage et même tout au long de la scolarité dans le parcours d'EPS, dans le cadre d'un « cahier virtuel de progression en sport ». De même, elle autorise l'extraction d'une typologie selon le profil du joueur et de l'apprenant utile pour différencier l'intervention. Cependant cette démarche appliquée aux techniques élémentaires (tir, passe...) et aux habiletés simples requiert une reprise en jeu, situation d'une complexité nettement supérieure. L'artéfact RA proposé dans ce cas prend une autre dimension.

2.2 Les artéfacts en situation complexe de jeu

La construction de compétences tactiques en jeu collectif d'opposition requiert une lecture interprétative du rapport de force prenant en charge la dialectique d'affrontement ainsi que les dynamiques variées des fenêtres temporelles décisionnelles. Ainsi, l'interprétation du jeu exige qu'une grille d'analyse soit élaborée en amont des faits observée afin d'orienter, par des attentes focalisées, le regard de l'observateur. En l'occurrence, l'enseignant du primaire qui intervient en EPS n'étant pas spécialiste ni de la discipline EPS, ni des APS sports collectifs, il est nécessaire de l'aider à construire son propre référentiel d'analyse au regard de la complexité de la situation de jeu collectif. L'enjeu de la RA consiste donc à orienter l'analyse de la systémique du jeu en autorisant une interprétation pour la décision, notamment pour permettre aux joueurs d'interagir de façon transformative.

Le dispositif P.L.A.Y. (***P**laying games; **L**earning focus; **A**ssessing project; **Y**es we've got it!*) est conçu pour apporter un cadre à la RA appliquée aux situations complexes de jeu collectif. En partant systématiquement des situations authentiques de jeu, une part large est octroyée à la phase active d'exploration et d'engagement moteur. L'enregistrement des phases de jeu est collecté sur un temps continu long et des extraits portant sur des «événements remarquables» sont répertoriés (Leutenegger, 2003). Ces événements remarquables correspondent à des moments-clefs dans les phases-mères du jeu ainsi qu'aux différentes «configurations du jeu» caractérisées par Gréhaigne (2007) et correspondant à des niveaux typiques de construction du joueur. La RA permet ainsi, au terme de l'analyse technologique de l'APSA, de passer à une phase didactique au cours de laquelle la collection des cheminements, opérés par les joueurs pour construire le jeu dans l'affrontement, sert de base pour le travail de « reconnaissance » déployé en formation des enseignants. En s'entraînant à re-connaître les configurations du jeu, les intervenants apprennent à analyser la structure typique signifiante à partir de laquelle les tactiques sont modélisées en fonction du niveau des joueurs.

Ainsi dans une classe de joueurs de BB (10 ans) en situation de 4X4 sur terrain réduit, le travail de « l'attaque rapide avec Joker » est collecté en RA pour une reprise à partir de l'expérience réelle vécue par les joueurs, et ce quasiment sans temps différé.

Figure 6. Contexte de mise en œuvre RA de la situation complexe de jeu 4X4

Munis de tablettes aimantées, les joueurs en situation de débat d'idées sont amenés à projeter dans cet espace représenté les événements passés et les tactiques à venir. En argumentant autour d'un outil de visualisation des placements et déplacements, ils inscrivent la mobilité des joueurs dans une dialectique fine propice à l'abstraction qui débouche sur la formulation des règles de l'action efficace, avant de repartir les éprouver par le retour au jeu.

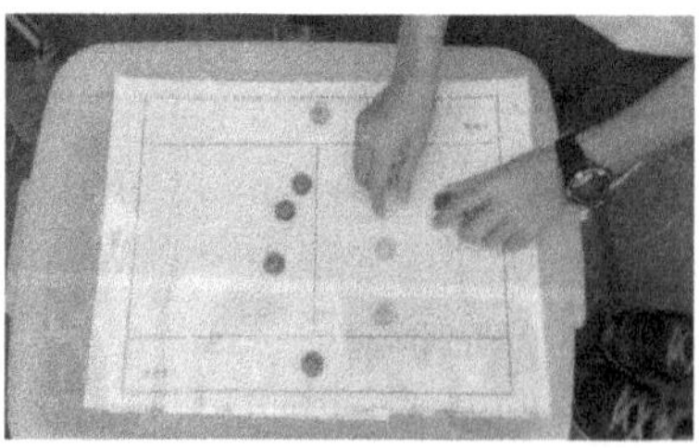

Dans ces conditions, en manipulant les pions magnétiques et en argumentant à propos des alternatives décisionnelles en contexte, les élèves apprennent à « lire » pour anticiper les issues plausibles du jeu.

Figure 7. RA produisant un artéfact de niveau 5 :
la conceptualisation formalisée de tactiques collectives

Dans cette situation, les élèves en débat d'idées (t = 5') sont filmés sur la tablette. Une fois qu'ils se sont mis d'accord grâce aux interactions formalisées sur tablette magnétique, le retour à la situation de jeu est repositionné par comparaison.

L'activité comparative entre les intentions partagées et négociées d'une part, et le réel du jeu en situation d'affrontement d'autre part, est menée par les élèves eux-mêmes. En identifiant les points similaires et divergents de l'action projetée/réelle, ils parviennent à mettre en mots les significations du jeu construites autour de configurations typiques.

Figure 8. RA produisant un effet différentiel et contrastif sur les tactiques collectives projetées/réelles

L'alternance de phases de jeu, de débat d'idées puis de reprise de l'interprétation avec retour au jeu autorise, outre la récupération physiologique du joueur, le déploiement d'une réflexivité orientée par la quête d'indices pertinents pour l'action. Ces indices permettent d'orienter l'action collective selon des principes et des règles d'action partagées et négociées - parfois âprement - surtout en début de cycle.

Dans cette situation d'observation active, l'élève qui enregistre les traces d'action pertinentes (bas du cliché) anticipe sur les événements qui se déroulent sous ses yeux: si "lire, c'est formuler des hypothèses de sens quant à l'issue plausible de l'action", le joueur devient alors un interprétant.

Figure 9. RA produisant un artéfact de niveau 6 ; la lecture orientée des tactiques collectives

2.3 Travailler les artéfacts pour aider à l'abstraction de l'action collective conceptualisée

Les élèves co-construisent progressivement, étape par étape, des configurations toujours plus élaborées et signifiantes. L'introduction ponctuelle de règles de jeu modifié (ex: introduction d'un Joker, limitation de l'espace de déplacement dans des couloirs, interdiction provisoire d'entrer dans le camp adverse en attaque...) oblige les joueurs à rediscuter l'état du rapport de force et la formulation tactique des intentions de jeu.

Afin de visualiser les relations des joueurs pour pouvoir identifier les configurations du jeu, il est possible de matérialiser sur l'image les positionnements des attaquants/défenseurs. Ces positionnements changent perpétuellement, amenant par alternance le déplacement du ballon en avant/arrière de l'espace du jeu effectif.

Figure 10. RA produisant un artéfact de niveau 7: les déplacements/replacements dans l'espace de jeu effectif

À ce stade de l›usage de la RA, il devient possible de munir les dossards de puces à GPS directement connectées aux tablettes. Le traitement informatique des déplacements réels des joueurs autorise la restitution des événements remarquables autour de la problématique de l›occupation de l›espace au regard des fenêtres temporelles plus ou moins ouvertes (Gréhaigne, 2009). L'artéfact permet ainsi au joueur de comprendre le lien entre positionnement spatial et fenêtre temporelle de la décision, ce qui l'amène à jouer sur «..».

Il apparaît ainsi, dans le dispositif RA expérimenté en jeu collectif, que l'élaboration des tactiques à partir des situations authentiques de jeu est favorisée par la co-construction d'images opératives dynamiques selon les niveaux de jeu moyennant une lecture interprétative toujours plus élaborée et orientée par des attentes précises.

3. Complexité et effets d'artéfacts : la co-construction du sens partagé en contexte

La RA autorise l'émergence de niveaux d'abstraction et de conceptualisation d'une complexité croissante. Selon les formes et les usages pris par les artéfacts présentés aux joueurs, le niveau de complexité du jeu est restitué dans un projet de lecture orienté. Non content de « reconnaître » les configurations typiques du jeu, le joueur devient pleinement un lecteur qui anticipe en formulant des hypothèses de sens quant à l'issue de l'action et qui valide - ou non - la valeur des décisions prises à l'aune des effets réels. Dit autrement, la RA permet au joueur sous conditions de co-construire son action au regard d'intentions explicitées et négociées et d'effets attendus/observés dans le jeu tout en collectant au fil de l'expérience les traces du cheminement historique.

Cette dialectique correspond bien aux idées déployées par Vygotsky qui considère qu'apprendre est un processus de socialisation, inscrit dans une historicité, dans lequel l'expérience façonne l'abstraction par la prise de conscience du jeu avec autrui. En changeant de point de vue, en subissant la récursivité des rôles lors d'une perte de balle, en discutant les interprétations plausibles des événements survenus dans le jeu, le joueur noue avec soi et autrui un dialogue signifiant par lequel il se transforme.

Le langage intervient comme une composante fondatrice de la rationalité du joueur, l'aidant à mettre en mots des faits et des intentions, à argumenter des points de vue à partager, à formuler des propositions à débattre, à synthétiser des règles collectives. En débattant hors du jeu et en dialoguant dans le jeu, les échanges deviennent constructifs et productifs. L'élévation progressive de la complexité des situations d'apprentissage amène progressivement le joueur à prendre en charge non pas « plus d'informations » mais des indices hiérarchisés selon une charge sémique différentielle : en apprenant à prioriser ses décisions, le joueur spécule sur les fenêtres temporelles en arbitrant l'urgent et l'important. Si la réalité du jeu n'est pas simplement « reflétée » dans la perception du joueur, elle l'impacte au point de le transformer : la connaissance abstraite est ainsi générée de la réalité interprétée et débattue dans et par une pratique orientée par des intentions explicites (Vygotsky, 2002, p. 112).

In fine, « Il n'y a pas la pensée, le langage (et l'action). Chacun des deux (trois) ordres à l'examen se dédouble et envoie un rameau dans l'autre... Les opérations expressives se passent entre parole pensante, (action en pensée) et pensée parlante (agie), et non pas, comme on le dit légèrement, entre pensée, (action) et langage » (Merleau-Ponty, 1960, p. 26).

Conclusion - Quand la pensée (verbale) devient actionnable et l'action conceptualisante

Le travail du chercheur sur des publics d'élèves jeunes a ceci d'intéressant que le langage n'est pas encore totalement décentré d'un point de vue égocentrique : il présente également un empan lexical encore fruste, limitant l'abstraction. En effet, le jeune joueur a tendance à considérer son interprétation comme le réel et le fait de découvrir pour lui qu'il existe d'autres réalités, via la RA, l'amène à prendre en charge - voire à contester - le point de vue d'autrui. En apprenant à mettre en mots des intentions, des ressentis et des impressions, le joueur élabore des niveaux d'abstraction croissants qui l'autorisent à formaliser sa pensée au-delà de sa propre expérience.

Dans une perspective développementale et émancipatrice, les apports de la RA, loin d'aliéner à une technologie bêtifiante parce que désambiguïsante ou démagogiquement esthétisante, peuvent être envisagés sur le mode collaboratif dématérialisé. En effet, c'est l'utilisation fonctionnelle des artéfacts de RA - et en fait leur potentiel transformatif - qui autorise la transformation : dit autrement, les conditions d'utilisation du langage, verbal dans le cas des débats d'idées, non verbal dans le cadre des actions de jeu collectif, donnent accès aux significations partagées et aux conceptualisation élaborées au sein de la communauté des pratiques. Les opérations mentales déployées s'inscrivent dans une variété d'activités ; s'exprimer, (se) raconter, (se) décrire, (s') exposer, (se) comparer, (contre-)argumenter, (s') inventer... Elles mettent en jeu une abstraction fondée sur l'analyse, l'induction, la déduction, l'abstraction, la synthèse, l'expérimentation (Vygotsky, 2002, p. 180) pour *in fine* partager, jouer ensemble et s'en trouver transformé.

Bibliographie

AVENIER, M-J., et SCHMITT, C. (2007). *La construction de savoirs pour l'action.* Paris : L'Harmattan.

BAKHTINE, M. (1929, 1977). *Marxisme et philosophie du langage.* Paris : Minuit.

BARAB, S., ZUIKER, S., WARREN, S., HICKEY, D., INGRAM-GOBLE, A., KWON, E.-J., KOUPER, I. and HERRING, S. C. (2007). Situationally embodied curriculum: relating formalisms and contexts. *Science Education, 91*(5), 750-782.

BOWKER, G., C. et STAR, S., L. (2000). *Sorting things out: Classification and its consequences.* Cambridge, MA, MIT Press.

BRONCKART, J.-P. (2002). La conscience comme «analyseur» des épistémologies de Vygoski et Piaget. In Y., Clot (dir.). *Avec Vygotsky.* Paris : La Dispute.

COOK, J. (2010). Mobile Phones as Mediating Tools within Augmented Contexts for Development. *International Journal of Mobile and Blended Learning, 2(3)*, 1-12.

FITZGERALD, E., ADAMS, A., FERGUSON, R., GAVED, M., MOR, Y., & THOMAS, R.. Augmented reality and mobile learning: The state of the art. Retrived January 10, 2017, from http://oro.open.ac.uk/34281/

GRÉHAIGNE, J.-F., (2007). *Configurations du jeu. Débat d'idées et apprentissage du football et des sports collectifs.* Besançon : PUFC.

GRÉHAIGNE, J.-F. (2009). *Autour du temps.* Besançon : PUFC.

GRÉHAIGNE, J.-F., Godbout, P. et Bouthier, D. (2001). "The teaching and learning of decision making in team sports", Quest, 53, p. 59-76.

HJELMSLEV, L. (1985). *Nouveaux essais.* Paris : Presses universitaires de France.

LACAN, J. (1949). *Le stade du miroir comme formateur de la fonction du Je telle qu'elle nous est révélée dans l'expérience psychanalytique.* XVIeme Congrès international de psychanalyse, Zurich.

LEUTENEGGER, F. (2003). Etude des interactions didactiques en classe de mathématiques : un prototype méthodologique. In A., Weil-Barais, A., Danis, & M-.L., Schubauer-Leoni (Ed.), *Numéro spécial du Bulletin de psychologie, 56*(4), 559-571.

MERLEAU-PONTY, M. (1960). *Signes.* Paris: Gallimard.

MILGRAM, P., TAKEMURA, H., UTSUMI, A. and KISHINO, F. (1994). Augmented reality: A class of displays on the reality virtuality continuum. *Proceedings of Telemanipulator and Telepresence Technologies,* (pp. 282-292) SPIE Press.

SATÔ, M. (2012). À la recherche d'une école pour le XXIe siècle. Quelles (réformes scolaires) alternatives aux politiques néolibérales ? *Les Dossiers de l'éducation, 27,* 37-54. [https://journals.openedition.org/dse/447]

SQUIRE, K. D. (2010). From information to experience: Place-based augmented reality games as a model for learning in a globally networked society. *Teachers College Record, 112*(10), 2565-2602

VYGOTSKY, L.S. (2002). *Pensée & langage*. Paris : La Dispute.

WALLIAN, N. (2015). Sémiotique de l'agir enseignant en Éducation Physique et Sportive : figures d'action et registres interprétatifs en milieu difficile. Revue *Carrefours de l'éducation, 40*(2), 63-80.

佐藤学(2012)。学校を改革する一学びの共同体の構想と実践。東京都：岩波書。

佐藤学(2015)。21世紀型の体育の学びへ。載於岡野昇與佐藤学編著，体育における学びの共同体の実踐と探究（227-234頁）。東京都：大修館書店。ＳＡＴＯＭａｎａｂｕ

岡野昇(2015)。体育における学びの移り変わり。載於岡野昇與佐藤学編著，体育における学びの共同体の実踐と探究（3-34頁）。東京都：大修館書店。**OKANO Noboru**

2.

JOINT ACTIVITY ORGANIZATION AND ITS EVOLUTION IN THE ZONE OF PROXIMAL DEVELOPMENT IN SPORT TEACHING. THE PROCESS OF TRANSFER OF RESPONSIBILITY AND CONTROL OF LEARNING

Víctor López-Ros, Bernat Llobet-Martí, & Bruno Avelar-Rosa, Spain
Educational Research Institute - Culture and Education Research Group
University of Girona (Catalonia, Spain)

Introduction

What do teachers and apprentices do daily in school, in normal and natural conditions, to favour the knowledge construction of the seconds? How is this complex process of multiple interactions articulated around tasks that need to be solved? This paper addresses these issues by showing how the joint activity between teachers and learners is articulated and is developed around specific contents throughout the Zone of Proximal Development. To this end, two concrete examples of teaching and learning processes of two team sports are shown, in which the attention is focused on the course of assignment of responsibility and the control of learning by the teacher to the apprentices. The analysis of the sequences highlights the importance of the semiotic resources used in the interaction and also that this process is not easy, neither fluid nor linear, and it is open to unpredictable events.

1. About the Zone of Proximal Development and the Joint Activity Organization (JAO)

The concept of Zone of Proximal Development (ZPD) (Vygotsky, 1978, 1993) is one of the most well-known notions of the rich Vygotsky's contributions (Daniels, 2001; Mahn, 2015), so it has attracted the attention of many scholars and researchers from the moment in which it appeared. There are, then, a vast number of works in this area since the 80s of the last century until the present (i.e., Chaiklin, 2003; Newman, Griffin and Cole, 1989; Moll, 1990; Veresov, 2017; Wertsch, 1985). This entails, in addition to a considerable number of contributions, the appearance and existence of interpretations that are not always coincident about this concept. One of the criticisms about some of the works on the ZPD is that they do not consider or interpret this concept in the entire context of Vygotsky's work or from a socio-historic and cultural perspective. Thus, some authors (Chaklin, 2003; Smagorinsky, 2017; Veresov, 2017) point out the need to review basic precepts of the ZPD concept with the intention of placing it in the theoretical perspective in which it was conceived. There are still controversies about how to consider the ZPD, and about the pedagogical derivations of the concept.

Although the idea of ZPD appears in different texts of Vygotsky[1], there is an enormous consensus in considering that the definition is specifically collected when Vygotsky writes about the relations between learning and development in the context of the development of higher psychological processes in the text translated as *Mind in Society* (1978). The concept of ZPD was originally defined as: *"It is the distance between the actual development as determined by independent problem solving and the level of potential development as determined through problem solving under adult guidance or in collaboration with more capable peers."* (Vygotsky, 1978: 86).

According this, the definition of ZPD underlies different ideas that are essential for its understanding (Chaiklin, 2003; Moll, 1990; Wertsch, 1985). In the first place, the concept of ZPD can be considered within the idea of showing, in a concrete way, the relationships established between

[1] See a complete revision in Chaiklin (2003).

interpsychological functioning and intrapsychological functioning in the framework of higher psychological processes development. This question is congruent with the genetic law of development that *"emphasized the primacy of social interaction in human development"* (John-Steiner & Mahn, 1996: 192). Secondly, in spite of some comments that criticize a certain reductionist vision, the ZPD highlights the distance between the level of real development of children manifested in the ability to autonomously solve a task and the potential level dependent on external aid, defining those functions that have not yet matured but that are in the process of maturing (Vygotsky, 1978). This distance shows the relations of interdependence between learning and human development, emphasizing that true learning always precedes development (Vygotsky, 1978). Third, it shows that the learning that drives development occurs when tasks with higher level of difficulty are solved than those solved individually. In some way, this shows that the difficulty of the tasks entails the development of the psychological functions in process of maturation. And, in fourth place, considering the social nature of development, it highlights the importance of the mediation procedures that appear throughout the interaction processes that turn possible the appropriation by the apprentice. Of these, language and other semiotic resources such as images are prominent.

Thus, the processes of interaction and communication between the apprentice and the teacher around an object of knowledge are at the centre of what happens in the ZPD. This negotiation necessarily involves a sufficient level of intersubjectivity (Bruner, 1997; Cole, 1996; Wertsch, 1985) that allows the participants to understand the mind of the other situated in the context of the activity in which they are involved (considering that the interaction does not guarantee the establishment of the communication itself).

According to Wertsch (1985), in source of Rommetveit and collaborators point of view, *"Intersubjectivity exists when interlocutors share some aspect of their situation definitions. Typically, this overlap may occur at several levels, and hence several of intersubjectivity may exist"* (p.159).

The achievement of high levels of intersubjectivity requires continuous adjustments of the contributions to the interaction, both on the part of the teacher and on the part of the apprentice (Wertsch, 1985; Smagorisnky, 2017). Or in other words, teacher and apprentice are involved in a joint activity in which each interlocutor influences and is influenced by the other and, therefore, this joint activity is not previously established completely (Rogoff, 1990, 1995). The joint activity can be understood as a system created actively and mutually by teachers and apprentices (Moll, 1990) who are mutually influenced. In this way, Newman, Griffin, & Cole (1989) mentioned ZPD as the Knowledge Construction Zone, emphasizing that the processes of cognitive change are constructed by the participants. That is, they are not given in advance and show a dynamic character.

The processes of interaction between participants in the ZPD are located in systems of broader activities (Cole, 1996, Rogoff, 1995) and are built through the establishment of better levels of intersubjectivity among them (Wertsch, 1985). This fact must do, also, with the domain of the semiotic resources that guarantee the mutual understanding and the adaptation of the participation of each interlocutor in the joint activity (Mercer, 1995; Vila, 1998). In this sense, we can consider that the processes of joint activity form a system of interactivity that takes into consideration the participation of each interlocutor in relation to a specific content and is part of a broader activity system that gives meaning to the actions that they are undertaken (Coll, Onrubia & Mauri, 2008; Cole, 1996; Rogoff, 1990, 1995). Thus, for example, a school has specific purposes that allow to understand and contextualize the activities carried out by the participants in its core. These purposes or socio-cultural reasons are not coincident, for example, with those who preside over a performance-oriented sports club. In the same way, what happens in a class or training session can only be understood if their context is taken into consideration. In other words, the learning and development processes of the participants in a specific context are conditioned by it.

We pointed out that interactivity considers the contributions of the participants in relation to a specific content or knowledge object. That means that the processes of joint activity established in the ZPD refer us to the relations of mutual influence and interdependence among the participants, as well as to the characteristics of the content or object of knowledge expressed in a given task. This idea is included in the concept of interactive triangle or didactic triangle (Cole, 1996), understood as the basic unit of interrelations between the elements involved in the teaching and learning process, and constituted in each of its vertices by the teacher, the apprentice and the content, respectively. The relationships maintained and developed by the three elements along the time are interdependent and the forms of organization of the joint activity throughout the ZPD cannot be understood if these mutual influences are not considered. (Coll et al., 2008). Thus, the teacher maintains an asymmetric relationship with the learner from his position of guide/instructor. However, their actions are influenced by the actions of the apprentice, by the understanding of the situation, by the contributions to the interaction, among others, and by the specific characteristics of the content that define the adequacy or not of the proposed tasks. In the case of the apprentice, their participation is conditioned by their ability to understand and resolve the tasks proposed by the teacher and the content characteristics, but simultaneously, their contributions modify the actions of the teacher and can demand or not modifications in the content. As several works indicate (Daniels, 2001, Frankel, 2012), the mutual influence among the participants in the interactive processes within the ZPD occurs even when the relationship can be clearly asymmetric. Finally, the particularities of the content object of learning and the tasks used for that purpose determine the teaching and learning process and its characteristics (Comino, 2017; López-Ros, 2001, 2013). Thus, the specific characteristics of a content such as, for example, climbing are different from those of swimming or team sports introduction. On the other hand, if we take the example of team sports, starting using tasks of a global and tactical nature has very different interactive consequences if, in opposition, we decide to use technical models based on the skill efficiency.

2. How is the Joint Activity Organization articulated during the process of transfer of responsibility and control of learning?

The emergence of the concept of ZPD in the Anglo-Saxon context has generated a considerable impact and gave rise to subsidiary concepts of it, among them the metaphor of *scaffolding* suggested by Wood, Bruner and Ross (1976). The initial idea of this metaphor pointed out that the interactive processes in the ZPD can be understood as the structure of a scaffolding in the sense that, at the beginning, there is a structure that guides and supports the wall. After that, progressively, this structure is going disappearing. In the same way, the teacher's guidance process in the context of the joint activity would be much more intense at the beginning and would be gradually withdrawn (Mercer, 1995; Vila, 1998). In this vein, the joint activity would show progressive modifications as the apprentice advances in the knowledge construction.

Although some works show that the metaphor of the scaffolding may not represent an adequate "reading" of the ZPD (Daniels, 2001; Smagorinsky, 2017), it has served as a reference for many works (Valsiner, 2005; Van de Pol, Volman, & Beishuizen, 2010). In general terms, and in accordance with the notion of ZPD, the scaffolding is interpreted as the process of systematic help offered by the most expert to the apprentice and that is progressively withdrawn as the apprentice becomes more autonomous in the resolution of a given task. Thus, the teacher acts as a guide in a process of joint activity that is, by definition, asymmetric and partially unpredictable in its development.

The joint activity organisation (JAO) in which the teacher adjusts the pedagogical help and gives the learner autonomy in the control of their learning is highlighted by several studies (Coll, Colomina, Onrubia, & Rochera, 1992). This clearly places this joint activity in the transition from the interpsychological to the intrapsychological processes and emphasizes the importance of semiotic resources during the interaction and the interactivity. The review work carried out by Van de Pol, Volman and Beishuizen (2010) points out the three main characteristics of the scaffolding process: the contingent support, the progressive withdrawal of support, and the process of transfer of responsibility.

The idea of the transfer of responsibility has also been collected by different works (Coll et al., 1992; Coll et al., 2008) that analyse how educational influence is exercised in the teaching and learning processes and how it produces the process of transfer of control and responsibility of learning in the ZPD, also in the field of physical education and sports (Comino, 2017; López-Ros, 2001; Llobet-Martí, 2016; Pradas, 2012). These works indicate the existence of two mechanisms of educational influence which are present in the teaching and learning processes, requires specific teaching devices, and that take place in the ZPD. Thus, the interactive processes that facilitate learning in the ZPD entail: a) a process of transfer of control and learning responsibility, and b) the establishment of a system of shared meanings increasingly more complex and richer. Both mechanisms are interrelated and show mutual interdependence although they can be analysed by focusing attention on one of them. That means that the joint activity carried out by the teacher and the apprentice will be modified while the apprentice becomes more autonomous. The ways in which this joint activity is organized will evolve from ways that show greater control and a higher level of regulation by the teacher towards forms that show an appropriation and a greater level of control by the learner. Thus, for example, it is reasonable to think that the forms of joint activity that indicate a strong presence of organizational aspects and control of development will have a greater predominance at the beginning than at the end of the teaching and learning process. Or, the period of autonomous practice of a learner of a specific motor skill will be greater at the end of a sequence of teaching and learning. These aspects will manifest themselves, also, through the differentiated use of certain semiotic resources as well as by the establishment of higher levels of intersubjectivity that will reveal a universe of a richer shared meanings (and probably greater) while the teaching and learning process advances.

Several works in the field of physical education and sport indicate some characteristics about the process of transfer of control and learning responsibility (Comino, 2017; López-Ros, 2001; Llobet-Martí, 2016; LLobet-Martí, López-Ros, & Vila, 2017; Pradas, 2012). Thus, they reveal that this process is dynamic and progressive, but it is neither linear, nor easy (nor fluid). Along the joint activity forms evolution, there are often moments of stagnation, regression, and ruptures. These moments are often associated with the necessity to renegotiate meanings and activities, and require a change in the intersubjectivity levels to allow and favour the reestablishment and advancement of shared knowledge. A detailed analysis reveals that such ruptures or setbacks are associated, among other aspects, with incomprehension and/or inadequate levels of contingency according to the complexity of the tasks.

3. Reviewing practical examples: analysis of the evolution of the Joint Activity Organization in two sports teaching sequences

In order to show how the joint activity is organised, and how it evolves along the process of transfer and cession of learning control, we use two examples of teaching sequences of team sports with novice learners. Once sequence corresponds to 4 sessions of a handball introduction unit with primary school students (11-12 years old), and the other corresponds to 11 sessions of rugby introduction in a sports club with novice players (17-19 years old). Both sequences are real, thus maintaining all the ecological validity, and use the Integrated Technical-Tactical Model (López-Ros, 2016; López-Ros & Castejón, 2005) as a model of sports teaching.

All the actions and conversations during these two sequences have been registered with video and wireless microphones. It allowed for obtaining all the information about what the participants do and say, and identifying and analysing the most generic forms of the JAO. Subsequently, all the contributions of the participants have been transcribed and analysed using a pragmatic perspective of discourse analysis.

It is possible to use different approaching levels to analyse of the JAO (Coll et al., 1992; Coll et al., 2008). In this work, and with the aim of obtaining generic evidence about the process of transfer of control and the learning responsibility through the evolution of joint activity forms, we only focus on the most general level (or macro level). We describe and analyse the interactivity among the participants seeing how it emerges, what characteristics it manifests, and how it evolves while the apprentices progress in their own learning. Apprenticeship learning has been corroborated in both sequences (López-Ros, 2001, 2013; LLobet, 2016; LLobet-Martí, López-Ros, & Vila, 2017), showing that the evolution of the JAO is directly linked to the appropriation and improvement of the content by them.

To determine the forms of JAO we have used the Segments of Interactivity (SI) as a unit of analysis. This unit has been used in other works (Coll et al., 2008; Comino, 2017; Pradas, 2012) with the purpose of studying the evolution of JAO in the process of transfer with different contents and in different settings. An interpretative methodology is used that, in the first place, establishes the SI that emerge and that make visible the forms of JOA among the participants. In accordance with the theoretical framework and with the methodological proposal used (Coll et al., 2008), each SI emerges considering: a) the range of possible actions in coherency with the activity that takes place; b) the instructional function that guides the activity where teacher and apprentice are involved.

Since the objective is to capture the forms of JAO that emerge, the establishment of the different SIs often requires a repeated process of "go and back" by the researchers until the final structure of each SI is delimited.

Each SI is constituted by different behavioural patterns of the participants (Teacher –T-, and Apprentices –A-). These patterns reveal the concrete forms taken by the joint activity of each participant in the context of a given segment. Thus, for example, an SI with a clear instructional function of practice organization that will be carried out next may imply that the teacher and the apprentices are involved in a joint activity that guarantees that the apprentices know the task to be carried out, and the conditions of it. This can lead to different behavioural patterns, for example: 1) (T) explanation, (A) follow up and question, (T) Answer; 2) (T) demonstration and explanation, (A) follow-up and questions.

At this point, what are the forms of JAO that can be seen in the two sequences analysed, that is, what does emerge? How do these forms evolve while learners improve in their "performance"? How is the joint activity articulated and evolved in these two sequences along the ZPD?

In the sequence of 4 sessions of handball we found five types of SI (López-Ros, 2001, 2013), each of them constituted by different behavioural patterns. These SI were: a) Segment of Activity Organization (SIAO), in which the teacher and the students are involved in the presentation of the tasks, as well as in the conditions of realization of the activity. b) Segment of Guided Practice (SIGP), in which the students are performing the task (i.e. 5 vs 5, maintaining possession of the ball), and the teacher offers help while the students are performing these tasks. c) Segment of Discussion (SID), in which the teacher and the students talk and discuss about events that happened in the task they were doing. d) Segment of Recapitulation (SIR), in which the teacher and the students discuss situations and events but in relation to other sessions contents or to the objectives of the session and the sequence (not in relation to the immediate task they have been carrying out). And e) Segment of Transition (SIT), which are moments and activities without instructional function.

In the 11 rugby sessions we found six types of SI (Llobet-Martí, 2016; Llobet-Martí, López-Ros, & Vila, 2017). Five SI are very similar to those indicated in the handball sequence, but in this sequence we highlight the emergence of a Segment of Autonomous Practice (SIAP) in which players practice under their own responsibility, without the help of the coach (who is usually preparing other activities in another area of the field). Probably, this SIAP is a nice example of the idea of "activity" beyond the "face-to-face interaction" pointed out by Rogoff (1995) in which the influence of the teacher exists even if it is not present.

Both sequences emphasize that the forms of JAO in sports situations developed using an integrated technical-tactical model presents strong similarities in its macro level. However, although the SI labels of both sequences may be similar, the behavioural patterns do not necessarily have to be coincident. Thus, the patterns that emerge in the SID of the handball sequence are not the same as those that appear in the rugby SID. It is reasonable if we consider, as we have indicated, that interactivity processes in the ZPD are built on the way and require high levels of intersubjectivity and negotiation. These features highlight their dynamic and unpredictable nature.

How does JAO evolve along the ZPD? What evidences can we begin to observe? In summary, in the handball sequence we found a progressive decrease in the number of SI while the sequence progresses. This shows that there are fewer ruptures in the JAO. In general terms, a lower level of ruptures in the interactivity is interpreted as an increase in the fluency of the process of transfer and of the appropriation by apprentices. Obviously, this would require a deeper analysis that exceeds this chapter.

More specifically, it seems that the ISAO decreases in number and time employed while the sequence progresses. That is, students are appropriating and constructing the knowledge related to the organizational and functional aspects of the tasks, so that it is unnecessary to renegotiate the conditions of the task, the rules of participation, and other aspects. This shows the process of transfer, as well as the establishment of a shared knowledge system. At the same time, the number of SIPGs decreases and the time spent in them. This fact could seem contradictory with the postulates of motor learning that assume that more and better practice time involves more learning. In this sequence the opposite happens, probably it can be understood linked to the increase in time of SID, that is, to the establishment of processes of dialogue and understanding about the practice carried out. The increase in time is also evident in the Recapitulation SI, which means that the process of transfer seems to be related to the knowledge appropriation about the conditions of tasks completion, and also about the reflective processes and the stimulation of the understanding of the practice, strengthening the relationship between procedural and conceptual knowledge. In other words, the progress made by the ZPD is distilling changes in the forms of JAO in which the teacher and the students are involved. However, this apparent progressive evolution of the different SI is broken in one of the sessions (session 2). This shows that the transit through the ZPD and the process of transfer is not easy, nor linear and often shows breakdowns and setbacks.

Some of the features observed in the 4 handball sessions also appear in a much longer sequence (11 sessions), with another sport (rugby) that shows different characteristics and in a different context (club) but using the same methodological model (the integrated technique - tactical model). Thus, for example, there is a decrease in the number of IS while the sequence progresses. There is also a slight decrease in the SIAO and SIGP, although no significant changes are observed in the SIAP, SID and ISR. However, a more detailed analysis of the dialogues and discussions held in the ISD shows how, at the beginning of the sequence, the coach created specific spaces or moments for debating around tactical aspects. As the SD progresses, the time spent in the IS is transferred to the ISGP. This could mean that, as players appropriate a higher level of knowledge, the coach can dialogue, support and discuss with the players while they are involved in the practice segment. This example suggests that some specific patterns of behaviour of the joint activity could be transferred between different IS during the process of transfer of control of learning responsibility.

Final comments

The analysis of the JAO in real processes of teaching and learning can offer us a more precise vision about what happens in normal conditions when teachers and apprentices move through the ZPD. An aspect that seems fundamental is linked to the capacity of the adjustment of the pedagogical support in each moment, considering that this adjustment only makes sense in a framework of intersubjectivity that facilitates a permanent communication. The evolution of the forms of JAO allows us to understand how pedagogical support is articulated in the context of an inseparable unit configured by teacher, apprentice and content. Far from being able to fully foresee the development of this activity throughout the ZPD, it seems that an important part of the process is not easy, or fluid and it requires permanent negotiations. The teaching and learning processes in the ZPD show a dynamic and interdependent nature and must be observed considering its complexity.

References

CHAIKLIN, S. (2003). The Zone of Proximal Development in Vygotsky's analysis of learning and instruction. In A. Kozulin, B. Gindis, V. Ageyev, V. & S. Miller. (Eds.) *Vygotsky's Educational Theory in Cultural Context*. (p. 39-64). New York: Cambridge University Press.

COLE, M. (1996). *Cultural Psychology. A once and future discipline.* Massachusetts: Harvard University Press.

COLL, C., COLOMINA, R., ONRUBIA, J., & ROCHERA, M.J. (1992). Actividad conjunta y habla: una aproximación al studio de los mecanismos de influencia educativa. *Infancia y Aprendizaje, 59-60*, 189-232.

COLL, C., ONRUBIA, J., & MAURI, T. (2008). Supporting learning in educational context: the exercise of educational influence and the analysis of teaching. *Revista de Educación, 346,* 33-70.

COMINO, J. (2017). *L'organització de l'activitat conjunta i la seva anàlisi en el procés d'ensenyament i aprenentatge de l'equilibri dinàmic en l'educació* física escolar. Universitat de Girona. Tesis doctoral no publicada. Girona.

DANIELS, H. (2001). *Vygotsky and Pedagogy*. London: Routledge Falmer.

FRANKEL, K. (2012). Coping with the double bind: Bidirectional learning and development in the zone of proximal development. *Learning, Culture and Social Interaction, 1*(3-4), 153-166.

JOHN-STEINER, V., & MAHN, H. (1996). Sociocultural approaches to learning and development: a Vygotskian framework. *International Psychologist, 31* (3/4), 191-206.

LLOBET, B. (2016). *Analysis of the interactivity in a teaching and learning sequence with novice players: the transfer of learning responsibility and control*. University of Girona. Unpublished doctoral thesis. Girona

LLOBET-MARTÍ, B., LÓPEZ-ROS,V., & VILA, I. (2017). The analysis of interactivity in a teaching and learning sequence of rugby: the transfer of control and learning responsibility. *Physical Education and Sport Pedagogy,* DOI: 10.1080/17408989.2017.1341472.

LÓPEZ-ROS, V. (2001). *L'organització de l'activitat conjunta en l'ensenyament escolar dels esports col·lectius*. Universitat de Girona. Tesis doctoral no publicada. Girona.

LÓPEZ-ROS, V. (2013). La organización de la actividad conjunta en la enseñanza escolar de los deportes colectivos. In Castejón Oliva, F.J., Giménez Fuentes-Guerra, F.J., Jiménez Jiménez, F.J., & López-Ros, V. (Eds.) *Investigaciones en formación deportiva* (pp. 41-64). Sevilla: Wanceulen.

LÓPEZ-ROS, V. (2016). El "modelo integrado técnico-táctico" de enseñanza deportiva. Origen, contextualización y características metodológicas. *eJRIEPS, 38,* 63-91.

LÓPEZ-ROS, V., & CASTEJÓN, F.J. (2005). L'ensenyament integrat Tècnic-Tàctic dels esports en edat escolar. *Apunts. Educació Física i Esport, 79,* 40-48.

MAHN, H. (2015). Classroom discourse and interaction in the Zone of Proximal Development. In N. Markee (Ed.) *The Handbook of Classroom Discourse and Interaction* (pp. 250-264). New York: John Wiley & Sons.

MERCER, N. (1995). *The guided construction of knowledge. Talk amongst teachers and learners*. Clevedon: Multilingual Matters Ltd.

MOLL, L. (1990). Vygotsky's zone of proximal development: Rethinking ints instructional implications. *Infancia y Aprendizaje, 50-51,* 157-168.

NEWMAN, D., GRIFFIN, P., & COLE, M. (1989). *The construction zone: working for cognitive change in school*. Cambridge: Cambridge University Press.

PRADAS, R. (2012). *L'organització de l'activitat conjunta I el pensament del professorat sobre l'acció docent en educació física escolar*. Universitat de Girona. Tesis doctoral no publicada. Girona.

ROGOFF, B. (1990). *Apprenticeship in thinking. Cognitive development in social interaction.* New York: Oxford University Press.

ROGOFF, B. (1995). Observing sociocultural activity on three planes: participatory appropriation, guided participation, and apprenticeship. In Wertsch, J., Del Rio, P., & Álvarez, A. (Eds.) *Sociocultural Studies of Mind* (pp. 139-164). Cambridge: Cambridge University Press.

SMAGORINSKY, P. (2017) (In press). Deconflating the ZPD and instructional scaffolding: Retranslating and reconceiving the zone of proximal development as the zone of next development. *Learning, Culture and Social Interaction.*

VALSINER, J. (2005). Scaffolding within the structure of Dialogical Self: Hierarchical dynamics of semiotic mediation. *New Ideas in Psychology, 23,* 197-206.

VAN DE POL, J., VOLMAN, M., & BEISHUIZEN, J. (2010). Scaffolding in Teacher-Student interaction: A decade of Research. *Educational Psychology Review, 22,* 271-296.

VERESOV, N.N. (2017). ZBR and ZPD: Is there a difference? *Cultural-Historical Psychology, 13*(1), 23-36.

VYGOTSKY, L.S. (1978). *Mind in Society: The development of higher psychological processes.* Cambridge MA: Harvard University Press.

VYGOTSKY, L.S. (1993). *Obras escogidas, II.* Madrid: Visor.

VILA, I. (1998). El espacio social en la construcción compartida del conocimiento. *Educar, 22-23,* 55-98.

WERTSCH, J. (1985). *Vygotsky and the social formation of mind.* Cambridge, MA.: Harvard University Press.

WOOD, D., BRUNER, J.S., & ROSS, G. (1976). The role of tutoring in problem-solving. *Journal of Child Psychology and Psychiatry, and allied disciplines, 17,* 89-100.

Práticas Físicas, Desportivas e Artísticas: uma perspectiva Vygotskiana

(PORTUGUÊS)

I. ANÁLISE TEÓRICA

1.

A PEDAGOGIA DE VYGOTSKY E O TREINO DESPORTIVO: UMA RELAÇÃO NÃO LINEAR

Carlos Eduardo GONÇALVES, Portugal.
Universidade de Coimbra, Faculdade de Ciências do Desporto e Educação Física

1. Aprendizagem no desporto

Vygotsky e o corpo: pode-se considerar que o desenvolvimento da escrita é comparável à forma como aprendemos tênis ou ciclismo, mas, para ele, interiorizar hábitos de movimento não tem nada em comum com desenvolvimento. Para um pesquisador e praticante no campo do esporte, tal afirmação é perturbadora.

Vygotsky destaca um outro ponto crítico para a pedagogia, quando escreve que a diferença entre aprender a datilografar e a escrever está no fato de que a primeira não permite melhorias, mesmo que sejamos profissionais. Já na segunda, aprendemos não só habilidades; nossa linguagem muda, para um uso consciente e pessoal. É possível encontrar similaridades com a aprendizagem de esportes, vista como mais do que uma repetição de técnicas padronizadas.

Além disso, na pedagogia contemporânea do esporte, o Construtivismo representa um palavra guarda-chuva, que cobre uma variedade de abordagens pedagógicas e atrai numerosos autores e variantes epistemológicas. Nesse ponto de vista, de certo modo, plástico, a aprendizagem dos atletas é encarada como um processo de interpretação e adaptação, no qual as ecologias reais do esporte são caóticas e o desenvolvimento individual é complexo e não linear.

Curiosamente, uma das referências, nessa eclética paisagem, é Vygotsky, um pesquisador quase desconhecido fora da Rússia até os anos 80 do século XX. Aparentemente, Vygotsky é um construtivista somente com crianças pré-escolares. De fato, há muitas semelhanças entre o Construtivismo e a teoria de Vygotsky:

- o desenvolvimento necessita de um ambiente ótimo para acontecer;
- o aprendizado se dá através da reorganização de funções psíquicas, mediadas por estímulos externos (no caso de Vygotsky, o uso de sinais).

Mas a recepção de Vygotsky nas ciências do esporte foi lenta e se deu através de fontes "de segunda mão", tomando pequenas partes de sua pesquisa e esquecendo de olhar criticamente para suas importantes conceitualizações e sua potencial utilidade no treino desportivo.

Ainda que Vygotsky não tenha se dedicado a pensar o exercício físico, a sua teoria sobre a imaginação e o seu estudo sobre o papel do jogo podem oferecer *insights* úteis e uma visão holística do esporte enquanto espaço de imaginação e performance. No entanto, a literatura e as práticas de treinamento contemporâneas parecem nunca reconhecer o esporte como um ambiente de performance no qual o tempo e a comparação social têm papéis cruciais. Mas Vygotsky nos faz, nos obriga a pensar sobre os problemas da aprendizagem no esporte, com: (a) exatidão racional; (b) lógica rigorosa; e (c) distância crítica diante de aspectos pessoais e afetivos.

Com essas premissas em mente, o propósito deste ensaio é olhar para alguns dos conceitos e teorias de Vygotsky e confrontá-los com a realidade do treinamento esportivo, argumentando que os pesquisadores e treinadores devem buscar e identificar coerência entre análises racionais e comportamentos. A postura crítica é importante porque, no desporto, aquilo que a maioria dos praticantes toma como conhecimento são apenas opiniões. Ainda reina uma convicção difundida de que o conhecimento existente reflete a realidade do treino.

Um dos maiores problemas para se lidar com essa "realidade do treinamento" é a ausência não de teorias, mas de teorização, enquanto reflexão sobre o que é interpretação e o que são fatos objetivos. No esporte, as dimensões emocional e social sempre estão presentes, e nosso cérebro está mais propenso a impor a narrativa errada, simplista, do que nenhuma narrativa, já que a mente não foi planejada para lidar com complexidade e incertezas não lineares.

Nós precisamos teorizar e refletir sobre a utilidade de meta-teorias (North, 2013), tomadas como suposições sobre a natureza do mundo social (ontologia), suposições sobre a natureza do conhecimento (epistemologia) e abordagens usadas para obter esse conhecimento (metodologia).

2. Ideologias hegemónicas

Desde a época da pesquisa de Vygotsky, as ciências do desporto enfrentaram diversas ideologias hegemônicas que moldaram nosso entendimento sobre treinamento e aprendizagem específica. Veremos esquematicamente as mais poderosas.

O cientificismo se caracteriza pela produção de conhecimento objetivo, livre de valores, sistemático, sobre fenômenos psicológicos "reais", baseado em leis/relações estatísticas/redutivas entre os fenômenos de maior ou menor ordem. O cientificismo psicológico também envolve eliminar influências contextuais dos seus sujeitos de pesquisa. Este conhecimento pode ser usado para identificar e solucionar problemas práticos, através de um processo de engenharia social racionalista.

Um corolário do cientificismo pode ser o reducionismo, por exemplo, a ideia de que fatores de primeiro nível (biológicos, psicológicos e ambientais) podem dar conta de problemas sociais complexos, de nível superior, simplificando as dimensões conscientes, intencionais, reflexivas dos comportamentos humanos, processos de grupos e relações sociais.

Do outro lado do espectro, o interpretativismo sugere que os objetos de análises sociais sejam fundamentalmente diferentes dos estudados através de ciências naturais. Indivíduos e grupos são autoconscientes, intencionais e reflexivos. Seus pensamentos e ações são carregados de valores e situados na experiência subjetiva vivida. A ecologia se torna um mecanismo explicativo central.

Dentro deste quadro, *saber* é visto como um verbo relacionado a ações na prática, ao invés de um substantivo (conhecimento formal). Existe um ceticismo em relação às leis e às soluções instrumentais e tecnocráticas. Para muitos, é mais apropriado falar em narrativas do que em teorias e, nesse ponto, começamos a questionar se tais modelos poderiam incluir a prática do treinamento de qualquer modo.

Nas variantes mais extremas, nada há além de construções, e não há meios de determinar seu valor epistêmico, todo conhecimento deve ser entendido como igual. Essa visão hegemônica molda a situação presente na pesquisa acadêmica sobre treinamento esportivo.

Existem autores que conectam Vygotsky, Paulo Freire e Construtivismo. É verdade que ambos rejeitam a abordagem do banco: a de que o professor deposita informações, as quais os aprendizes devem coletar de maneira acrítica. (Spaaj, Oxford & Ruth, 2016) Contudo, diferentemente de Vygotsky, Freire parece acreditar que a crítica garante a transição para o desenvolvimento, sem esquecer os conteúdos, mas ele também parece negligenciar o papel do professor. E podemos sempre pensar sobre o que realmente queremos dizer com democracia no esporte, e se existe um papel para o treinador enquanto crítico. Nos debruçaremos sobre essas questões no próximo subcapítulo.

Essa virada da psicologia comportamental para a cognitiva, em meados do século XX, foi acompanhada por um "abrandamento" da estratégia conceitual e metodológica. Os pesquisadores agora estavam "autorizados" a teorizar sobre os mecanismos, processos e conceitos menos objetivos, verificáveis, observáveis subjacentes à cognição, e a utilizar uma gama mais ampla de métodos, incluindo projetos de pesquisa qualitativos e introspecção. No entanto, todo este processo se deu em um mundo acadêmico que nada sabia sobre Vygotsky.

3. O papel do treinador

Se aceitarmos que a contradição entre as reais habilidades do atleta e as potenciais habilidades que ele pode atingir no futuro representa o motor do desenvolvimento, então nós temos que aceitar também que a mediação de adultos e pares representa um fator chave para o acesso completo aos processos de desenvolvimento. Vygotsky postula claramente que não é o encontro diário aleatório com a atividade que impulsiona o desenvolvimento, mas sim uma abordagem sistemática, planejada, de cima para baixo, através da qual os alunos possam performar em níveis mais altos.

Assim, parece claro, para a maioria dos estudiosos, que devemos encorajar o pluralismo disciplinar, meta-teórico e metodológico. O debate entre os lados deve ser visto como dialético e construtivo. Aqui, as concepções de Vygotsky sobre dialética na pesquisa podem ser úteis, em um campo que pouco reconhece esse recurso intelectual: como ir além de teses contrastantes.

Crianças são capazes de imitar ações que estão acima de suas verdadeiras capacidades e, sob supervisão de adultos, elas fazem coisas que não fariam de outra maneira. O que uma criança pode fazer com ajuda de adultos indica a zona de desenvolvimento proximal. Usando essa metodologia, é possível avaliar o real nível de maturidade e também possibilidades futuras.

A ideia de que treinadores podem desenhar um planejamento, mecanismos de tomadas de decisão e repertórios em diferentes níveis – macro, médio e micro – e de que isso responde às complexidades sociais e políticas trazidas por outras abordagens, traz consigo algumas sugestões interessantes, mas, ao final, é somente uma reafirmação estendida de velhas ideias, que focam em uma camada do treinamento (por exemplo, o(a) treinador(a) e suas estratégias cognitivas). No entanto, as abordagens cognitivas (Schön, 1987; Vygotsky, 1980) falham em dar conta das fontes de conhecimento e sua formação e transformações no mundo social.

Vygotsky coloca diversos desafios ao entendimento atual do enquadramento do papel dos treinadores. Consideremos apenas alguns. Primeiramente, a função da linguagem. Richards e colaboradores (2012) falam sobre conhecimento declarativo e aprendizagem lenta como ferramenta para desenvolver a aprendizagem processual. Consequentemente, a linguagem tem um papel instrumental: tudo tem um nome e saber os nomes aumenta as habilidades táticas. Mas Vygotsky não está de acordo com os treinadores; para ele, o raciocínio e a linguagem têm raízes genéticas diferentes.

Em segundo lugar, vem a questão do crescimento e da maturação. Para os técnicos, esses são obstáculos à aprendizagem e criam problemas sérios em relação ao avanço do nível de habilidade e à coesão do time. No entanto,

Vygotsky considera a puberdade uma época de estabilidade, porque é uma fase de ganhos maiores de personalidade, e considera esta uma condição e não o motor do desenvolvimento. Se o desenvolvimento não é linear, então a pedagogia tem que ser não-linear. Nós temos que entender o conceito de conflito. A maturidade e a cultura reorganizam profundamente o conteúdo natural do comportamento e o curso do desenvolvimento da criança é reestruturado de um jeito totalmente novo. Em certas "idades críticas" o desenvolvimento é mais destrutivo do que construtivo. E reconhecer isso é uma tarefa árdua para os treinadores.

Terceiro, Vygotsky não limita o desenvolvimento individual ao nível atingido nos estágios maduros, porque isso significaria recusar a dinâmica do desenvolvimento intelectual e motor. O paradigma hegemônico no esporte se baseia em modelos de desenvolvimento ancorados em estágios de acordo com idades cronológicas. Para os treinadores, cada estágio tem seus próprios conteúdos, bem como a especialização no esporte é vista como caminho para a *expertise*. Para eles, a verdadeira contradição e poderosa fonte de tensão é o fato de que a maior parte da literatura coloca performance e resultados em perspectiva, enfatizando o papel do técnico como um facilitador e não como um *expert* em conteúdos específicos do esporte e na entrega desses conteúdos em uma sequência. Assim, vale a pena explorar o conceito de zona de desenvolvimento proximal.

O último tópico que atrai atenções é o papel da imaginação no esporte. O desenvolvimento do pensamento criativo vai do pensamento à ação, não da ação ao pensamento, e esse conceito é particularmente importante para os esportes e a aprendizagem tática. Vygotsky não destaca sua importância, mas o tema permanece longe de um entendimento unificado no treinamento esportivo. O esporte moderno constantemente se refere à criatividade e à consciência tática na tomada de decisões como fatores chaves do sucesso, especialmente em esportes de equipe. Mas os passos e recursos necessários para otimizar a criatividade ainda são um problema não resolvido para técnicos e pesquisadores. Em diferentes momentos, Dewey (1933), Kolb (1975) e Gibbs (1988) teorizam sobre ciclos de reflexão como uma maneira de melhorar a criatividade dos aprendizes: é uma via interessante de pesquisa, que pode ser associada ao trabalho de Vygotsky.

4. Semiótica da aprendizagem

Para Vygotsky, os processos psíquicos são genéticos e, ao mesmo tempo, resultantes de relações sociais. Este é um tópico controverso nas ciências do esporte. Aqui, é importante fazer a referência a Bloch (2012) e seu argumento sobre genética e aprendizagem: é estupidez ignorar ambas.

Vygotsky acrescenta que a principal diferença entre os estágios do desenvolvimento não é a transição para novas funções, mas que normalmente lidamos com mudanças intra-funções. É uma característica de sistemas de dinâmica complexa. Ele aponta, de maneira crucial, que a atividade humana media dois processos: o uso de instrumentos e de sinais. Devido ao papel de mediação dos sinais é que as funções psíquicas maiores aparecem. Ao mesmo tempo, a memorização através de sinais está intimamente ligada à importância da linguagem. É possível especular que se crianças não dominarem a linguagem com proficiência, elas estejam menos aptas a aprender através de sinais e a desenvolver o pensamento lógico.

5. O ritmo do desenvolvimento

Aprendizagem significa o processo de desenvolvimento que se expressa através da aquisição de novos hábitos e através da capacidade de resolver problemas. Para Vygotsky, aprendizagem e desenvolvimento são coincidentes. Seu contemporâneo, Piaget, acreditava ser impossível estabelecer conexões causais antes dos 11 anos de idade. Para o esporte, este é um argumento importante, pois os treinadores buscam ensinar a separação entre esforço e habilidade desde muito cedo. Mas, para Vygotsky (1980), os estágios de Piaget são abomináveis, pois erguem uma barreira entre aprendizagem e desenvolvimento intelectual. Vygotsky escreve sobre cultura, mas podemos transferir seus conceitos para o esporte.

Existem períodos ótimos para aprendizagens específicas, nem cedo demais, nem tarde demais. Crianças são capazes de aprender línguas quando têm cerca de um ano e meio, quando é muito mais fácil do que mais tarde. Por isso, a aprendizagem deve colocar desafios sempre maiores, e focar em funções ainda em um estado de amadurecimento.

Se ler demanda o entendimento completo de cada palavra, não significa que devamos ensinar dessa maneira. É útil traçar um paralelo com a maneira que ensinamos jogos. Porque aprender se torna efetivo no momento em que vai além do desenvolvimento.

O pedagogo planta suas sementes e abre caminhos de desenvolvimento os quais devem seguir seus próprios ciclos para produzir resultados. É impossível ensinar novas formas de raciocínio a aprendizes que evitam o ritmo do desenvolvimento. Para criar a zona desenvolvimento proximal, por exemplo, para criar múltiplos processos de desenvolvimento interno, precisamos de um processo de aprendizagem construído corretamente.

A autoconsciência se desenvolve muito rapidamente porque não é um processo solitário, mas social. As crianças não criam significados, elas assimilam os significados determinados por seu uso social. Mais uma vez, salientamos o quanto é importante que o conhecimento declarativo seja assimilado pelo aprendiz no momento certo.

6. Formal vs. informal

Uma característica controversa do trabalho de Vygotsky é sua defesa dos currículos formais, vistos como essenciais para o desenvolvimento intelectual global, mesmo que não tenham valor prático. Uma ideia importante é a de que Vygotsky rejeitou o conceito de desenvolvimento enquanto processo determinado a partir do interior. Para ele, programas de aprendizagem vêm antes, e depois as micro-culturas. A contradição com a não linearidade defendida pela pedagogia contemporânea é evidente, assim como a necessidade de novas pesquisas na área do esporte. Para Vygotsky, as crianças adquirem conhecimento porque suas relações e ligações com o mundo são mediadas pelos adultos. No processo da comunicação oral entre crianças e adultos, os significados de "real" e "ideal" se relacionam e interagem. Uma vez que se tenha em mente a complexidade do caminho até a expertise em um dado campo, é totalmente compreensível que o professor/treinador deva ter a palavra final.

Se Vygotsky estiver certo quando afirma que a palavra é o fim que completa a ação, então a verbalização, no processo de treinamento, se torna um fator chave para o progresso em direção a níveis mais altos de *expertise*.

Para Vygotsky, todas as formas de vida psíquica da criança se formam no processo da comunicação. Ele também argumenta que uma forma inicialmente compartilhada entre duas pessoas se torna uma função psíquica interiorizada e que o fator mais importante no processo de desenvolvimento é a assimilação da experiência humana como um todo. Todo conhecimento novo reorganiza processos mentais, criando novas formas específicas de atividade cognitiva e volitiva. Esse entendimento materialista do desenvolvimento é pouco reconhecido nas ciências do esporte, especialmente por treinadores.

Foi William James (2017) que identificou a aprendizagem como desenvolvimento e como formação de reflexos condicionados. Vygotsky seguiu esse caminho e acreditamos que seja hora de olhar mais de perto para a aquisição de habilidades, sua sequência e sua evolução.

7. Cognição e emoções

A separação do lado intelectual dos lados afetivo e volitivo é uma das maiores fraquezas do treinamento esportivo tradicional. Quarenta anos depois da publicação dos trabalhos de Teodorescu (2003), Mahlo (1974) ou Knapp (1963), a maior parte dos praticantes ainda ignora a cognição e/ou tende a rejeitar emoções. Assim, o raciocínio é transformado em um fluxo de pensamentos autônomos, sem contato com a plenitude da vida real. Para muitos treinadores, bons atletas não pensam.

Vygotsky nos ensina que o raciocínio não é o nível final, porque o pensamento não nasce de outro pensamento, mas de nossa motivação e consciência, incluindo nossas preferências e necessidades, afetos e emoções. Sem comprometimento emocional e sem desejo de participação, o esporte é uma coreografia vazia.

A principal força que conduz o desenvolvimento é a contradição entre as capacidades técnicas do atleta e sua motivação. Permanece o problema de como transformar atividades práticas em mecanismos de socialização e assimilação de normas.

8. Desafios do nosso tempo

Vygotsky introduz uma metodologia para avaliar o desenvolvimento, apoiada na relação entre: (a) como o aprendiz resolve um problema por si mesmo; (b) como o aprendiz resolve o mesmo problema com ajuda de um adulto (aqui temos o papel do treinador revisitado).

O papel central deferido às ferramentas externas no processo de aprendizagem está na sua capacidade de transformar funções psicológicas externas. Para Vygotsky, o desenvolvimento é realizado através da internalização dos sinais, e as ferramentas/artefatos utilizados por treinadores têm um papel crucial nesse complexo sistema de semiótica.

Tome um exemplo de um atleta que tenta pegar uma bola. Para um pesquisador, parece que ele/ela se comportou como se tivesse resolvido um conjunto de equações diferenciais para prever a trajetória da bola e parece que, em um nível subconsciente, algo equivalente a cálculos matemáticos está acontecendo. Mas os praticantes sabem que algo realmente diferente está acontecendo, e atletas confiam em outros recursos. Se a bola já está alta no ar, atletas fixam o olhar na bola, começam a se mover e ajustam sua velocidade de forma que o ângulo do olhar permaneça constante. Um atleta capaz de fazer isso pode ignorar todas as variáveis causais necessárias para computar a trajetória da bola. Prestando atenção a apenas uma variável, o atleta vai terminar no lugar onde a bola vem. Através de um longo processo de aprendizagem, o atleta interpreta os sinais relevantes necessários para ter sucesso, sem computar um número alto de variáveis (Taleb, 2012).

No esporte, o conhecimento declarativo permite que o aprendiz análise, transforme e reconstrua seu conhecimento prévio. A teorização de Vygotsky sobre a relação entre a linguagem oral e escrita representa um exemplo impressionante do valor pedagógico de suas ideias para os pesquisadores e praticantes do esporte contemporânco.

9. Barreiras epistemológicas que devem ser superadas

A crítica de teorias pedagógicas baseadas em estruturas de conhecimento ou em situações de solução de problemas é clara e dura. Para Vygotsky, se o aluno não é confrontado com formas alternativas de pensar ou buscar por conhecimento, resulta impossível formar novas zonas de desenvolvimento proximal. Ao mesmo tempo, ele argumenta que o conhecimento deve ser sistemático e geral, para que tenha um efeito transformador, o que significa que o professor precisa ser um *expert* em conteúdos e metodologias do assunto que ele ensina.

Recusando uma concepção linear de desenvolvimento, Vygotsky conecta a aprendizagem com o raciocínio reflexivo, contrastando com uso espontâneo do conhecimento e ferramentas pedagógicas. Contra o construtivismo, Vygotsky destaca as dimensões social e histórica que impedem a redução da aprendizagem cognitiva à mera construção de conceitos.

As ideias de Vygotsky levantam questões epistemológicas interessantes que parecem estar em desacordo com as teorias contemporâneas de pedagogia do esporte. Tanto a abordagem construtivista quanto as baseadas em restrições (Renshaw et al., 2016; Pill, 2017) alegam ter bases científicas robustas para explicar a aprendizagem no esporte, mas falham em dar conta de todas as facetas do problema. O potencial explicativo das zonas de desenvolvimento proximal, o uso de funções semióticas, a importância do conhecimento declarativo ou o papel reflexivo do treinador abrem vias promissoras de pesquisa, mas demandam considerações cuidadosas.

Repetidamente, Vygotsky (1986) nos lembra que a aprendizagem não pode ser limitada às habilidades motoras, mas à habilidade de dar ao aprendiz oportunidades de acessar níveis de conhecimento mais altos e mais complexos. O processo de aprendizagem sempre vai ter alguns efeitos, mesmo que o professor/treinador não esteja consciente deles.

Para os pesquisadores contemporâneos, o desafio ainda está no caminho aberto por Vygotsky, com necessidade de desvelar os efeitos e transformações causados pelo processo de aprendizagem em **cada** participante em atividades esportivas. No mundo da vida, existe apenas sujeitos e eles estabelecem relações de significância, não de causalidade. Os conceitos de (a) passar do exterior para o interior e (b) zonas de desenvolvimento proximal ainda estão distantes para que os pesquisadores explorem e reorganizem nosso entendimento sobre a aquisição de *expertise* no esporte.

Vygotsky mostrou, *avant la lettre*, o que Latour (2010) afirmou cerca de 70 anos mais tarde: "precisamos transformar nossos recursos em tópicos." (p. 37). Ele sempre seguiu a lógica da pesquisa, começando pelos dados disponíveis e não saltando para conclusões pré-definidas. Deste ponto de vista, sua epistemologia não é de forma alguma construtivista, dada dimensão social e histórica que impede de reduzir o desenvolvimento cognitivo à mera construção de conceitos. O mundo não é feito de conhecimento e menos ainda de conhecimento unificado. Podemos tentar conhecê-lo, mas não é a mesma coisa.

Referências

Bloch, M. (2012). Anthropology and the cognitive challenge. Cambridge: University Press.

Dewey, J. (1933). How We Think: A Restatement of the Relation of Reflective Thinking to the Educative Process. Boston, MA: D.C. Heath & Co Publishers

Gibbs, G. (1988). Learning by Doing, Oxford, Oxford Polytechnic.

James, W. (2017). The will to believe. Akron, Midwest Journal Press.

Kolb, D.A. & Fry, R.E. (1975). Toward an applied theory of experiential learning. In C. Cooper (ed.), Theories of Group Processes (33-57). New York, John Wiley & Sons.

Knapp, B. (1963). The attainment of proficiency. London, Routledge & Kegan Paul PLC.

Latour, B. (2010). Cogitamus. Paris, La Découverte.

Mahlo, F. (1974). L'acte tactique en jeu. Paris, Vigot Frères.

North, J. (2013). Philosophical underpinnings of coaching practice research. Quest, 65:3, 278-299.

Pill, S. (2017). Using Appreciative Inquiry to explore Australian football coaches' experience with game sense coaching Using Appreciative Inquiry to explore Australian football coaches' experience with game sense coaching. Sport, Education and Society, 20(6), 799–818. http://doi.org/10.1080/13573322.2013.831343

Renshaw, I., Araújo, D., Button, C., Chow, J. Y., Davids, K., & Moy, B. (2016). Why the Constraints-Led Approach is not Teaching Games for Understanding: a clarification. Physical Education and Sport Pedagogy, 21(5), 459–480. http://doi.org/10.1080/17408989.2015.1095870.

Richards, P., Mascarenhas, D., & Collins, D. (2012). Developing rapid high-pressure team decision-making skills. The integration of slow deliberate reflective learning within the competitive performance environment: a case study of elite netball. Reflective Practice: International and Multidisciplinary Perspectives, 13:3, 407-424.

Schön, D. (1987). Educating the reflective practitioner. San Francisco: Jossey-Bass.

Spaaj, R., Oxford, S., & Ruth, J. (2016). Transforming communities through sport. critical pedagogy and sport for development, Sport, Education and Society, 21(4): 570-587.

Taleb, N. N. (2012). Anti-fragile. London: Penguin Books.

Teodorescu, L. (2003). Problemas de teoria e metodologia nos jogos desportivos. Lisboa, Livros Horizonte.

Vygotsky, L. (1986). Thought and Language. Cambridge, MA: MIT.

Vygotsky, L. (1980). Mind in Society. Cambridge, MA: Harvard University press

2.

OS ATLETAS SÃO LIVRES NAS SUAS ESCOLHAS?

Pascal SÉVÉRAC, França
Universidade Paris-Leste, LIS (EA 4395)

Serge ÉLOI, França
Universidade Paris-Leste, LIRTES (EA7313)

Introdução

A questão das escolhas está no coração das práticas esportivas. Mas o que quer dizer escolher, já que o tempo dedicado a esta atividade é reduzido ao mais justo? O que quer dizer escolher quando sua própria escolha depende da atividade de outrem (parceiros ou adversários) e terá consequências sobre o futuro coletivo? É para avançar nesta reflexão que nós nos propusemos confrontar nossos pontos de vista: de um lado, um filósofo que conduz pesquisas sobre Spinoza e Vygotsky; de outro, um praticante (professor e treinador)/pesquisador, também Vygotskiano, que toma os esportes coletivos como uma prática social constituída por elementos culturais dignos de serem transmitidos. No coração da decisão, e notadamente aquela que deve ser considerada em plena urgência, encontra-se a incerteza.

1. A incerteza: propriedades e paradoxo

O que é a incerteza? Podemos realmente criá-la e, se sim, para que ela pode servir? No quadro das práticas esportivas, que consequência tem esta incerteza sobre a relação de oposição ataque/defesa? Eis algumas questões essenciais nas quais é necessário se fixar se quisermos apreender as práticas esportiva sem alterar sua complexidade. Definindo a incerteza como estado no qual nos encontramos quando não sabemos que evento pode acontecer, começamos a capturar os problemas ligados à tomada de decisão.

Constatemos primeiramente que, nos esportes coletivos, os protagonistas de um jogo não param de tentar colocar seus adversários em uma situação desconfortável. Para fazê-lo, eles tentam tornar equiprovável a aparição dos eventos que eles controlam, isto é, eles se organizam para que seus adversários estimem que cada possibilidade tem a mesma possibilidade de acontecer. Quanto mais a probabilidade de dois eventos acontecerem for igual, mais a incerteza ligada a um desses eventos aumenta. Para a equipe que ataca, criar incerteza manipulando a informação mergulha a equipe rival em um estado de dúvida: os jogadores, na defesa, tentam decifrar a situação imposta pelos adversários, e esse estado de precariedade os obriga a aguardar, a mudar o momento da decisão. Eles precisam acumular uma quantidade suficiente de indícios que confirmem qual é o evento que vai se produzir, para entrar em ação. A propriedade essencial da produção da incerteza é, então, colocar o adversário em atraso.

Mas tal situação nos reserva algumas surpresas, pois, cansada de ser manipulada, a equipe em defesa pode, por sua vez, usar estratagemas para sair dessa situação delicada. É o que denominamos "paradoxo da incerteza".

Nos esportes coletivos, há sempre, de um lado, uma equipe que toma iniciativa e outra que a suporta. No voleibol, por exemplo, a equipe que está sacando vai lutar, não sem correr riscos, de colocar a equipe que está na recepção numa situação ruim. Se ela tem sucesso nisso, o esquema ofensivo (dessa equipe adversária) se torna irrealizável. A incerteza para a equipe na defesa (que acabou de sacar) se reduz à sua expressão mais simples. Um bloco coletivo pode se configurar.

Contudo, no voleibol, as estatísticas mostram que em seis em cada dez casos, o sacador não pode impedir que a recepção chegue nas mãos do passador (Éloi, 2011). Nessas condições, é a equipe na recepção que tem a iniciativa na troca. Escolhendo um esquema ofensivo particular, o passador coordena os movimentos sem bola de quatro jogadores que se engajam em tempos e espaços de ataque diferentes. É isso que chamamos de "alternativas espaciais e temporais de ataques". Os atacantes propõem, mas é o passador que dispõe. O objetivo do passador é colocar o atacante escolhido em posição de "um contra um". Com efeito, é constatado que, em dois a cada três casos, quando o atacante tem apenas um bloqueador de frente para ele, ele marca o ponto. Já quando o atacante se encontra de frente para dois bloqueadores, ele só marca o ponto em um a cada três casos.

Trata-se então de propor esquemas táticos (combinações de ataques) que semeiem a dúvida entre os três bloqueadores adversários, assim como de escolher o atacante que ele finalmente deverá arrebatar. Como a iniciativa é do passador, o bloqueador central do adversário está sempre atrasado. Ele se submete ao jogo do passador adversário.

No entanto, o bloqueador central pode escolher retomar a iniciativa. Cansado de correr aqui e ali sem sucesso, ele pode decidir fazer uma aposta. Certamente, essa tomada de decisão é ousada. Mas entre correr atrás da bola sem nunca tocá-la ou tomar uma opção e, uma vez, ultrapassar o jogado que ataque, existe apenas um passo que esses jogadores darão, de tão mais dispostos a superar os eventos precedentes que eles estarão. É assim que os defensores podem derrubar a tendência. Ou pelo menos são levados a crer. No lugar de se submeter, eles tomam a frente. Evidentemente, eles podem fazer uma má escolha. Mas se sua escolha for a boa, eles emboscam, vigiam o atacante, e são eles que o surpreendem.

Assim, criar incerteza no adversário é correr o risco de ter que responder, à sua vez, a uma reação imprevisível ou ao menos pouco previsível e, então, assumir o risco de ser colocado na incerteza. Daí uma dialética de produção de incerteza recíproca entre os adversários.

2. Compreender o que está em jogo no jogo

Como sair do círculo da incerteza? É possível? Como pelo menos reduzir essa incerteza, quando se é o dono da escolha, para não ser submetido ao paradoxo da incerteza, pra não ficar preso na dialética, apesar de tudo arriscada, de produção de incerteza?

O ponto de partida da nossa reflexão será esclarecido pelo dilema do burro de Buridan. Recuperada por Vygostky no seu estudo sobre o domínio do próprio comportamento (especialmente no capítulo 12 do seu *História do desenvolvimento das funções psíquicas superiores*), essa situação coloca em cena um burro que, sofrendo tanto de fome quanto de sede, se encontra à igual distância de um balde de água e de um saco de aveia. Na impossibilidade de escolher, o burro termina morrendo de fome e de sede.

Figura 1: A parábola do burro de Buridan

Apoiado em Spinoza, Vygotsky analisa essa situação – que ele aplica no caso da escola como campo de experimentação – para concluir que um homem, em circunstâncias semelhantes (circunstâncias de dilema ou de "duplo constrangimento"), encontrará ou inventará um motivo (dito "auxiliar") para tomar uma decisão: diferente do animal, o homem sai do dilema pela força de seu pensamento, nos diz Vygotsky. Este homem, por exemplo, porque se trata de uma situação radicalmente indecidível e urgente de ser desemaranhada, escolhe tirar a sorte – ou, como dissemos, fazer uma aposta: este pode não ser o meio mais elaborado de decidir, mas às vezes é a única solução. Vygotsky se opõe, em todo caso, à ideia de que homem, diferentemente do animal, consegue decidir porque é dotado de livre arbítrio, isto é, de uma faculdade absolutamente indeterminada de se autodeterminar: ele então rejeita a solução tradicional para o problema do burro de Buridan, que é uma solução espiritualista que consiste em dizer que o homem tem uma natureza diferente da do animal, porque ele é capaz, devido ao seu livre arbítrio, de produzir *ex nihilo* uma nova situação – como Deus foi capaz de criar o mundo a partir do nada.

Mais exatamente, para contrariar a tese espiritualista do livre arbítrio, Vygotsky se serve paradoxalmente de uma citação de um trabalho de juventude de Spinoza (os *Princípios da Filosofia Cartesiana*), no qual o filósofo não desenvolve seu próprio pensamento, mas apresenta o de Descartes (o do seu *Princípios da Filosofia*): Spinoza retoma a afirmação cartesiana de acordo com a qual o homem, à diferença do animal (do burro), pode se desvencilhar de uma situação de dilema equilibradamente porque ele é uma "coisa pensante". Vygotsky, no entanto, interpreta essa afirmação não da maneira cartesiana de que a essência da alma é o livre arbítrio, isto é, que o espírito é dotado de uma potência de vontade absolutamente indeterminada, mas sim de que o espírito é uma potência de pensamento no sentido de uma potência de agir, de uma potência de compreender. Ou, é justamente aí que está o sentido propriamente spinozista da ideia de que o espírito é uma coisa pensante. O espírito é aqui entendido como alguma coisa que, por sua potência de pensamento, tem a capacidade de resolver os problemas produzindo ideias adequadas. Isso não é o pensamento como livre arbítrio, mas o pensamento como atividade de conceitualização, potência de ligação (entre um problema e uma solução), reivindicada por Vygotsky, o qual está totalmente consciente de que Spinoza não pode ser incluído entre os defensores de uma substância da alma, que agiria fundamentalmente por si mesma, sem ser determinada por nada.

Vygotsky faz uso da referência a Spinoza para sustentar uma reflexão sobre a memória, de que o espírito não está livre dessa liberdade de indeterminação: "Que procedimento então nos recomenda a técnica mnemônica? Cada um de nós escolhe mais ou menos inconscientemente suas maneiras de fazer. O talento de quem se lembra consiste em capturar, em um fragmento de prose, ideias que se sobressaem, breves frases, palavras simples que atraem para si páginas inteiras. Aproximamo-nos aqui de um ponto da mais alta importância a partir do qual se abre toda uma perspectiva filosófica, que não vamos explorar de maneira tão aprofundada. Lembremo-nos somente *en passant* que um outro grande filósofo – Spinoza – via justamente na memória uma prova de que nosso espírito não é livre. Nós não podemos fazer nada de acordo com o que decreta o espírito, dizia ele, se nós não lembrarmos dele [a fórmula vem da nota da proposição 2 da terceira parte de *Ética*]. Efetivamente, o papel decisivo da memória no estudo da intenção mostra a que ponto todas as nossas intenções estão ligadas a um dispositivo da memória que deve em seguida realizá-las (Vygotsky, 2014, p. 436).

O espírito não é livre, nem se torna livre, tanto para Spinoza como para Vygotsky, sem que haja poder de pensar ou de compreender: "A liberdade humana consiste precisamente em que pensa, quer dizer, em que toma consciência da situação criada." (Vygotsky, 2014, p. 470).

O paradigma cartesiano do livre arbítrio a partir de então rejeitado por Vygotsky, através da figura de W. James, que ele critica por recorrer a um "fiat!" divino para explicitar a liberdade: "[...] é algo como o ato de criação do mundo que se repete aqui, a partir de uma escala microscópica. É isso que volta a dizer, para explicar um ato voluntário, um homem de ciência, alguém que está no terreno do empírico, e traz pura e simplesmente o discurso bíblico sobre a criação do mundo." (Vygotsky, 2014, p. 482).

Vygotsky contesta então, resolutamente, que a solução do problema da liberdade não possa ser encontrada "no terreno de um estudo científico determinista da vontade". (Ibid.) A solução é conceber a liberdade a partir do determinismo, em seu seio, e fazê-lo com atenção à potência de agir do espírito que se encontra na situação de escolher. De acordo com Vygotsky, essa potência já existe no nativo da África do Sul do qual Lévy-Bruhl fala, que, ao responder a pergunta do missionário sobre mandar seu filho para a escola, responde "Verei isto em sonho". (Vygotsky, 2014, p. 176). Vygotsky afirma que certamente não se trata de um pensamento racional, mas de um pensamento que, contudo, tem sua positividade, já que ele envolve "um início de autocontrole consciente". (Ibid.) Vygotsky vai ainda mais longe no caso, também relatado por Lévy-Bruhl, do *kaffir* que, para memorizar um sermão, utiliza primeiramente somente sua memória, para depois utilizar um instrumento, um bastão, no qual ele faz entalhes. Vygotsky contesta a interpretação de Lévy-Bruhl, para quem essa solução marca uma impotência do espírito, que se refugia mais na memória do que na reflexão: "[...] nós somos inclinados a ver ali justamente o inverso: um exemplo de como o intelecto do homem o leva a criar novas formas de memória. Quanto pensamento é necessário para gravar um discurso com a ajuda de entalhes em um pedaço de madeira! Mas, dito isso *en passant*, o que é essencial e nos interessa é a diferença entre uma memorização e a outra." (Vygotsky, 2014, p. 185)[1].

A primeira forma de memória, que não usa instrumentos, está totalmente submissa ao princípio do estímulo-reação; ela não passa de efeito de uma causa exterior, e a potência do pensamento do *kaffir* não faz nada além de participar residualmente da causalidade desse efeito. Na segunda forma de memória, no entanto, ele tem uma atividade verdadeira, que toma corpo com o bastão, formando uma causa comum com ele, ou seja, faz do estímulo exterior uma forma de autoestímulo. Logo, ter uma causa comum com uma alteridade, tornar-se uma causa adequada com seus próprios efeitos, enquanto permanece uma causa causada, quer dizer, produzir efeitos que se explicam por sua própria potência, mesmo quando essa potência resta integralmente inscrita no determinismo causal, tal é a definição de Spinoza de liberdade.

Acontece o mesmo, explica Vygotsky, com uma criança que é, de forma experimental, colocada em condições próximas às do burro de Buridan: ela talvez não encontre sozinha a solução – a de tirar na sorte –, mas se for colocada no caminho por outro, então uma verdadeira atividade é suscitada, uma atividade adequada ao sentido do termo para Spinoza. "O sujeito demonstra irresolução, ele hesita, pesa os motivos, tenta colocá-los numa balança. Às vezes a escolha demora e se torna extremamente difícil. Nesses casos, nós introduzimos um novo elemento complementar, que constitui o centro de nossas experiências: nós sugerimos à criança em dificuldade a ideia de fazer sua escolha na sorte. Para sugerir essa ideia, existem diversos meios, começando por simplesmente colocar à mesa um dado a ser jogado, ou deixar a criança brincar com este dado antes da experiência, para depois colocar diretamente a pergunta: ela não quer tirar na sorte? Ou ainda, apelar à imitação direta, com a criança vendo como outro resolve o mesmo problema." (Vygotsky, 2014, p. 467).

---

[1] Também teria que ser considerado (especialmente a partir do *Tratado da Reforma do Entendimento*, bem como da quinta parte de Ética) como Spinoza pensa essa relação – essa relação interfuncional, diria Vygotsky – entre intelecto e memória.

Sobre essa criança que pouco a pouco toma consciência de que deve escolher, e que passa a utilizar esse meio – tirar na sorte – a partir da sua própria potência de pensamento, Vygotsky afirma: "sua liberdade é a consciência da necessidade" (Vygotsky, 2014, p. 471). Ele usa ainda uma expressão mais forte, no caso do homem que decide fazer uma greve de fome para defender uma causa ou de permanecer numa mesa de cirurgia para que seu braço seja operado (exemplo tomado de W. James): "A liberdade de que então se trata, tanto no caso de um como de outro, não é entendida como liberdade em relação à necessidade, é a liberdade enquanto necessidade compreendida. Neste plano, a expressão "pegar pela mão" pode ter um sentido literal, como também a expressão "suportar a dor apertando os dentes". O que significa que, na base de tal liberdade, assim como na base da liberdade em relação ao mundo exterior, há a inteligência da necessidade." (Vygotsky, 2014, p. 484).

"A inteligência da necessidade": uma fórmula perfeitamente *Spinozista* para definir a liberdade. Poderíamos até afirmar: a liberdade, segundo Spinoza, é a força afetiva que causa a inteligência da necessidade – uma definição que serviria muito bem para Vygotsky, já que mostra a ligação entre função cognitiva e função afetiva.

Ele reencontra a concepção de liberdade de Spinoza como compreensão das lógicas que conduzem uma situação – essas lógicas podem por sua vez surgir da história da situação: a inteligência da necessidade, a inteligência da situação tal como é determinada pode se nutrir, com efeito, do conhecimento sobre a história do *set* ou da partida jogada, ou ainda da análise de outras partidas jogadas pelos mesmos adversários, ou mesmo da análise das tendências dos jogadores adversários de acordo com a configuração do jogo na qual eles são levados a operar.

Essa oposição entre livre arbítrio e inteligência sobre a situação pode, então, remeter, em certa medida, à oposição entre, de um lado, teorias da ação situada, de acordo com as quais, tudo apareceria aos atores aqui e agora, tudo se decidiria *in situ*, na qual somente a situação presente *hit et nunc* permitiria determinar, decidir; e, de outro lado, o que nós chamamos de inteligência sobre a situação, que existe, ao mesmo tempo, que se conheça a história pregressa dessa situação, e capturar seus fatos presentes. De acordo com essa segunda teoria, o que está em jogo no jogo é sempre determinado pela complexidade da situação, a qual se caracteriza pelo emaranhamento de uma pluralidade de elementos às vezes muito diferentes, e pela imprevisibilidade do que esse sistema complexo produzirá *in fine*. Nessa perspectiva, a complexidade só pode modelar. É ilusória pretender resolvê-la. Há então um interesse maior em modelar um sistema complexo, porque a possibilidade de injetar nesse sistema elementos que controlamos pode potencialmente conduzir a saídas favoráveis.

3. A aptidão para a pluralidade simultânea

Mas até onde pode ir essa inteligência sobre a situação em circunstâncias de prática esportiva, nas quais cada decisão deve ser tomada em um estado de pressão maior ou menor? Até onde pode ir, na urgência de uma situação de jogo, essa modelização da complexidade? O que se faz de nossas decisões em situações em que a oposição de protagonistas é direta e interdependente?

Para encarar a urgência de uma situação, na prática esportiva, parece necessário formar jogadores aptos à "pluralidade simultânea". O que entendemos sobre isso? Tomemos exemplos: no voleibol, o estrategista do ataque é o passador. É ele que recebe todas as bolas destinadas a serem atacadas. Ele é o distribuidor de passes, permitindo ataques cravados. Formar um passador apto à pluralidade simultânea é formar um passador que, ao mesmo tempo que olha a bola que ele se apressa em passar, vê – com ajuda de sua visão periférica – o movimento, ou a espera, do bloqueador central do adversário. Se, na urgência da situação, o passador alcança essa pluralidade simultânea de percepções e afetações, ele sempre dá a bola ao atacante diante do qual só há um bloqueador, ele estará em uma situação de sucesso total.

Nós compreendemos melhor assim o que significa, para nós, decidir através da "inteligência sobre a situação" e não do "livre arbítrio": se existisse, o livre arbítrio produziria o arbitrário. Ora, tal arbitrário, por acaso, pode ser um sucesso, mas pode também estar destinado ao fracasso. A inteligência sobre a situação, ao contrário, permite reduzir a incerteza e os riscos de fracasso. Mas vemos que essa inteligência não deve ser entendida em um sentido intelectualista: como diria Spinoza, a inteligência é a atividade de um espírito que tem lugar simultaneamente à atividade de um corpo.

Essa atividade do corpo, de acordo com Spinoza, se define por sua aptidão para ser afetado e afetar, de várias maneiras e ao mesmo tempo – na urgência de uma situação esportiva, por exemplo: é nessa condição que o espírito compreenderá o que é melhor fazer.

Spinoza, em *Ética*, define dois critérios a partir dos quais podemos dizer que um corpo é mais ativo que o outro e, consequentemente, a partir dos quais podemos dizer que um espírito é mais ativo que outro (o espírito definido como "a ideia de um corpo", como sua consciência viva). Esses critérios são a multiplicidade e autonomia (ver a nota da proposição 13 da parte II de *Ética*).

De acordo com o primeiro critério, um corpo ativo é um corpo capaz de construir múltiplas relações com os outros, um corpo aberto aos encontros diversos e variados. A multiplicidade é boa, para Spinoza, pois ela é compatível com a simultaneidade. O corpo passivo é o corpo fechado em si mesmo, congelado em suas experiências de tal maneira que é pouco afetado pelos outros e que eles pouco lhe afetam: o corpo passivo experimenta pouca plasticidade e pouca adaptabilidade; o corpo ativo é um corpo altamente lábil.

Logo, um corpo sensível, um corpo plástico, é um corpo que dá ao espírito uma multiplicidade de coisas para pensar. Para que um espírito compreenda qualquer coisa, para que ele se torne verdadeiramente ativo, é preciso começar dando-lhe material para pensar: ele precisa de sensações, percepções, imaginações, como diz Spinoza, mesmo que no começo essas ideias sejam confusas, imprecisas, parciais. De qualquer maneira, para Spinoza, um espírito ativo pode ter tantas ideias inadequadas quanto um espírito passivo (ver a nota da proposição 20 da parte V de *Ética*), e isso não só não é grave, mas – nós mesmos podemos acrescentar – é absolutamente indispensável. Todo o problema é saber o que faz o espírito desse rico material para pensar. Daí a intervenção do segundo critério, o da singularidade da ação corporal, correspondente, no espírito, à formação de uma compreensão distinta.

O segundo critério de definição de um corpo superior aos demais é, com efeito, que a ação de tal corpo dependa o máximo possível somente dele mesmo. Como alcançar essa autonomia corporal? Como compreender essa fraca participação dos outros corpos na produção de uma ação por um corpo ativo? Poderíamos interpretar esse segundo critério imaginando a necessidade de uma certa separação desse corpo em relação aos outros: o corpo cujo espírito compreende distintamente seria assim "um grande corpo solitário", impermeável às influências mundanas – imperturbável, ele se fecharia em si mesmo, por exemplo, durante a partida de voleibol, se deixando perturbar o mínimo possível pelas solicitações exteriores. Esse corpo seria como um centro de movimentos realizados com todo o domínio, sem ajuda de outros. A distinção das percepções do espírito viria justamente da distinção corporal, que se obteria pelo afastamento ou pela separação do corpo em relação aos demais. Haveria, aqui, nessa ideia, uma espécie de resíduo de cartesianismo: certamente, não é porque o corpo está inerte ou passivo que o espírito pensa bem (a atividade mental resta correlativa a uma atividade corporal), mas é quando o corpo age sozinho, de uma certa forma retirada do mundo ou autossuficiente, que o espírito poderia se dedicar a compreender as coisas distintamente, notadamente as ações do próprio corpo. A força da alma de um jogador, sua fortaleza, para usar uma palavra antiga, requereria a solidão do corpo.

É justamente para desmontar tal interpretação que o primeiro critério interveio antes do segundo: um corpo tanto mais independente na produtividade de suas ações quanto não esteja fechado às afetações dos outros corpos. Aqui temos todo o paradoxo da atividade corporal e toda a dificuldade de articular os dois critérios de superioridade de um corpo em relação aos outros.

A questão para Spinoza é pensar a autonomia do corpo no determinismo: melhor, se trata de mostrar que um corpo é tão mais forte quanto ele faça corpo com outros corpos. E fazer corpo não significa se dissolver ou se dispersar na multidão de outros, corpos, mas tornar-se independente em suas ações, singularizar-se graças a eles.

Reformulemos o paradoxo: um corpo superior é um corpo que age só com o outros. É a alta plasticidade do corpo que garante sua alta independência.

Não se deve opor, mas sim articular, multiplicidade simultânea a autonomia, determinismo plural e independência: para Spinoza, só somos ativos quando, produzindo um efeito, não somos determinados por outros. Somos ativos simplesmente quando a explicação do efeito que produzimos não necessita recorrer a outras causas, diferentes de nós, para ser estabelecida.

Para Spinoza, é ativo, ou causa adequada, aquela cujo efeito pode se compreender por si mesmo. Isso não significa que sejamos então uma causa não causada, uma causa não determinada ou não afetada por outros, mas que somos ativos quando basta não levar em conta que a causalidade de que somos portadores pode dar conta do efeito produzido. Isso só é possível se agirmos através de uma causalidade comum às causas que nos determinam, que nos afetam. É nesse sentido que um corpo é uma causa singular, independente, distinta: porque ele forma uma causa comum com a causalidade de outros corpos. E mais uma vez, essa causalidade comum não significa que o corpo é somente uma parte da causalidade total que explica sua ação, mas que essa causalidade total que explica sua ação atravessa por inteiro esse corpo que é ativo, assim como os demais corpos que o afetam. Isso só é possível em virtude do primeiro critério, a saber, que corpo agindo de forma autônoma está altamente apto a ser afetado. O primeiro critério de superioridade de um corpo é na verdade a condição do segundo critério: somente um corpo apto a ser afetado de várias maneiras ao mesmo tempo pode agir através das propriedades que ele tem em comum com outros corpos, em outras palavras, somente um corpo superiormente sensível é capaz de agir sozinho, de produzir ações que não necessitam do concurso de outros corpos para serem compreendidas.

Os dois critérios de superioridade de um corpo e de um espírito, então, não formam um só, eles se enriquecem mutuamente. O primeiro mostra que não saberíamos compreender a singularidade da ação do corpo como exclusão pura e simples dos outros corpos: pelo contrário, um corpo não age sozinho, sem concurso de outros corpos, se não estiver apto a ser afetado por eles de numerosas maneiras ao mesmo tempo. Reciprocamente, um corpo apto a ser muito afetado não é um corpo que se dispersa, se espalha ou se diverte nas conexões que estabelece com os outros corpos: é um corpo cuja quantidade de afetações simultâneas lhe dá potência para produzir uma ação que só depende dele mesmo.

Vemos deste então que as ideias de atividade e passividade devem ser redefinidas: a atividade não se define mais como movimento obrigado, forçado, quer dizer, como agitação. Pelo contrário, o corpo ativo pode ser um corpo que espera o movimento do adversário para se decidir (como o passador no vôlei). O jogador ativo é aquele que age percebendo a multiplicidade dos movimentos no jogo, compreendendo de uma vez sua lógica, que parte sabendo qual gesto é melhor para a necessidade da situação. O jogador passivo, por sua vez, não é necessariamente o jogador imóvel, em repouso: é o jogador que age, mas que é colocado em ação pelo outro, que faz sem compreender, ao acaso, sendo causa somente parcial ou inadequada, nas palavras de Spinoza, de seu próprio gesto – enquanto que o jogador ativo é causa total ou adequada de seu gesto, e isso não porque ele é determinado a agir por alguma coisa, mas porque ele se determina de acordo com a lógica da situação. A atividade, nesse sentido, se caracteriza por uma alta aptidão para a recepção de informações, uma alta sensibilidade às questões do jogo. Atividade é o outro nome da liberdade, de acordo com Spinoza, assim como com Vygotsky, que afirma ao fim do capítulo 12 de *História do desenvolvimento das funções psíquicas superiores*: "Nós não podemos não observar que chegamos à própria concepção de liberdade e de domínio de si que desenvolveu Spinoza em sua *Ética*." (Vygotsky, 2014, p. 488)

É porque não é tanto o jogador, mas a própria situação, que decide: ou melhor, é o jogador, como parte integrante da situação, um jogador que faz corpo com uma necessidade, ainda mais que ele age na urgência, sem defasagem em relação ao jogo.

Conclusão

Para concluir, diremos que o apropriado para uma boa decisão, no momento muito breve em que o gesto se torna decisivo para marcar um ponto, um gol etc., consiste em produzir, no adversário, o inesperado, a novidade, a tal ponto que o adversário fica como estupefato, atordoado, impedido. Resta impossível, para ele, o reflexo de automatismo de desencadear tal ou tal movimento para agir de forma eficaz: o bloqueador não sabe mais o que fazer. Os jogadores ficam como "pregados no chão", seu movimento de pensamento e de ação parece bloqueado: é correto falar em proibição. É esse fenômeno físico-psíquico que Spinoza chama de admiração, e que considera como negação a potência de agir, como corte na atividade, psíquica e física. A decisão eficaz em urgência, portanto, é aquela que, no jogador ativo, não surge da memória, do puro automatismo mnemônico, mas de uma compreensão que ultrapassa o encadeamento ordinário, automático, de movimentos e que, de uma só vez, no jogador passivo, impede qualquer recurso a um encadeamento mnemônico de movimentos. E se dizemos que as teorias da ação situada não são suficientes para dar conta dessa atividade de produção novamente adequada à inteligência sobre a situação, é porque é preciso mais trabalho – de formação de jogadores e de preparação de jogo – para alcançar decisões eficazes em um contexto de urgência.

Referências

Spinoza, (1988). Éthique. Traduction Bernard Pautrat. Paris, Seuil.

Clot, Y. (2003). Vygotsky, la conscience comme liaison. Préface à la 1re édition de *Conscience, inconscient,* émotions, Lev S. Vygotsky, Paris, La Dispute.

Clot, Y. (2017). L'affect et sa signification. Postface à la 2e édition de *Conscience, inconscient,* émotions, Lev S. Vygotsky, Paris, La Dispute.

Éloi, S. (2011). Analyse technologique du rôle de libéro en volley-ball : une influence paradoxale sur le jeu. *EJRIEPS*, (23), 46–75.

Sévérac, P. (2005). *Le devenir actif chez Spinoza*. Paris, Honoré Champion.

Spinoza (1964). *Principes de la philosophie de Descartes* dans Œuvres I, traduction Charles Appuhn. Paris, GF-Flammarion.

Vygotsky, L. S. (2014). *Histoire du développement des fonctions psychiques supérieures*. Traduction de Françoise Sève, édition préparée par Michel Brossard et Lucien Sève. Paris, La Dispute.

II. DA TEORIA À PRÁTICA

1.

CONSTRUIR UMA FERRAMENTA DE OBSERVAÇÃO DO JOGO DE RUGBY DE 7 POR ESTUDANTES FUTUROS EDUCADORES: UMA ATIVIDADE INSTRUMENTAL MEDIATIZADA

Gilles UHLRICH, França
Universidade Paris Sul, Paris Saclay, CIAMS (ED566)

Resumo

As pesquisas que convocam os trabalhos de Vygotsky evocam o desenvolvimento dos sujeitos não como um processo baseado em etapas a cumprir de acordo com uma lógica que obedece a leis naturais, mas através de crises e saltos qualitativos. Esses estados são difíceis de serem apreendidos e de controlar pelo educador, porque estão muito ligados com os meios materiais e sociais colocados. Eles são também inferidos da história e da vivência dos sujeitos. Vygotsky (2014) exprime a ideia de que é pela implementação de atividades instrumentais mediatizadas que o desenvolvimento dos sujeitos é estimulado. Essas atividades, mediadas por ferramentas, contribuem para a construção de instrumentos psicológicos apropriados para cada sujeito. Nessa lógica, nós mostraremos aqui como a mobilização de uma ferramenta considerada como um artefato material (Éloi & Uhlrich, 2011), o *software* Sportscode de construção de observação de jogo, integrado em um dispositivo de formação em observação para estudantes em formação de educadores em esporte, provoca, entre eles, o desenvolvimento a partir dos conflitos que gera.

Introdução

O sistema escolar francês parece estar, há algum tempo, no centro de profundas mutações, as quais intrigam especialistas e pesquisadores (Van Zanten, 2000). A escola funciona há muito tempo tomando emprestados certos conceitos piagetianos sem apreciar limites, frequentemente evocados pelo próprio autor. Por exemplo, os estágios do desenvolvimento distinguidos por Piaget, principalmente a primeira infância, parecem organizar o conjunto do sistema escolar francês em diferentes níveis de escola (maternal, primária, colégio, liceu), de acordo com um princípio de progressão quase natural e linear. No entanto, certas proposições, em termos de educação, levam a uma outra perspectiva e tendem a ganhar importância. Falar de perspectiva sócio-construtivista ao invés de construtivista é considerar a aprendizagem de um aluno como condição de desenvolvimento ao invés do contrário não é mais absurdo. Essas ideias são largamente emprestadas dos trabalhos de Vygotsky mesmo que seja conveniente ser muito prudente quanto a uma utilização abusiva desses conceitos. Sem entrar em uma descrição detalhada das fundações das teorias piagetianas e vygotskianas, e destacando o papel principal dos trabalhos de um depois do outro, na reflexão sobre aprendizagem e desenvolvimento, nós mesmo assim distinguimos duas posições. Parece que em Piaget, se as estruturas cognitivas individuais são bem solicitadas na relação do sujeito com seu ambiente, as ferramentas de pensamento repousam sobre uma construção em grande parte autônoma e funcionalmente endógena. O desenvolvimento de um indivíduo está então condicionado à sua estrutura interna, que parece ser o berço da construção e da estabilização de invariantes operatórias ou de esquemas. Essa estrutura interna estável condicionaria a relação do indivíduo com seu ambiente. Já em Vygotsky, o desenvolvimento cognitivo propriamente humano é primeiramente condicionado por sua relação com o exterior. É justo pela dinâmica de interação entre um meio social culturalmente rico e as funções psicológicas superiores de um indivíduo que se constrói o desenvolvimento. Essa dinâmica é alimentada pela utilização de signos e de instrumentos de pensamento que, partindo do exterior, vão ser interiorizados pelos indivíduos em desenvolvimento. Tomando essa perspectiva, parece então sábio para um instrutor pensar a proposição de instrumentos na atividade de um sujeito. Mas convém sobretudo considerar sua atividade de utilização no que ela permite o desenvolvimento do signo que alimenta então um instrumento psicológico. É esse posicionamento teórico que nós vamos interrogar na ocasião da implantação de um dispositivo de formação em observação de jogo de Rugby de 7 por estudantes destinados a se tornar profissionais de intervenção educativa em esportes.

1. Vygotsky e a educação

Vygotsky questiona a educação não como um fenômeno natural de desenvolvimento de um indivíduo que se vai preencher com conhecimento, mas a definindo como "o desenvolvimento artificial da criança" (2014, p. 572). Ele acrescenta que a educação é "o domínio artificial dos processos naturais do desenvolvimento" e não faz senão "exercer sua influência sobre tal ou tal processo de desenvolvimento" (2014, p. 573). Nessa dinâmica, Vygotsky questionar a teoria dos "dons naturais" ou ainda do desenvolvimento de um indivíduo que obedece a passagens lógicas por estágios que limitariam a atividade dos aprendizes ao longo de sua evolução no tempo.

Considerando essa orientação, Vygotsky precisa o que ele entende por desenvolvimento. "No processo de desenvolvimento, a criança é equipada e reequipada com ferramentas as mais variadas; entre a criança mais velha e mais jovem, o que faz a diferença ainda é o nível e o caráter de seu ferramental, de sua instrumentalização, quer dizer, o nível de domínio de seu próprio comportamento" (2014, p. 573). A maior ou menor capacidade de fazer uso de suas funções naturais e apropriação de ferramentas psicológicas são determinantes essenciais de todo tipo de desenvolvimento da criança. A concepção do desenvolvimento da criança de Vygotksy é então "uma concepção histórico-cultural ligada a pensar como a apropriação e o uso de ferramentas e técnicas culturais, de natureza semiótica e/ou instrumental, conferem ao desenvolvimento suas formas, seus conteúdos e suas contradições, através de atividades, frequentemente de natureza assimétrica, compartilhadas com outrem" (Rochex, 2003, p. 5). É com base nessas ideias que nós conduzimos nossos trabalhos de pesquisa, evocando mais precisamente a noção de atividade instrumental mediatizada, de acordo com o princípio da dupla estimulação. Nós buscamos compreender como, "adicionando, aos estímulos naturais, estímulos artificiais bem escolhidos" (Sève, 2014, p. 54), os estudantes produzem uma atividade instrumental que possa ser significativa para um desenvolvimento cultural. Nós evocamos então o conceito de atividade instrumental mediatizada.

2. Determinar uma atividade instrumental mediatizada

De acordo com Sève, a atividade instrumental mediatizada "é interposição de um instrumento mediador – ferramenta, signo – entre o sujeito e seu objeto, que não só aumenta sua eficácia, mas modifica qualitativamente a estrutura, a qual se tornou triangular" (Vygotsky, 2014, p. 54). Nós decididamente nos inserimos nessa perspectiva, ao analisar o funcionamento dessa estrutura triangular na qual consideramos o funcionamento do instrumento como artefatual. Agora, vamos precisar o que entendemos por atividade instrumental mediatizada.

2.1 Atividade, ações, operações

Com base nos conceitos da teoria da atividade desenvolvidos por Vygotsky (1978) e Léontiev (1981), nós consideramos a atividade como toda ação humana mediada por artefatos portadores de uma dimensão histórica e cultural que ligam o pensamento do indivíduo ao da sociedade na qual ele vive. Convém, nesse quadro, considerar não somente o indivíduo, mas também a natureza coletiva dessa atividade. A atividade se realiza então em um ambiente social. Léontiev determina a atividade como o conjunto das ações humanas que se desenrolam em um dado contexto, baseadas em motivos para agir particulares, ações realizadas de acordo com um objetivo fixado pelo sujeito e operações consideradas então como meios mobilizados para agir. Nessa organização em sistema, o instrumento mobilizado pelo sujeito responde às suas funções de incitação e orientação, tanto quanto às de realização. Assim, o indivíduo pode articular, em toda atividade, sentido e eficiência.

2.2 O instrumento em uma lógica de gênese instrumental (Rabardel, 1995)

Para determinar esse conceito de instrumento, nós nos inspiramos nos trabalhos de Rabardel (1995), os quais fundamentam uma teoria instrumental que distingue a ferramenta técnica e o instrumento. Ele então caracteriza o processo de gênese instrumental. Um sujeito que toma para si uma ferramenta, qualquer que seja ela, começa um duplo movimento de instrumentação e instrumentalização. A ferramenta, por sua mobilização, se torna um artefato, no sentido de que provoca um incidente na atividade do sujeito. A instrumentação corresponde à exploração de potencialidades da ferramenta proposta, que nós então consideramos como um momento de "tomada nas mãos" (Uhlrich & Éloi, 2016). Esse primeiro movimento leva o sujeito a dar sentido e orientação para a atividade que ele realiza. O artefato se torna instrumento. O segundo movimento corresponde à instrumentalização. O sujeito faz evoluir seus modos de utilização para "colocar em sua mão". Ele então determina sua atividade a partir de novas ações, as quais precisam de outras operações, precisas e identificáveis. Para o pesquisador, esses dois movimentos devem ser caracterizados considerando-se que exprimem desde o início a mobilização da ferramenta, mas que existem certamente momentos decisivos a se observar. Com base na dinâmica de gênese instrumental, nós introduzimos, na atividade de nossos estudantes, ferramentas tecnológicas então consideradas como artefatos. O artefato é um incidente introduzido voluntariamente na atividade do aprendiz, de modo a fazer evoluir sua experiência. Nós então buscamos compreender o efeito desse artefato na atividade de formação e, mais particularmente, a evolução deles na conceitualização do que fazem em sua própria prática. Nós nos localizamos, assim, em uma postura dupla, que questiona a atividade instrumentada. Por um lado, "a cada artefato correspondem possibilidades de transformação dos objetos da atividade, os quais foram antecipados, pesquisados deliberadamente, e estão suscetíveis a se atualizar no uso" (Rabardel, 1995, p. 60). Por outro lado, ignorar as modificações conduzidas pela introdução de um artefato nas interações leva o educador a correr o risco de participar somente de uma reprodução do idêntico (Rochex, 2003). O artefato tem a vocação de produzir um efeito propício. Ele é finalizado porque visa trazer uma solução vantajosa a um dado problema. Ele é evolutivo e pode se aperfeiçoar com o tempo. Mas ele também é imprevisível, porque colocá-lo à prova não prediz os usos futuros que se pode fazer dele (desvio, catacrese). Nosso trabalho consiste então em distinguir momentos particulares que correspondem a momentos de dúvidas, de questionamento das controvérsias entre os formandos, postulando que o desenvolvimento de um indivíduo não se dá de maneira linear, mas em momentos de crise e de "saltos pedagógicos" repentinos. Nós então nos juntamos à posição de Vygotsky, conforme descrita por Sève, quanto à educação: "De encontro às ilusões da educação sem esforço, é preciso organizar os saltos que não podem faltar a nenhum aluno, para que alcancem níveis de desenvolvimento superiores" (Sève, 2014, p. 56). Esses saltos se organizam ao propor dispositivos que impliquem em uma necessária mediatização.

2.3 Em torno do conceito de mediatização

Etimologicamente, mediato se opõe a imediato. A mediatização implica, então, em agir indiretamente, a atividade do sujeito só está em relação com outra coisa por um intermediário, de jurisdição mediada, de conhecimento mediado, abstrato ou intelectual, em oposição ao conhecimento imediato. Logo, a mediatização corresponde a uma mediação técnica. Mediatizar consiste em oferecer suporte para atividades de sujeitos que vão ajudar na sua conceitualização: esquemas, grades, ajudas à realização. Assim, em cada ação de mediatização existe o conceitual. A partir de então, as operações de mediatização que dizem respeito à cenarização de conteúdos deve considerar a mediatização de relação que se instaura entre o emitente e o destinatário. Se a mediatização pode se conceber como uma forma de mediação, ela não o será concretamente se não for conduzida de maneira profissional, dentro do conhecimento e do domínio das especificidades das ferramentas empregadas e seus usos. Sève (2014, p. 63) considera a mediatização no coração da psicologia vygotskiana. Além do curso "natural" da atividade operada pelo sujeito, desenvolve-se, através da mediatização do instrumento, uma significação da ação vetor de um pensamento conceitual.

Com esse posicionamento teórico interpretado a partir dos trabalhos de Vygotsky, vamos apresentar sucintamente aquilo a que dedicamos nossa atenção há mais de 10 anos. (Uhlrich, 2005; Éloi & Uhlrich, 2011; Uhlrich, Éloi & Bouthier, 2011; Uhlrich & Éloi, 2016) Nós analisamos o impacto da introdução de um artefato material na formação dos futuros educadores esportivos e, particularmente, na sua capacidade de observar e interpretar o jogo de rugby que se desenrola diante de seus olhos.

3. Estudo da atividade instrumental mediatizada em um dispositivo de formação para a observação do jogo de Rugby de 7

Nós funcionamos profissionalmente em uma situação particular, já que intervimos junto a estudantes de uma instituição de formação de futuros educadores. Assim, não somente convém, em um primeiro nível, formar os estudantes em novos conceitos que lhes permitam ao mesmo tempo descrever práticas físicas e esportivas com precisão, mas trata-se também, em um segundo nível, de interpretar o comportamento dos outros (os jogadores) com vistas a lhes propor situações que vão permitir sua própria transformação. O futuro educador deve ser capaz de "dizer sobre o fazer" dos outros. Então, é necessário, para nós, considerar o desenvolvimento desses estudantes com base nas perspectivas vygotskianas evocadas acima. Temos nós mesmos que nos colocar no lugar de situações de aprendizagem, consistindo não em reproduzir receitas, mas possibilitando a mobilização de signos com fins de desenvolvimento de instrumentos psicológicos pelos estudantes. Enfim, existe um terceiro nível que nos interessa profissionalmente, que é o fato de os dispositivos utilizados questionam de acordo com uma lógica científica. No quadro de um procedimento tecnológico, trabalhos de pesquisa sobre essas mesmas situações de aprendizagem colocam a questão de sua eficácia e a identificação do "movimento" dos sujeitos, permitindo-nos, assim, distingui-lo do "desenvolvimento" (Uhlrich, Éloi & Bouthier, 2011). Nós então questionamos o uso de artefatos no desenvolvimento da atividade humana. Questionamos a aprendizagem requerida para dominar esses objetos técnicos de acordo com um processo de gênese instrumental. É por isso que instalamos os estudantes dentro de uma "atividade instrumental mediatizada".

3.1 A tomada nas mãos do *software*, o período de instrumentação

Propusemos a estudantes futuros educadores esportivos inscritos em um curso universitário de STAPS (*Sciences et Techniques des Activités Physiques et Sportives* – Ciências e Técnicas de Atividades Físicas e Esportivas) mobilizar uma ferramenta de informática para descrição das ações de jogo no Rugby de 7. Eles mobilizam o *software* Sportscode, considerado um artefato material (Éloi & Uhlrich, 2014). O objetivo inicial da formação é fazer funcionar minimamente essa ferramenta técnica. Os estudantes devem tomar nas mãos o *software* de descrição do jogo, que lhes permite, ao longo de todo o desenrolar de uma partida, distinguir ações de acordo com um guia preciso (Anexo 1). Nossa primeira intenção é que os estudantes em questão se apropriem dos indicadores que lhes permitem distinguir as ações do rugby umas das outras, para melhor identificar o jogo que se desenrola diante de seus olhos. Essa atividade tem, então, como função, permitir aos estudantes iluminar aquilo que se passa de maneira efêmera e complexa, para que possam qualificá-lo. Essa atividade cultural lhes permite construir signo, particularmente quando devem distinguir os momentos de equilíbrio e desequilíbrio, para qualificar a evolução de uma relação de força entre duas equipes que se enfrentam. O *software* de observação é feito de modo a orientar o olhar do treinado para levar em conta sistematicamente essa relação de oposição em rugby, considerando a ação dos atacantes em relação às reações dos defensores que os encaram.

Durante o primeiro período de mobilização do *software*, os sujeitos efetuam uma "tomada nas mãos" do artefato. Os estudantes testam "rotinas de captura" que dão resultados mais ou menos conclusivos. Eles se instalaram em uma situação de simulação sob a forma de binômios, o que inevitavelmente engaja uma mediação. O trabalho de observação se desenvolve numa sala, diante de uma partida projetada em uma tela. Essa configuração permite observar momentos de experimentação e incerteza, que levam a suspender a retransmissão. Os estudantes ocupam, alternativamente, dois papéis:

- O papel do secretário que coleta os dados: ele captura, com a ajuda do *software*, as informações que lhe são comunicadas em voz alta por seu colega. Ele olha apenas para a tela do computador.
- O papel do comentarista (informante): ele descreve as ações do jogo, que ele observa durante o desenrolar da partida, e as comunica a seu colega. Ele olha apenas para o jogo (tela de televisão ou ao vivo, desde a beira do campo).

Esse trabalho colaborativo leva os estudantes a mobilizar o instrumento de acordo com tarefas distintas que não deixam de provocar controvérsia. Com efeito, ao longo do trabalho de observação, nenhum dos protagonistas pode se limitar estritamente a seu papel. Nós observamos a partir de imagens gravadas que o informante não consegue se impedir de verificar a exatidão da coleta, realizada pelo parceiro. Por sua vez, o secretario controla que o informante caracterize corretamente as ações do jogo a serem capturadas, olhando para a tela do vídeo que passa a partida. Instalam-se a partir de então trocas que levam à controvérsia sobre a qualificação das fases do jogo. A ferramenta do vídeo permite então efetuar um retorno para trás e submeter ao debate os momentos característicos que precisam de um esclarecimento sobre as fases de jogo observadas. As trocas se referem aos indicadores recolhidos sobre os jogadores, que permitem a qualificação da fase do jogo. Depois, para fazer um acordo, os estudantes voltam à definição isolada da modelização do jogo, que alimenta um guia de descrição. Eles se posicionam, colocando em relação as atitudes dos jogadores, as trajetórias das corridas de atacantes de defensores ou ainda dos gestos do árbitro. O momento da controvérsia é especialmente frutífero, por trazer à luz concepções que fundamentam sua observação do jogo de rugby. Ao longo das trocas, se constrói então uma linguagem comum sobre a descrição do jogo. Eles desenvolvem uma nova interpretação do jogo. Os signos sobre o jogo se tornam signos para eles mesmos, alimentando, de fato, seu instrumento psicológico.

3.2 O período de instrumentalização

O período de instrumentalização constitui um prolongamento do período de instrumentação. Aqui, o sujeito constrói para si um referencial dos usos adequados ou ineficazes da ferramenta. Ele coloca o instrumento "em sua mão". No nosso caso, esse segundo tempo se realiza na fase de finalização do módulo de formação para a observação. A fase de instrumentalização corresponde à necessidade sugerida pelo formador, de fazer evoluir a ferramenta dentro da perspectiva de sua utilização ao vivo em um torneio internacional universitário de Rugby de 7 (o Central Seven). O fato de dever mobilizar a ferramenta na situação de uma partida real leva os estudantes a se concentrar em seu caráter ergonômico, para deixá-la mais adaptada para uma coleta rápida e eficiente. Com efeito, eles não poderão mais fazer parar a imagem, nem voltar atrás para qualificar as ações que acontecem diante de seus olhos. Eles deverão mobilizar seus instrumentos psicológicos no calor da realidade. Eles não estarão mais em uma atividade simulada. As observações realizadas serão comunicadas aos treinadores das equipes em questão, o que implica em um relatório fiel ao "cenário da partida". Ao longo do trabalho de reorganização ergonômica da coleta, eles têm a liberdade, oferecida pelo *software*, de modificar a disposição dos ícones. Eles são igualmente levados a acrescentar ícones que lhes faltarem. O processo de gênese instrumental aqui é impulsionado a um outro nível. Os estudantes capazes de provocar evolução no dispositivo original, respeitando as concepções iniciais, mostram que compreenderam a lógica da modelização subjacente proposta, a qual contribuiu em parte para a construção do artefato material. Eles então se descolam de uma simples execução de tarefas impostas pelo instrumento, para questioná-lo. Aqui, encontramos o que Brossard (2018) considera como uma inversão de interpretação do funcionamento humano pela utilização de mediadores ou de meios artificiais. "Ao invés de serem dependentes das leis naturais, os indivíduos agora estabelecem objetivos para si mesmos e são capazes de produzir e transformar em permanência não só seu meio exterior, mas também seu próprio modo de funcionamento. A atividade se torna um momento de uma história humana e não o simples resultado de processos naturais" (Brossard, 2018, p. 19). Esse estabelecimento de um novo objetivo em sua atividade, assim como a liberdade ou a ultrapassagem de função que foram concedidas aos estudantes, leva-os a, por um lado, personalizar o instrumento que eles mobilizam e, por outro, os conduz a novos questionamentos sobre o desenrolar do jogo nessa perspectiva de descrição da relação de oposição entre ataque e defesa. Aqui, mais uma vez, observamos essas evoluções a partir de questões que eles se colocam e proposições que fazem, em vista da modificação do *software*. O obstáculo que eles tentam novamente ultrapassar provoca o desenvolvimento da observação que fazem do jogo de Rugby de 7.

Conclusão

O recurso ao artefato material revela-se, então, particularmente pertinente nessa fase de formação inicial. Trata-se, para o estudante, de transformar a identificação de uma situação de jogo através de um clique em uma tecla do computador. Há a transformação do estudante porque uma fase de jogo realizada por outros é identificada, depois interpretada, para tornar-se uma ocorrência em uma grade de observação. E é justamente o problema de identificação das evoluções do estudante que está no coração dessa formação para a observação. Nessa dinâmica, em que a mobilização de artefatos permite esse movimento? É, nos parece, o modo de utilização do artefato que permite contribuir para essa evolução. Com efeito, longe de encerrar o observador em um funcionamento estereotipado, colocar a prova o artefato o obriga a fazer idas e voltas entre a lembrança do que vem de acontecer diante de seus olhos e as possibilidades de caracterização que lhe são ofertadas. Todo o interesse é o de tomar partido de eventuais dissonâncias e conseguir a possibilidade de fazer evoluir o artefato. Essa capacidade de criar sentido sobre o jogo observado alimenta uma nova significação. Essa significação que alimenta a concepção do treinado é bem compreendida em conexão com a subjetividade de cada ator e não é desejável que generalizemos essas evoluções. Mas, a partir desse exemplo, a questão pode realmente se colocar, sobre saber como a atividade instrumental mediatizada tem como consequência favorecer, no aluno, a construção de uma conceitualização na ação (Vergnaud, 1996), permitindo utilizar com eficiência o artefato material. Nós formulamos a hipótese de que a mobilização do artefato material conduz à construção "indireta" de um artefato cognitivo (Éloi & Uhlrich, 2011) favorável à construção de um verdadeiro instrumento de pensamento.

Bibliografia

Brossard, M. (2018). Vygotsky aujourd'hui. *In EPS et culturalisme* : jeux, arts, sports et *développement humain*. Contrepied hors-série n° 20-21, centre EPS et société.

Éloi, S. & Uhlrich, G. (2011). La démarche technologique en STAPS : analyse conceptuelle et mise en perspective pour les sports collectifs. *eJRIEPS, 23.* 20 – 45

Éloi, S. & Uhlrich, G. (2014) : Utilisation d'artefacts dans le domaine des pratiques physiques, sportives et artistiques (PPSA). *TrasnFormations, Recherches en* éducation *et formation des adultes, 12, 117 – 137.*

Leontiev, A. N. (1981). The problem of activity in psychology. *In* J.V.Wertsch (ed.), *The concept of activity in Soviet psychology.* Armonk, NY : M. E. Sharpe.

Rabardel, P. (1995). *Les hommes et les technologies, approche cognitive des instruments contemporains.* Paris : Armand Colin.

Rochex, Y. (2003). La théorie Vygotskienne n'est pas un temple mais un chantier. *In Vygotsky et l'éducation.* Ss la dir. de A. Kozulin et al. Ed. Retz, pp; 4 – 6.

Sève, L. (2014). Présentation. In Brossard et Sève. *Histoire du développement des fonctions psychiques supérieures.* Paris : La Dispute.

Uhlrich, G. (2005). *Rôle des artefacts matériels et cognitifs dans le développement des compétences de l'intervenant* éducatif *et rugby.* Thèse non publiée. Université Bordeaux 2, V. Segalen.

Uhlrich, G., Éloi, S. & Bouthier, D. (2011). « La technologie dans le contexte des STAPS : de la conception d'outils à la conceptualisation… et réciproquement », *eJRIEPS 23*, p. 4-19.

Uhlrich, G & Éloi, S. (2016). Formation à l'observation de futurs intervenants éducatifs en rugby : quelles conséquences pour leur conception du jeu ? *Revue des sciences de l'éducation, 42/2,* 123 -147.

Van Zanten, A. & al. (2000). *Les transformations de l'école.* Ed. La Découverte, 2000, 415 p

VERGNAUD, G. (1996). « Au fond de l'action, la conceptualisation ». In J.-M. Barbier, *Savoirs théoriques et savoirs d'action.* Paris : PUF. p. 275-292.

VYGOTSKY, L. (1978 / 1930). *Mind in society: The development of higher psychological processes.* Cambridge, MA : Harvard University Press.

VYGOTSKY, L. (2014). *Histoire du développement des fonctions psychiques supérieures.* Paris : La Dispute.

Anexo 1: guia de utilização do software Sportscode

***CAP INDEX* em 7:** *Cada ação caracterizada abaixo associa a qualidade técnica e energética da realização e a relevância da escolha tática do ataque.*

Contexto	Pontuação	Tentativas Transformação Penalidades		
Fase estática	CE/CR			**CE / CR +:** recuperação de balão **CE / CR -:** recuperação do adversário e desequilíbrio **CE / CR Neutro:** recuperação do adversário com equilíbrio
	Penalidade			**Penalidade +:** criação de desequilíbrio ou ganho significativo de terreno. **Penalidade -:** escolha inadequada colocando a equipe sob pressão da defesa adversária ou perda da bola (chave não encontrada ...) **Penalidade Neutra:** criação de nenhum desequilíbrio, ganho de terreno insignificante.
	Toque			**Toque +** : ganho da bola e aproveitamento com possibilidade de desequilíbrio imediato. **Toque -** : perda da bola. **Toque Neutro** : ganhar a bola com circulação obrigatória em equilíbrio.
	Corpo a corpo			**Corpo a corpo +:** pegue a bola e use-a com a possibilidade de criar um desequilíbrio imediato. **Corpo a corpo -** : perda da bola **Corpo a corpo neutro** : ganhar a bola com a obrigação de um movimento equilibrado.
	Na frente da defesa	Jogo de mão	Contournant	*Passe (s) longo (s) ao longo da largura para passar a extremidade defensiva (intervalo entre o toque e o último defensor)* **Déployé Contournant +** : criação de um desequilíbrio do lado de fora, estouro. **Déployé Contournant -** : jogo de estouro e perda da bola. **Déployé Contournant Neutre** : movimento da bola ao longo da largura sem desequilíbrio
			Penetrante	*Iniciativas do corredor ou passe (s) na largura com cruzamento da defesa em intervalo.* **Déployé Pénétrant +** : criação de um desequilíbrio diferente do exterior, cruzamento. **Déployé Pénétrant -** : intervalo de ataque e perda da bola. **Déployé Pénétrant Neutre** : ataque um intervalo e não crie nenhum desequilíbrio.
		Chutando	Liberação	*Chute que alivia a pressão da equipe ao ganhar terreno.* **Folga com os pés +**: ganho significativo em terreno com reversão de pressão **Folga com os pés -** : ganho insignificante de terreno, nova pressão sobre sua equipe **Jogo de chute neutro**: ganho significativo de terreno, nova pressão sobre sua equipe
			Ofensiva	*Jogo de chute com intenção de recuperar a bola da queda.* **Jogo de chute ofensivo +** : recepção da bola por sua equipe. **Jogo de chute ofensivo -** : recepção da bola pelo adversário e colocando sua equipe em dificuldade. **Chute ofensivo neutro**: recepção da bola pela equipe adversária sem criar desequilíbrio

Fase de movimento total	**Em contato com a Defesa**	Bloqueio longo	*Ruck ou maul long, a defesa posiciona-se na saída da bola.* **Bloqueio longo +** : conservação da bola, progressão e criação de um desequilíbrio explorável. **Bloqueio longo -** : perda da bola **Bloqueio longo neutro** : conservação da bola sem criar desequilíbrio.
		Bloco Curto	*Ruck ou maul court, o desequilíbrio é preservado na saída do balão.* **Bloqueio curto +** : conservação da bola, progressão e criação de um desequilíbrio explorável. **Bloqueio curto -** : perda da bola. **Bloqueio curto Neutro** : conservação da bola sem criar desequilíbrio
		Pivô Axial	*Passe profundo no eixo para estender o movimento em andamento ou para transformá-lo.* **Pivô Axial +** : No passe, distância da bola dos zagueiros com criação de desequilíbrio **Pivô Axial -** : Pelo passe a perda da bola **Pivô Axial Neutro** : No passe, distância da bola dos zagueiros sem criar desequilíbrio
	Em defesa	Duelo 1/1	*A cortina está cruzada, duelo de homem a homem contra o líbero.* **Duelo 1/1 +** : oponente eliminado individualmente, ganho significativo de terreno. **Duelo 1/1 -** : perda da bola **Duelo 1/1 neutro** : adversário não eliminado individualmente, fica com a bola
		Manobra Coletiva	*A cortina passa, 2 ou mais atacantes contra o líbero.* **Manobra Coletiva +** : oponente eliminado por uma manobra, ganho significativo de terreno. **Manobra Coletiva -** : perda da bola. **Manobra Coletiva Neutro** : adversário não eliminado por uma manobra, ficar com a bola.
	Contra-ataque		*Recuperando a bola da linha de frente ou atrás.* **Contra-ataque +** : criação ou uso de um desequilíbrio com ganho significativo de terreno. **Contra-ataque -** : Perda de bola e / ou perda significativa de terreno. **Contra-ataque Neutro** : Sem criação de desequilíbrio e sem ganho de terreno.

2.

APRENDER A FAZER ESCOLHAS EM VOLEIBOL EM SITUAÇÃO DE 2 CONTRA (1+1). CONTRIBUIÇÃO DA TEORIA INSTRUMENTAL DE VYGOTSKY

Serge ÉLOI, França
Universidade Paris-Leste, LIRTES (EA7313)

Introdução

As práticas esportivas e artísticas se manifestam em diferentes setores: o do ensino (escolar, universitário), o do treinamento (federação, clubes), o da recreação (centros de lazer, colônias de férias) e até o dos encontros auto-organizados em que os praticantes se encontram a partir de acordos mútuos, sem que nenhuma estrutura identificada coordene as práticas. Qualquer que seja o setor, a questão da transmissão, mais ou menos racionalizada, dos saberes ligados a essas práticas continua uma preocupação permanente (Éloi & Uhlrich, 2011). Nós queremos explorar aqui uma situação já bem descrita (Éloi & Uhlrich, 2013; Éloi & Uhlrich, 2014; Éloi, 2017), a dos 2 contra (1+1) no voleibol. Nós nos propomos a precisar as etapas do processo de gênese instrumental (Rabardel, 1995), anteriormente descrita nos textos já citados, alimentando-nos da teoria instrumental de Vygotsky. Nós nos focaremos mais especificamente no conceito de signo, tal qual ele foi conceitualizado por Vygotsky em diferentes obras (1978; 1934/1997; 1935/1997; 2012; 1931/2014), para compreender como, nessa situação particular, ele tem um papel preponderante. Este estudo se apoia em experimentações realizadas no ensino do voleibol, no quadro da formação inicial de estudantes universitários de 2° ano, os quais pretendem se tornar professores de educação física.

1. A situação de 2 contra (1+1)

O objetivo deste curso de voleibol no 2º ano da Licenciatura visa mobilizar tanto os recursos motores dos estudantes quando suscitar sua reflexão sobre o ensino dessa disciplina esportiva. Esse curso tem, então, um valor duplo de "Prática de voleibol – Reflexão didática sobre o voleibol". As características dos grupos de estudantes que se sucedem todo ano não mudam fundamentalmente. As mesmas observações podem ser renovadas. Os mesmos obstáculos podem ser identificados. É necessário explicar que esses estudantes não são especialistas em voleibol. Ao longo dessa prática, o professor pode observar um estereótipo que se apresenta sistematicamente, compreendido em uma situação efetivamente reduzida como o 2 contra 2. Pode-se descrever esse estereótipo assim: ao longo de uma rotação, quando um aluno recebe a bola, ele utiliza invariavelmente e independentemente da estrutura da oposição (posicionamentos e deslocamentos do parceiro e dois adversários) uma das duas escolhas seguintes:

- A escolha "coletiva": pode-se observar porque os alunos fazem invariavelmente o passe a seu parceiro.
- A escolha "individualista": pode-se identificar quando os alunos mandam a bola sempre diretamente ao adversário.

Assim, a eficácia da resposta encontra sua justificativa na adaptação de sua própria ação à relação de oposição do momento. Assim, nem uma nem outra dessas escolhas é *a priori* melhor. Às vezes, é preciso fazer um passe, em outras, é preciso devolver a bola diretamente. Na prática de esportes coletivos, nada está escrito antecipadamente. Como relação de força é flutuante, é preciso "ler" a situação para jogar sabiamente.

Aqui, nos interessamos pelos problemas das escolhas táticas. Como liberar os alunos desse estereótipo de decisão? Pode-se transmitir a capacidade de escolher? Pode-se definir o que é uma boa escolha? Notaremos que essas questões ultrapassam largamente a simples formação de futuros professores de educação física. Elas se juntam a uma problemática cultural mais geral: a da tomada de decisões.

2. A gênese instrumental

É para tentar remediar esse problema dos estereótipos que nós introduzimos a situação dos "2 contra (1+1)" no voleibol (Éloi & Uhlrich, 2013). A situação recorre a um artefato, quer dizer, um incidente, o qual podemos caracterizar "como utilização de um objeto material ou não, voluntariamente introduzido pelo educador na atividade do sujeito, visando a modificação do curso normal de sua prática, com o objetivo de provocar uma compreensão nova de sua atividade" (Éloi & Uhlrich, 2011, p. 30). Aqui, trata-se de um artefato regulamentar. Nós falamos de artefato regulamentar porque se trata de uma regra nova que será introduzida na situação do jogo. A regra oficial vai então sofrer uma "transformação transitória" e é pela mediação dessa nova regra que o educador vai buscar provocar uma mudança na atividade dos sujeitos.

Na continuidade dos trabalhos de Rabardel (1995), nós pensamos que, no quadro do ensino ou do treinamento esportivo, a introdução de um artefato desencadeia um processo de gênese instrumental, e que esse processo se realiza em uma sucessão de períodos de instrumentação e instrumentalização cíclico. Esses ciclos podem então se reproduzir tanto quanto for necessário, ao longo do desenvolvimento do sujeito. É isso que nós mostramos com essa situação dos "2 contra (1+1)" no voleibol (Éloi & Uhlrich, 2013).

2.1. A instrumentação

A instrumentação corresponde a um período durante o qual o sujeito "toma na mão" o artefato (Éloi & Uhlrich, 2013). Ele testa seus possíveis usos, efeitos, limites. "Nós utilizaremos o termo instrumentação... para designar aspectos do processo de gênese instrumental orientados na direção do próprio sujeito" (Rabardel, 1995, p. 137). O sujeito deve encontrar os recursos nele mesmo, para utilizar *a minima* a ferramenta proposta. "A instrumentação é então esse processo através do qual as restrições e as potencialidades de um artefato vão condicionar de forma durável a ação de um sujeito para resolver um dado problema" (Trouche, 2005, p. 274).

2.2. A instrumentalização

Na sequência dessa fase de maneira mais ou menos imbricada, vai suceder uma outra frase, dita de instrumentalização. Ela corresponde a "tomar em suas mãos" (Éloi & Uhlrich, 2013) do artefato pelo sujeito. Aqui, o sujeito vai de qualquer maneira dominar o artefato para adaptá-lo a seu uso pessoal. "Nós reservamos este (o termo) instrumentalização para o processo dirigido ao artefato" (Rabardel, 1995, p. 137). Essa "retomada nas mãos" pode ir até a modificação do artefato. Aqui, a atividade do sujeito está voltada na direção do artefato.

2.3. O processo de apropriação: um duplo movimento

É então esse duplo movimento que, para nós, caracteriza a gênese instrumental. Notemos que Félix & Vérillon (2017) evocam dois eixos de desenvolvimento: "A partir de então, vemos se desenhar, para os instrumentos, dois eixos distintos, sejam mais ou menos solidários, de desenvolvimento potencial: um eixo de desenvolvimento operatório centrípeto, de instrumentação (desenvolvimento esquemático, representacional...), ao curso do qual os usuários tentam 'tomar na mão' (Éloi & Uhlrich, 2013; 2014) o artefato; e um eixo de desenvolvimento artefatual centrífugo, dito de instrumentalização (desenvolvimento das funcionalidades do artefato), no curso do qual os usuários se esforçam para 'colocar em sua mão' (ibidem), em uma perspectiva continuada do artefato" (Félix & Vérillon, 2017, p. 19). Trata-se agora de apresentar o artefato regulamentar e a maneira como ele opera.

2.4. Divergências científicas

Nós queremos sublinhar aqui um ponto de discussão com a tese inicial de Rabardel, que sugere que "a descoberta progressiva das propriedades (intrínsecas) do artefato pelos sujeitos é acompanhada da acomodação de seus esquemas, mas também de mudanças de significação do instrumento resultante da associação do artefato a novos esquemas" (Rabardel, 1995,

p. 116). Os esclarecimentos que nós vamos desenvolver se distanciam das teorias da escola piagetiana e do recurso ao esquema. Nossos trabalhos encontram um caminho de desenvolvimento no que julgamos mais fecundo, com base nos textos de Vygotsky e especialmente no caráter dialético de sua teoria instrumental. Essa tese não é então a de Rabardel. Para ele, instrumentação e instrumentalização podem se apresentar não importa em qual ordem e até uma sem a outra. Elas não constituem fases bem identificadas. De nossa parte, nós consideramos que uma vez lançado o processo de gênese instrumental, as fases vão se suceder em alternância. Nós pensamos que é aqui que o esclarecimento de Vygotsky pode nos abrir novas perspectivas científicas. O fato é que a intuição de Rabardel, de uma gênese instrumental estruturada por momentos de instrumentação de instrumentalização abre horizontes heurísticos dos mais entusiasmantes.

3. O artefato regulamentar dos 2 contra (1+1)

O artefato regulamentar é introduzido pelo educador quando os estereótipos (coletivo versus individualista) são flagrantes numa situação de 2 contra 2. Como tirar os estudantes de seus estereótipos de decisão?

A inspiração dessa situação nos veio dos jogos eletrônicos. O artefato regulamentar é apresentado como uma fábula, o que não deixa de desafiar o pesquisador em relação às emoções suscitadas pelo estabelecimento dessa situação (Prot, 2017). Essa metáfora é construída sobre a ideia de eu não se é jamais eliminado do jogo. Os protagonistas dispõem de um estoque ilimitado de vidas. O princípio do jogo é de fato bastante simples. O jogador que manda a bola para o adversário está provisoriamente "morto". Para recuperar sua "vida", ele deve ir tocar um dos pilares que delimitam os fundos de seu campo (conforme Figura 1). Uma vez tocado esse pilar, o jogador pode voltar na rotação com as mesmas prerrogativas. Evidentemente, se um jogador for pego jogando a bola quando ainda estiver "morto", a rotação é parada e o ponto é dado ao adversário. Simbolicamente, é ele que tenta "matar" seus adversários e paga com sua "vida" pela iniciativa, tal qual uma abelha que pica, perde seu ferrão e morre. Essa disposição provoca subsequentemente um encaixe de configurações mais ou menos fugazes de

"2 contra 1+1" (o "+1" representando o jogador que saiu para tocar o pilar). É aí que os efeitos dessa medida levam a transformar o objeto da atividade dos sujeitos, isto é, do que ela se trata, e esses objetos vão variar no curso da aprendizagem.

As tentativas realizadas com o objetivo de ganhar a rotação estão agora subordinados ao respeito a uma nova disposição (a nova regra), que vai inicialmente desorientar os praticantes. A atividade dos jogadores é então massivamente redirigida no sentido de respeitar esse novo elemento regulamentar, em detrimento da eficácia do retorno. Esse desvio pode parecer paradoxal e tedioso, já que o objetivo anunciado do professor é tornar os estudantes capazes de se adaptar aos adversários. Na verdade, perdemos tempo para ganhá-lo melhor. É um passo obrigatório para reviver a motricidade "esclerosada" dos estudantes. A introdução do artefato regulamentar se revela como ponto de partida de um processo de causas e efeitos em cascata, que vai levar a tornar indispensável levar em conta posicionamentos e deslocamentos dos adversários. Reconstituir os caminhos do desenvolvimento necessita considerar as mudanças iniciadas pelo artefato desde sua introdução, sem omitir nenhuma das etapas, sob pena de estudar "a reação complexa em sua forma morta, como uma coisa já feita, depois que seu processo de desenvolvimento é alcançado" (Vygotsky, 1931/2014, p. 229).

3.1. Os dois versus (1+1): uma experimentação multidimensional

A experimentação conduzida no curso de um ciclo de ensino no qual a situação é renovada sobre uma sequência de 10 a 15 minutos em cada uma das duas dez sequências necessita uma análise multidimensional.

É preciso, com efeito, indicar quatro dimensões:

- A dos pontos de vista: educador – praticante.
- A das fases: instrumentação – instrumentalização.
- A dos estatutos: atacantes – defensores.
- A da localização do signo: externa – interna; o sujeito, outrem.

3.2. Os pontos de vista

Na nossa situação, é o educador que decide introduzir o artefato regulamentar. Ele escolhe o momento dessa introdução em vista do comportamento de seus aprendizes (alunos, estudantes, jogadores). No entanto, a introdução de um artefato no processo ensino-aprendizagem não passa de uma proposição estabelecida pelo educador, o qual busca seus objetivos. Isso não prediz nada sobre o uso que será feito desse artefato pelos aprendizes.

3.3. Instrumentação – Instrumentalização

A questão dessa dimensão consiste em observar as duas fases. Como garantir que aquilo que se observa se trata de instrumentação ou de instrumentalização? O que permite a passagem de um ao outro?

3.4. No ataque – Em defesa

A particularidade dos esportes coletivos de oposição direta (basquete, futebol, handebol, rugby, voleibol, hockey...) é que os protagonistas podem alternar do status de atacante ao de defensor em um instante. Essa especificidade leva a considerar que a gênese instrumental se desenrolará tanto para uma quanto para outra dessas prerrogativas.

3.5. Onde está o signo? Qual é seu papel?

Vygotsky enuncia uma regra geral: "em uma estrutura superior, o que é o maior determinante funcional ou o início de todo o processo, é o signo e seu modo de utilização." (Vygotsky, 1931/2014, p. 246) Seremos levados a identificar o signo utilizado, mas também a discernir seu lugar ao longo de todo o processo analisado. Qual signo é utilizado e com quais fins? Como ele é emitido? Quem o recebe?

4. O processo de gênese instrumental e seus efeitos sobre o jogo

Nós devemos agora proceder à descrição mais fina do encadeamento das fases que estão ligadas a essa situação. Tudo começa quando o professor introduz o artefato regulamentar e expõe seu princípio.

4.1. Instrumentação defensiva: ir tocar o pilar

O professor propõe um exercício sob a forma de uma situação de 2 contra 2, mas com uma regra diferente que estipula que depois de ter atacado (mandado a bola ao adversário), "se está morto". É impossível jogar de novo na rotação sem ter "recuperado sua vida".

Nessa primeira fase de instrumentação defensiva, os estudantes devem realizar um trabalho de "tomar na mão" essa nova regra. Ela constitui inicialmente uma restrição, um obstáculo inédito. Esse caráter de obstáculo pode ser objetivado pelas observações recorrentes dos jogadores que esquecem de ir tocar o pilar ou ao contrário, que vão tocar o pilar quando recém fizeram um passe a um parceiro (e não quando recém devolveram a bola para o adversário). O praticante esquece que nesse momento de sua progressão no exercício nada o recorda da nova regra, enquanto ele está envolvido na ação. Ele está a partir de então implicado demais na ação para se abrir a outra coisa. É aí que o caráter coletivo da tarefa vai participar do desenvolvimento de cada um. Com efeito, os pontos de vista são diferentes, entre o que deve intervir sobre a bola e é "sob pressão" e seu parceiro que constata que só resta ele como válido em campo (já que imediatamente seu parceiro "morre"). Então é o parceiro que vai lembrar com uma ordem ao que acaba de devolver a bola para o adversário, gritando "Vai tocar!" ou "O pilar!". A situação particular dos 2 contra (1+1) contribui para despertar solidariedades adormecidas no jogo convencional do 2 contra 2. Torna-se então possível ultrapassar o obstáculo. O parceiro pensa pelo outro e o adverte quando toma consciência, ao longo das rotações que seguem, que ele vai ficar sozinho se seu companheiro de equipe não for rapidamente tocar o pilar.

Vejamos o que evolui nessa fase: no início do exercício, nem uma palavra. Depois, ouve-se pouco a pouco os jogadores interpelarem seus parceiros: "Vai tocar!" ou "O pilar!" A alternância de papéis – o que intervém sobre a bola/o parceiro – está ligada aos perigos do jogo. Ela permite que os protagonistas compreendam através da posição do companheiro de equipe o que ele mesmo deve fazer quando se encontrar em seu lugar. Como destaca Vygotsky, "é por intermédio dos outros que nos tornamos nós mesmos." (Vygotsky, 1931/2014, p. 285)

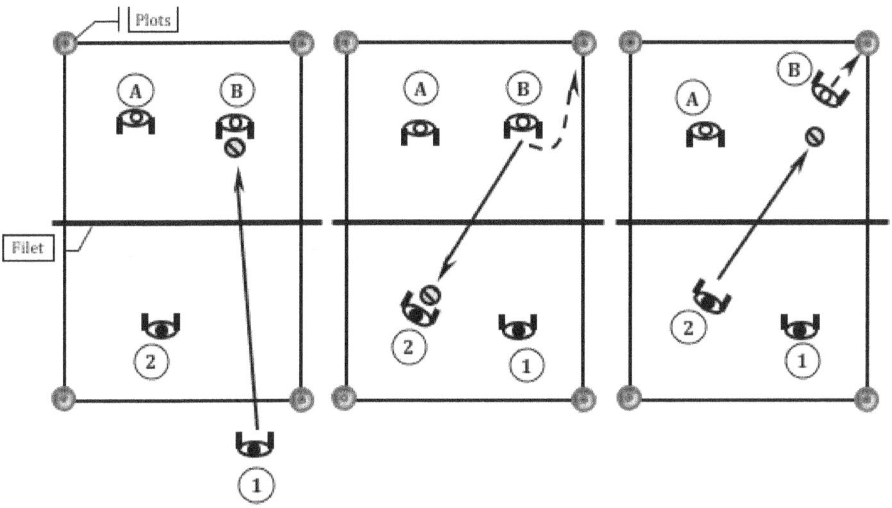

Figura 1: Situação típica de jogo em 2 contra (1+1) no voleibol. Os 3 campos correspondem a 3 momentos do desenrolar da mesma rotação. Campo da esquerda - o jogador **1** serve, o jogador **B** recepciona. Campo do centro - **B** lança na direção de **2** e deve se virar para ir tocar o pilar atrás dele. Campo da direita - **2** lança diretamente na direção de **B**, que deve ir tocar o pilar. Fim da rotação.

4.2. Instrumentação ofensiva: devolver diretamente sobre o adversário morto

Pouco a pouco, as advertências somem. Os jogadores interiorizam que devem ir tocar um pilar. Mas os estereótipos ficam no lugar (coletivo versus individualista). Coloca-se então a questão da resolução estratégica do problema. O professor impulsiona a verbalização dessa solução, mas certos estudantes a colocam já a colocam no lugar. A resolução estratégica do problema é verbalizada coletivamente. Reagrupa-se os participantes e se questiona: "como fazer para ter certeza de ganhar a rotação?" É necessário pouco tempo para que os estudantes elaborem a resposta: "Devemos visar diretamente o adversário 'morto.'" Mas falar não é fazer. Com efeito, tão objetivo requer levar em conta a trajetória da bola que se dirige a si, tomar a informação sobre os adversários e devolver a bola com uma certa precisão, na direção de um ponto particular do campo.

Nessa fase de instrumentação, os estudantes devem "tomar na mão" um novo artefato, cognitivo: a solução estratégica-tática. Ela é aplicável em todos os casos ou quase. Não é mais necessário se perguntar se é necessário fazer um passe ou se é necessário devolver a bola. A devolução direta é sempre a boa solução porque permite pegar os adversários com velocidade. Resta lembrar disso e determinar em qual direção fazê-lo. E, para isso, é preciso parar de jogar às cegas.

Vejamos o que evolui nessa fase: Num primeiro momento, as devoluções diretas aumentam, mesmo que a direção pareça secundária. Depois, progressivamente, a precisão se refina. Primeiramente, o lado bom do campo, aquele do adversário "morto". Depois, busca-se visá-lo. É mesmo um jogo muito divertido fazer cair a bola nas suas costas, enquanto ele se abaixa para tocar o pilar e está a dois dedos de recuperar sua vida. A efetiva tomada na mão do artefato regulamentar pode ser concretamente observada nos dois planos. No plano defensivo, pelas incessantes idas e vindas na direção dos pilares e, no plano ofensivo, por um aumento significativo das devoluções diretas na direção do adversário "morto". A "bomba" da situação é detonada e as instrumentalizações defensivas e ofensivas que vão se seguir não necessitam mais da intervenção do professor. O novo estímulo então é apenas o efeito de causas desencadeadas anteriormente pelo artefato regulamentar (a nova regra) e pelo artefato cognitivo (a solução estratégica-tática do problema).

4.3. Instrumentalização defensiva: compensar a ausência de seu parceiro "morto"

Ao longo das confrontações, as devoluções sobre o parceiro "morto" são cada vez mais frequentes. As perdas de pontos (para a equipe em defesa) se reproduzem frequentemente nas mesmas condições. Com efeito, é preciso compensar a ausência do parceiro que saiu para tocar o pilar. Os ataques sistematizados dos adversários na direção do espaço deixado provisoriamente livre pelo parceiro mergulham o defensor que fica só em um dilema.

- Ou ele permanece no seu lado e deixa um espaço muito aberto para os adversários;
- Ou ele vai para o meio de seu campo para tentar proteger ao mesmo tempo o seu lado e o lado abandonado pelo parceiro.

Vejamos o que evolui nessa fase: é a segundo solução que é pouco a pouco retida pelos estudantes. Vê-se então uma sistematização dessa cobertura defensiva, essa compensação que necessita, para o defensor deixado sozinho, um deslocamento na direção do eixo do campo. Essa adaptação defensiva necessita simultaneamente, entre os atacantes, uma devolução cada vez mais precisa, porque a faixa do campo inacessível ao defensor adversário se reduz drasticamente. É importante assinalar que o educador não deve solicitar essa compensação.

4.4. Instrumentalização ofensiva: pegar a informação e até jogar "ao contrário"

Mais uma vez, é através do coletivo e notadamente pelo intermediário dos comportamentos defensivos que vão ser solicitadas as adaptações ofensivas. Os estudantes são colocados diante de um problema. Quanto mais eles aplicam a instrução estratégica-tática elaborada coletivamente, que consiste em devolver sobre o adversário "morto", mais a bola volta instantaneamente. É porque ao mesmo tempo, o defensor adversário, que ficou sozinho, tomou parte na proteção do lado do campo deixado por seu parceiro "morto". Alguns se posicionam diretamente sobre a metade deixada pelo colega de equipe que partiu para tocar o pilar. Outros podem até ir além do eixo medial do seu campo. Essa cobertura de espaço deixado livre só tem um objetivo: antecipar o ataque dos adversários e se posicionar idealmente sobre a trajetória da bola inicialmente destinada a "finalizar" seu parceiro. Assim, então, a pertinência da solução estratégica-tática adotada encontra seus limites. A constatação de certa perda de confiança é tão fácil que dos dois lados do campo se "compensa" da mesma maneira. É preciso então encontrar uma solução para essa nova situação. Aqui, é no segundo grau que o artefato cognitivo (a solução estratégica-tática) continua a exercer seu papel. Com efeito, são os comportamentos que ele engendra (a compensação) e não mais o artefato como tal (a devolução direta sobre o adversário "morto") que necessitam de uma nova adaptação dos protagonistas.

Vejamos o que evolui nessa fase: o artefato cognitivo, isto é, o plano estratégico-tático adotado coletivamente é agora aplicado por todos quando isso é possível. Mas os jogadores são pegos cada vez mais frequentemente em sua própria armadilha, já que todo mundo conhece essa solução estratégico-tática e pode então antecipá-la, incluindo quando é o adversário que a utiliza. Essa constatação leva, num primeiro momento, a refinar as devoluções. A melhor solução consiste então em "ver" qual é o lado para onde o adversário foi tocar o pilar e devolver a bola nesse lado e o mais próximo do limite lateral do campo adversário. O aumento das bolas que caem desse lado ou justo fora do campo é um bom revelador dessas tentativas. No entanto, pudemos observar que entre alguns estudantes particularmente perspicazes, uma nova solução aparece. Para esses, trata-se de garantir que o adversário vai reagir "normalmente". Eles se dedicam então a confortá-lo em seu julgamento inicial, sabendo que é exatamente a solução da devolução em direção do parceiro "morto" que eles vão utilizar. Esses jogadores particularmente astutos vão se dedicar a enganar seus adversários. Tudo em seu comportamento (deslocamento, posição do corpo, posição das mãos, olhar...) é feito para confortar o adversário em sua crença inicial. Ele deve permanecer persuadido de que a devolução tentará atingir seu parceiro "morto". Um jogo de mímica precede então o toque da bola e depois, no último momento, o jogador com a bola muda bruscamente de orientação e desvela sua verdadeira intenção devolvendo a bola ao contrário do deslocamento do seu adversário.

O laço está enlaçado: O professor, depois de um desvio que pode parecer tedioso, atingiu seus fins. Mudando momentaneamente a regra do jogo, ele estabeleceu condições que permitiram aos alunos abrir os olhos, olhar através, examinar além do seu próprio campo, para levar em conta o jogo dos adversários. O artefato regulamentar criou uma verdadeira encenação da oposição, ao mesmo tempo em que ele desenhou caminhos para uma concepção dialética para gerar tais aprendizagens. Deleplace indica que "o processo pesquisado é fazer descobrir logicamente, dentro da oposição vivida, a relação com o parceiro como uma consequência da relação com o adversário, a trama de fundo do comportamento adequado podendo se enunciar na alternativa:

- Ou posso atravessar eu mesmo uma parte do obstáculo (ou mesmo tudo o que resta do obstáculo a atravessar) e eu devo atravessar, imediatamente, com toda minha energia e toda minha determinação.
- Ou eu não posso, ou não posso mais, atravessar eu mesmo o obstáculo adversário e devo fazer um outro ou certos outros dos meus parceiros atravessarem, sem esperar mais, colocando toda a minha energia e toda a minha determinação em ajudá-los ao máximo." (Deleplace, 1979, p. 101) Coloca-se agora a verdadeira questão que consiste em decidir se a devolução direta é possível ou se é necessário fazer um passe a seu parceiro. O artefato regulamentar se comporta, aqui, como o iniciador de um processo que necessita em seguida da elaboração de um artefato cognitivo (a solução estratégica-tática) cuja aplicação provoca, por sua vez, adaptações relativamente autônomas (quer dizer, sem que elas sejam suscitadas pelo educador). Esse artefato é construído sob a direção do educador. Mas como os sujeitos integram suas novidades? Como eles se tornam capazes de sair de seus estereótipos iniciais? O desvio pelo conceito de signo pode nos fornecer algumas explicações.

5. O signo de acordo com Vygotsky

Para entender o que é o signo em Vygotsky, é preciso considerá-lo como fazendo parte de um sistema: o da significação. "Se a atividade fundamental e a mais geral dos grandes hemisférios nos animais e nos homens é a sinalização, a atividade fundamental e mais geral do homem, que o distingue em primeiro lugar do animal, do ponto de vista psicológico é a significação, isto é, a criação e utilização de signos. [...] A significação é a criação e utilização do signo, isto é, de sinais artificiais." (Vygotsky, 1931/2014, p.192) É, então, para Vygotsky, uma especificidade dos serres humanos dispor de um processo através do qual ele se assinala suas próprias restrições (a ele mesmo e aos outros), para se afastar dos perigos da vida. Sève destaca o modo de pensamento dialético posto aqui: "O que faz do processo de Vygotsky um processo dialético não é simplesmente sua preocupação constante e universal com a essência histórica do psiquismo humano, é sempre se fixas em compreender essa história como um tecido de contradições e tratá-la como tal." (Sève, 2018, p. 56) Não podemos então fazer economia para tratar dessas contradições, se quisermos compreender o processo de desenvolvimento estabelecido na nossa situação. Para Vygotsky, todos os meios artificiais introduzidos pelo homem em situações usuais e que preenchem a função de estimulação de outrem ou de autoestimulação são signos. "De acordo com nossa definição, é um signo todo estímulo convencional, artificialmente criado pelo homem, que seja um meio de dominar o comportamento – o do outro e o seu próprio." (Vygotsky, 2014, p. 190) Assim, então, e contrariamente ao animal, o humano tem a capacidade de se autoestimular, de se autossinalizar, de inventar seus próprios meios de agir, mas também de agir sobre os outros. "Se eles agem como os outros, esses estímulos provêm de uma fonte inteiramente diferente. Eles não são mais dados pela natureza, mas produzidos pela invenção humana, o que muda tudo: a estimulação se converte em autoestimulação [...]" (Sève, 2008, p. 325)

Como tirar partido dessa capacidade humana quando se é educador?

Eis o desafio mais apaixonante que tentamos enfrentar no quadro de nossos ensinos das práticas físicas esportivas e artísticas. É nessa perspectiva que nós vamos retomar a situação dos 2 contra (1+1), nos dedicando a observar a evolução dos signos usuais do educador ou dos estudantes ao longo de todo o processo de gênese instrumental.

6. Metamorfose e migração de signos

A ambição desse parágrafo é seguir o itinerário dos signos ao longo da evolução da situação dos 2 contra (1+1), observando quem os introduz, como eles evoluem, quem os utiliza e para quais fins. Às vezes esses signos são ostensivos, às vezes, invisíveis. Isso se deve à especificidade das funções psicológicas superiores. Vygotsky propõe uma lei geral: "Ao longo do desenvolvimento cultural da criança, toda função entra em cena duas vezes, em dois planos – numa primeira vez social, em seguida psicológica, uma primeira vez entre os indivíduos a título de categoria interpsicológica, em seguida no interior da criança." (Vygotsky, 1931/2014, p. 547)

Um primeiro movimento do signo do exterior em direção ao exterior pode ser notado através da função de significação. "Para nós, dizer, a respeito de um processo, que ele é exterior, é dizer que ele é social. Toda função psicológica superior foi exterior – o que significa que ela foi social; antes de ser uma função, ela foi uma relação social entre duas pessoas. Os meios de agir sobre si foram inicialmente meios de agir sobre os outros, e dos outros sobre a pessoa. (Vygotsky, 1929/2014, p. 545)

Um outro movimento do signo também pode ser acompanhado: o da sua transformação no interior. "Nós chamamos a reconstrução interna de uma operação externa, internalização." (Vygotsky, 1978, p. 56) O trabalho que precisaria ser conduzido consistiria em identificar as etapas do processo de internalização. "A internalização das formas de comportamento cultural implica na reconstrução da atividade psicológica na base das operações de signo." (Vygotsky, 1978, p. 57) Com efeito, para compreender o processo de desenvolvimento em seu conjunto, é preciso identificar cada etapa, pois "a internalização das atividades socialmente enraizadas e historicamente desenvolvidas é a característica discriminante da psicologia humana, a base do salto qualitativo entre a psicologia animal e a psicologia humana." (Vygotsky, 1978, p. 57) Vygotsky faz referência a Janet nessa análise, citando, na nota 7 de *História do desenvolvimento das funções psicológicas superiores* (1931/2014, p. 280): "Todas as leis psicológicas têm dois aspectos: um aspecto referente aos outros homens, um aspecto interior referente a nós", sendo essa segunda forma "posterior à primeira", consistindo em "aplicar a si mesmo o comportamento dos outros entre eles ou em relação a nós mesmos." (Janet, 1929, p. 521)

7. Diferenciação signo-ferramenta

As atividades mediatizadas têm algo em comum, que é tomar caminhos tortuosos. É o caso tanto para o signo quanto para a ferramenta. Vygotsky chama nossa atenção para a importância de diferenciar uma ferramenta e um signo mesmo se "a analogia fundamental entre signo e ferramenta estiver na função de mediação que caracteriza cada um deles." (Vygotsky, 1978, p. 54) No entanto, essas duas entidades são muito diferentes e confundi-las nos condena a não compreender as funções psíquicas superiores. Para Vygotsky, "uma diferença essencial entre signo e ferramenta, que é base de uma divergência real entre as duas linhas, se constitui em diferentes maneiras de orientar o comportamento humano. A função da ferramenta é agir como condutora da influência humana sobre o objeto da atividade; ela é direcionada ao exterior; ela deve conduzir a mudanças nos objetos. É um através do qual a atividade humana externa visa dominar e triunfar na natureza." (Vygotsky, 1978, p. 55) A ferramenta permite ao humano transformar o mundo em que ele vive. Sua utilização conduz à observação de fatos ostensivos que ela permite produzir. "O signo, ao contrário, não muda nada no objeto da operação psicológica. Ele é um meio de atividade interna que visa o domínio de si; o signo é direcionado ao interior." (Vygotsky, 1978, p. 55) O signo é dedicado ao nosso próprio controle. O comportamento humano ao qual ele conduz é apenas a consequência de uma atividade psicológica, a qual não é visível. Para Vygotsky, "essas atividades são tão diferentes umas das outras que a natureza dos meios que elas utilizam não pode ser a mesma nos dois casos." (Vygotsky, 1978, p. 55) É preciso então discernir, no processo de desenvolvimento implementado nos 2 contra (1+1), o que se refere à ferramenta e o que se refere ao signo. Onde estão os signos? O que eles engendram? Que são os utilizadores do signo? Como eles são construídos? Como eles se impõem?

7.1. Durante a fase de instrumentação defensiva do artefato regulamentar

Quando o professor introduz o artefato regulamentar, ele o utiliza como uma ferramenta didática, cuja ambição é mudar o universo no qual evoluem seus alunos. Sua missão é transformar os aprendizes. Ele vai utilizar diferentes ferramentas de desenvolvimento. O artefato regulamentar não é, então, um signo, mas uma ferramenta. Exatamente como o pedreiro utiliza uma espátula, como o marceneiro utiliza uma plaina, o professor de educação física utiliza situações de aprendizagem, quer dizer, ele coloca seus aprendizes em um contexto com vocação para incitá-los a agir diferentemente. No nosso caso, trata-se de uma situação de oposição, apresentada sob a forma de uma fábula e para a qual o professor procedeu em algumas medidas regulamentares. Nosso artefato regulamentar é uma ferramenta que vai transformar a relação com os adversários de um lado, e a relação com o parceiro de outro. É essa situação que vai provocar a aparição dos signos que vamos descrever.

Nessa situação, trata-se de ir tocar um pilar. Porém, o fato de ir tocar um pilar é um signo diferente para os diferentes atores da situação.

- Inicialmente, para o jogador que recém atacou e que está "morto", tocar o pilar é o sinal de que ele pode voltar à vida, voltar ao jogo.
- É também um signo para o professor, que pode então decretar que os estudantes entrem na situação e comecem a "tomar na mão" o artefato regulamentar.

No entanto, a ida a tocar o pilar não acontece sozinha. Bem no começo, a maior parte dos protagonistas esquecem.

- Curiosamente, sem que o professor peça, produz-se um evento notável. É o jogador que vai se encontrar sozinho para jogar que vai fazer sinal ao seu parceiro, de ir tocar o pilar, gritando: "Vai tocar! Vai tocar!" ou "O pilar! O pilar!" Então, em um primeiro momento, é o parceiro do atacante "morto" que o lembra que ele deve tocar o pilar. Com efeito, a atividade do atacante "transborda" suas capacidades de tratamento. Ele não está em condições de assumir ao mesmo tempo sua intervenção sobre a bola e o respeito à nova regra do jogo. Na nota 17, Vygotsky (1931/2014, p. 546) se refere a uma nova citação de Pierre Janet: "No início, a palavra e o ato eram inseparáveis, a palavra era apenas o começo da ação, o grito que o chefe dava, começando um ato para tornar a execução mais fácil. Mas já no comando a palavra se separou do ato, pois a palavra existia para um, o chefe, e o ato existia para outro indivíduo, aquele que obedecia." (Janet, 1926, p. 220) É a mesma situação que encontramos aqui, em que, alternativamente, os dois parceiros assumem o papel do "chefe".

- Esse papel de "chefe" é redobrado aqui, devido à particularidade das situações de oposição esportivas. O não cumprimento da regra é uma falta que pode ser sinalizada pelo parceiro, mas também pelos adversários. Para cada um dos protagonistas, trata-se de, pouco a pouco, verificar se a equipe adversária respeita a nova regra. Pode acontecer que os quatro jogadores não vejam que um entre eles esqueceu de ir tocar o pilar. No início, trata-se realmente de um esquecimento de boa-fé. Eles ainda não estão trapaceando. Para trapacear, é preciso dominar a regra, o que poderá aparecer mais tarde. O educador deve então focalizar a atenção dos praticantes na direção de uma arbitragem sem concessão.
- Com efeito, essas deficiências de arbitragem são um sinal para o professor, que as identifica e constata que a "tomada na mão" do artefato regulamentar ainda não foi atingida.

É mais tarde que a observação metódica pelos protagonistas desse esquecimento (ir tocar o pilar) se revelará, por sua vez, um indicador confiável.

- *A contrario*, a sinalização sistemática pelos adversários desse descumprimento da regra constitui o sinal, para o professor, de que a fase de instrumentação relativa à introdução do artefato regulamentar está na fase de aperfeiçoamento. É também o sinal de que é hora de introduzir o artefato cognitivo ligado à resolução estratégica-tática do problema colocado pelo artefato regulamentar. Vemos então, aqui, que os signos se constroem coletivamente e têm uma vida antes de serem internalizados.

7.2. Durante a fase de instrumentação ofensiva do artefato regulamentar

A partir do momento em que o professor constata uma certa sistematização do respeito à regra (há cada vez menos descumprimentos da regra, e eles são sistematicamente sinalizados pelo parceiro ou pelos adversários), ele vai introduzir o artefato cognitivo. Aqui, novamente, essa situação de reagrupamento dos praticantes, com o fim de enunciar uma solução estratégica-tática para o problema, é uma ferramenta. Não se trata de uma situação de jogo, mas uma situação de reflexão coletiva. Essa situação é provocada pelo professor, que convida os estudantes a proceder em uma análise da situação, a debatê-la e adotar a solução adequada, isto é, a situação estratégica-tática que consiste em devolver a bola diretamente na direção do adversário "morto". Mas essa devolução direta é ainda difícil de ser executada. É preciso novamente, para os estudantes, entrar em uma fase de instrumentação do novo artefato. No início, eles persistem em seus estereótipos. Mais frequentemente, observamos um passe na direção do parceiro. Depois, com o impulso dos parceiros e do professor, que deve regular incessantemente as fases do jogo que ele observa, aparecem timidamente devoluções diretas ao campo adversário. Notaremos que o educador desempenha um papel determinante na ativação do processo. É a sua obstinação que permite manter os estudantes sob tensão, lembrando sem parar, *in situ*, que a solução é devolver sobre o adversário morto. Ele produz o signo do que o estudante deve realizar, sob a forma de uma análise, que acompanha uma situação de "flagrante delito". Trata-se então de observar os casos em que a devolução direta era facilmente realizável, de parar o jogo (inclusive durante a rotação) e de questionar o jogador em questão. Você lembra do que acabou de fazer? Isso corresponde ao que você devia fazer? O que você podia fazer de outro jeito? Frequentemente, é preciso tempo para que o estudante em questão rememore a rotação, para tomar consciência da ocasião perdida. O testemunho dos outros protagonistas às vezes é útil. Essa rememoração da rotação também constitui um signo para eles. Ainda que no início dessa nova fase a precisão não esteja sempre lá, o professor deve encorajar as tentativas, direcionando a atenção dos jogadores para a destinação de suas devoluções. Como consequência, a necessidade de tornar adequadas as tomadas de informações e a realização material leva o praticante a desenvolver não só uma forma gestual "canônica", mas uma motricidade que se adaptará a cada nova situação. Porque devolver sobre o adversário que ficou no jogo é arriscado, é se expor a um retorno tão instantâneo quanto fatal. *A contrario*, devolver sobre o alvo correto, isto é, o adversário "morto", é a garantia de um sucesso imediato, que leva a um grande júbilo, sobretudo se a bola cai no momento em que ele toca o pilar. Então aqui é o adversário "morto" que sai para tocar o pilar que se torna o estímulo que permite dominar seu comportamento. No entanto, contraditoriamente, o signo mais forte é certamente o que se materializa no adversário que devolve a bola. Com efeito, é porque nos enganamos de adversário (o adversário "com vida" toma o lugar do adversário "morto") que a bola volta tão rápido quanto partiu. Novamente, um signo que um outro pode transmitir (aqui, os oponentes) e que, nesse caso específico, desenvolve progressivamente mais precisão. Mais um sinal dado pelo adversário, que não se pode subestimar. O júbilo de uns provoca a frustração de outros e seus diferentes sentimentos indicam o que é preciso fazer e não fazer. O jogo é pretexto para atribuir aos signos o estatuto de verdadeiro estímulo que permite mobilizar recursos insuspeitos pelo próprio sujeito, recursos que finalmente levam a implementar os meios para uma ação eficaz. Os protagonistas são pegos em um turbilhão de questões que estimula sua imaginação e, mais além, seu engajamento na ação. "O poder de agir é heterogêneo. Pode-se dizer que ele aumenta ou diminui em função da alternância funcional entre o sentido e a eficiência da ação, em que se desempenha o dinamismo da atividade..." (Clot & Simonet, 2015, p. 40)

7.3 Durante a fase de instrumentação defensiva: a compensação

Agora, a situação de desenvolve de maneira autônoma, o professor não deve intervir. A ausência do parceiro se torna o sinal de que algo de perigoso pode acontecer e que um espaço deve ser preenchido. A potencialidade do retorno de uma bola em uma área deixada pelo parceiro que partiu para tocar o pilar coloca um dilema para o jogador que ficou sozinho. Ele deve se contentar em proteger seu lado do campo esperando seu par ou deve proteger todo o campo? Esse dilema se resolve bem mais facilmente quando as vontades dos adversários se afirmam. Quanto mais os retornos diretos da bola na área do parceiro são frequentes, mais essa compensação "espontânea" se sistematiza. É uma conjunção de signos que funciona aqui: de um lado, a retirada do parceiro (que foi tocar o pilar); de outro, a ameaça cada vez mais premente do retorno imediato da bola em sua área.

7.4. Durante a fase de instrumentação ofensiva: jogar "ao contrário"

Como que presos em uma engrenagem, os alunos avançam na situação, que oferece aos poucos todas suas potencialidades. Doravante, os estereótipos se apagam, em proveito de uma necessária leitura da situação. Quanto mais os estudantes são capazes de devolver sobre o adversário "morto", mais a compensação "espontânea" se automatiza. É o ataque do parceiro que a agora é o sinal da compensação. Constata-se até que alguns antecipam radicalmente a devolução direta do adversário, posicionando-se no lugar dela. Eles esperam assim surpreender o adversário que, no entanto, aplica ao pé da letra a solução estratégica-tática combinada. Porque as coisas não podem parar por aí. Assim, para alguns estudantes particularmente perspicazes, a constatação da antecipação surpreendente do aniversário se torna o sinal de que se deve jogar de outra maneira. Na sua vez, eles vão dar ao adversário o sinal do que eles esperam, a saber, um deslocamento, uma orientação do corpo, uma fixação do olhar, que leva a crer que é exatamente sobre o adversário que saiu para tocar o pilar que eles vão devolver a bola. Tudo em seu comportamento incita a proteger a área momentaneamente abandonada. O "antecipador" é então pego na armadilha. Cheio de certeza, ele se precipita ao espaço provisoriamente deixado por seu parceiro (que saiu para tocar o pilar), a ponto de ser levado pelo seu impulso. A armadilha preparada pode se fechar. O adversário observa essa precipitação e de repente, no último momento, muda sua opção de jogo, para devolver a bola ao lado oposto, isto é, na zona agora deixada libre pelo "compensador". Esse tipo de ação é a mais bela prova de que os protagonistas do jogo deixaram seu estereótipo no vestiário e agora jogam olhando além. Nessa primeira etapa da situação, é o movimento de compensação do jogador que ficou sozinho que se torna o sinal da pertinência de jogar "ao contrário".

8. Aporte da teoria instrumental

O processo de desenvolvimento que implantamos na nossa experimentação do 2 contra (1+1) pode se explicar através do prisma da teoria instrumental de Vygotsky. Isso requer, em primeiro lugar, fazer a distinção entre ferramentas e signos. As duas ferramentas implementadas pelo educador são o artefato regulamentar (a regra específica para essa situação) e o artefato cognitivo (a resolução estratégica do problema colocado por essa nova regra). Os signos são numerosos e têm diferentes destinatários: o parceiro, os adversários, o educador. Mas em que os signos e as ferramentas se diferenciam em termos de funções no processo de desenvolvimento? Vygotsky é muito claro a esse respeito, em sua tese 13 da metodologia instrumental em psicologia. "A diferença essencial da ferramenta psicológica (o signo) para a ferramenta técnica reside na orientação de sua ação na direção do psiquismo, do comportamento, enquanto que a ferramenta técnica, que também se insere como meio termo entre atividade do homem e objeto exterior, é orientada na direção da obtenção de tal ou tal mudança no próprio objeto. A ferramenta psicologia não modifica em nada o objeto, ela é um meio de influência sobre si mesmo (ou sobre outrem) – sobre o psiquismo, o comportamento – e não um meio de ação sobre o objeto. No ato instrumental, se manifesta, consequentemente, uma atividade em relação não com a coisa, mas consigo mesmo." (Vygotsky, 1930/2014, p. 571) A essência do método instrumental reside na capacidade dos humanos de se autoestimular ou estimular os outros, usando signos. A consequência de tal possibilidade "é que em um mesmo estímulo estão presentes estímulos de duas ordens, ao mesmo tempo do objeto e da ferramenta, então, cada um desempenha qualitativa e funcionalmente um papel diferente." (Vygotsky, 1930/2014, p. 570) O signo constitui então um fator determinante do ato instrumental, no que se torna uma operação intelectual. Mas para que um signo preencha seu papel, ele deve mostrar sua capacidade de influência sobre o psiquismo e o comportamento. Em numerosas reprises, ao longo de todo este texto, nós apontamos os diferentes signos que se sucedem na situação dos 2 contra (1+1): o pilar, a sinalização do parceiro de "Vai tocar! O pilar!", o adversário momentaneamente "morto"; e para o professor, a observação, pelos estudantes, dos esquecimentos do adversário, a devolução sistemática sobre o adversário morto... Todos esses signos têm capacidade de influenciar o psiquismo e, por consequência, o comportamento dos protagonistas: lembrar-se de que deve ir tocar o pilar, saber em que direção do campo devolver a bola, saber que é preciso devolver o mais rápido possível (em devolução direta). "O método instrumental é um modo de investigação do comportamento e de seu desenvolvimento que se apoia na atualização das ferramentas psicológicas utilizadas no comportamento e da estrutura dos atos instrumentais que elas engendram." (Vygotsky, 1930/2014, p. 574) É dessa experiência que nós quisemos participar, com essa contribuição.

Referências

CLOT, Y. & SIMONET, P. (2015). Pouvoirs d'agir et marges de manœuvre. *Le travail humain* 2015/1, (Vol. 78).

DELEPLACE, R. (1979). *Rugby de mouvement rugby total.* Paris : Ed. EPS

ÉLOI, S. (2017). Genèse instrumentale et activité médiatisante : introduction d'un artefact réglementaire en volley-ball ? Dans S. Éloi et G. Uhlrich (s/d), *De l'usage des artefacts dans les métiers de l'intervention* (p.119-138). Toulouse : Octares

ÉLOI, S. & UHLRICH, G. (2011). La démarche technologique en STAPS : analyse conceptuelle et mise en perspective pour les sports collectifs. *eJRIEPS*, 23, 20-45.

ÉLOI, S. & UHLRICH, G. (2013). La mobilisation d'un artefact réglementaire dans le cadre de la formation d'étudiants en STAPS. Une illustration en volley-ball. *Recherche et formation*, 73, 73-88.

ÉLOI, S. & UHLRICH, G. (2014). Utilisation d'artefacts dans le domaine des pratiques physiques, sportives et artistiques (PPSA). *Transformation*, 12, 117-135.

FÉLIX, M-C. & VÉRILLON, P. (2017). Pilotage à distance de l'activité par les dispositifs : dilemmes professionnels, pouvoir d'agir et renormalisation du milieu de travail. Dans S. Éloi et G. Uhlrich (s/d), *De l'usage des artefacts dans les métiers de l'intervention* (p.139-149). Toulouse : Octares

JANET, P. (1926). *De l'angoisse à l'extase*, Alcan, Paris, Tome I.

JANET, P. (1929). *L'évolution psychologique de la personnalité*, Chanine, Paris.

PROT, B. (2017). Le plaisir du contre-pied - Deux interprétations de l'usage d'un artefact pour développer des gestes techniques. Dans S. Éloi et G. Uhlrich (s/d), *De l'usage des artefacts dans les métiers de l'intervention* (p.139-149). Toulouse : Octares

RABARDEL, P. (1995). *Les hommes et les technologies. Approche cognitive des instruments contemporains*. Paris : Armand Colin.

TROUCHE, L. (2005). Des artefacts aux instruments, une approche pour guider et intégrer les usages des outils de calcul dans l'enseignement des mathématiques ». Université d'été « *Le calcul sous toutes ses formes* », Saint-Flour, France

SÈVE, L. (2008). *Penser avec Marx aujourd'hui*. « L'Homme », tome 2. Paris : La Dispute.

SÈVE, L. (2018). Vygotsky : une démarche dialectique en psychologie. Dans J-Y. Rochex, C. Joigneaux et J. Netter (dir.) *Histoire, culture, développement* : questions *théoriques, recherches empiriques*, Actes du 6e séminaire international Vygotsky, pp. 51-65. Équipe CIRCEFT-ESCOL, Université Paris 8 Saint-Denis et CRTD - CNAM Paris.

TROUCHE, L. (2005). Des artefacts aux instruments, une approche pour guider et intégrer les usages des outils de calcul dans l'enseignement des mathématiques, Université d'été « *Le calcul sous toutes ses formes* », Saint-Flour, France.

VYGOTSKY, LS. (1978). *Mind in Society: The Development of Higher Psychological Processes*. Michael Cole et al., eds. Cambridge: Harvard University.

VYGOTSKY, LS. (1934/1997). *Pensée et langage*. Traduction de F. Sève. Paris : La dispute.

VYGOTSKY, LS. (1935/1997). Le problème de l'enseignement et du développement mental à l'âge scolaire. Dans B. Schneuwly & J-P Bronckart (Ed), *Vygotsky aujourd'hui*, pp. 95-117, Lausanne : Delachaux et Niestlé.

VYGOTSKY, LS. (2012). *Vygotsky, une théorie du développement et de l'éducation*. Recueil de textes et commentaires. Sous la direction de Frédéric Yvon et Yuri Zinchenko. Moscou MGU.

VYGOTSKY, LS. (1929/2014). Sur la conception historico- culturelle du psychisme humain. Dans F. Sève (Trad), M. Brossard et L. Sève (Ed) *Histoire du développement des fonctions psychiques supérieures*, pp. 543-564 Paris : La dispute.

VYGOTSKY, LS. (1930/2014). La méthode instrumentale en psychologie. Dans F. Sève (Trad), M. Brossard et L. Sève (Ed) *Histoire du développement des fonctions psychiques supérieures*, pp. 567-574 Paris : La dispute.

VYGOTSKY, LS. (1931/2014). *Histoire du développement des fonctions psychiques supérieures*. Traduction de F. Sève. Édition préparée par M. Brossard et L. Sève. Paris : La dispute.

3.

AS CONTRADIÇÕES COMO FORÇA MOTRIZ DA ZONA DE DESENVOLVIMENTO PROXIMAL: APRENDIZAGEM, ENSINO E DESENVOLVIMENTO DA ATIVIDADE

Yannick LÉMONIE, França
CNAM, CRTD, (EA. 4132)

Introdução

Se o trabalho de Vygotsky teve uma influência importante no campo da Educação Física (EF), através da criação de currículos baseados em perspectivas construtivistas (Rovegno & Dolly, 2006), ou no quadro da promoção de processos de aprendizagem cooperativos (Dyson & Casey, 2012), seu trabalho teórico, no entanto, recebeu pouca atenção empírica no campo da EF. (Barker, Quennerstedt & Annerstedt, 2015) Pode-se ver aí uma dificuldade em trabalhar com Vygotsky no campo da EF?

Trabalhar com e a partir de Vygotsky confronta o pesquisador com múltiplos obstáculos, para tirar proveito da profundidade teórica de seus conceitos. Entre esses obstáculos, Kozulin (2016) identifica três problemas maiores, associados à publicação e à tradução dos textos de Vygotsky. O primeiro problema diz respeito ao fato de que Vygotsky não pôde ou não desejou publicar em vida. Assim, é impossível saber se a maior parte do trabalho publicado depois de sua morte está na forma desejada pelo autor. É difícil para quem deseja trabalhar com Vygotsky de distinguir "que escreveu Vygotsky e o que Vygotsky realmente escreveu". (Yasnitsky & Van der Ver, 2016, p.73)

Aqui surge um segundo problema ligado à difusão do trabalho de Vygotsky: os tradutores buscaram ajustar os textos de Vygotsky ao que eles consideram como "aceitável" em relação ao público-alvo desses textos. Neste cenário, frequentemente os editores buscaram adaptar o texto de modo a encaixá-lo em enquadramentos preexistentes (cognitivos ou sócio-construtivistas), os quais o próprio Vygotsky teria rejeitado. (Jornet, 2018; Setstensko, 2008)

Assim, certamente é possível afirmar que o trabalho de Vygotsky não pode exprimir plenamente todo seu potencial sem uma compreensão expandida do contexto ontológico/epistemológico que deu origem a conceitos amplamente difundidos na literatura (mediação, zona proximal de desenvolvimento).

O terceiro problema, mais profundo, se refere às dificuldades ligadas à tradução dos textos. Cole (2009), editor da versão inglesa de *Mind in Society*, evoca assim a simplificação do termo russo *Obuchenie*. A tradução do ensaio foi publicada em 1935, depois da morte de Vygotsky, sob o título *Ensino/aprendizagem (obuchenie) e desenvolvimento na criança em idade escolar*, o qual foi traduzido como *interação entre aprendizagem e desenvolvimento*, no capítulo 6 de *Mind in Society*. Porém, na língua russa, o termo *Obuchenie* se refere a um processo de duas faces: uma voltada à aprendizagem, outra voltada à organização do ambiente pelo adulto. Mais adequadamente, o termo *Obuchenie* se refere a um processo complexo de ensino-aprendizagem. Schneuwly (1995) explica, de qualquer maneira, que essa simplificação do termo *Obuchenie* por *aprendizagem* se encontra nas edições francesas, alemãs, espanholas e inglesas. Dessa simplificação na tradução, resultam implicações profundas na maneira de apreender e trabalhar com Vygotsky. Como nota Cole, a posição de Vygotsky em relação aos laços entre aprendizagem e desenvolvimento é conhecida e se opõe tanto às concepções de Thorndike quanto às de Piaget: "Nosso conceito de desenvolvimento implica na rejeição à opinião frequentemente difundida de acordo com a qual o desenvolvimento cognitivo resulta da acumulação progressiva de mudanças distintas. Nós cremos que o desenvolvimento da criança é um processo complexo, caracterizado pela periodicidade, a desigualdade no desenvolvimento de diferentes funções, a metamorfose ou a transformação qualitativa de uma forma em outra, o entrelaçamento de fatores externos e internos e os processos adaptativos que permitem superar os obstáculos que a criança encontra." (Vygotsky, 1978, p. 73) A verdade é que a relação entre aprendizagem, desenvolvimento e ensino permanece largamente inexplicada. Como observa Cole (2009, p.294), "o que continua inexplicado nessa definição explicita de desenvolvimento é a natureza das relações complexas entre ensino, aprendizagem e desenvolvimento que têm lugar no contexto da educação formal." (Cole, 2009, p. 294)

Ao contrário de uma acepção usual do conceito de Zona de Desenvolvimento Proximal (ZDP), nós buscamos, com esta contribuição, reintegrar o ensino à análise das aprendizagens e do desenvolvimento nas práticas de EF. Com base nos resultados de uma pesquisa sobre ensino-aprendizagem de dança na educação física, nós mostraremos que as aprendizagens e o desenvolvimentos da atividade dos dançarinos se apoiam em contradições entre a atividade de ensino e atividade de aprendizagem. Engajados em pesquisas que visam melhorar ou transformar as atividades de ensino, nós discutiremos então a necessidade de analisar as contradições inevitáveis entre atividade de ensino e atividade de aprendizagem, de maneira a conceber uma zona de desenvolvimento proximal para os professores.

Buscamos, assim, nesta contribuição, responder três perguntas:

- Como mobilizar o conceito de ZPP para investigar as aprendizagens em EF?
- Quais evidências para argumentar que são as contradições entre atividade de ensino e atividade de aprendizagem que são o motor das aprendizagens e do desenvolvimento da atividade dos dançarinos em EF?
- Como nós podemos estender o conceito de ZDP para estimular o desenvolvimento profissional dos professores que colaboram conosco no contexto das nossas pesquisas?

Para responder a essas questões, nós nos apoiaremos em um estudo conduzido em EF em uma unidade de ensino de dança. Esses dados provêm de um projeto mais amplo, que buscava dar conta do uso, pelos professores, de prescrições oficiais, em um momento de reescrita dos programas de EF para o colégio. O professor possui uma experiência de 10 anos no ensino de educação física, mas ensina dança pela primeira vez em sua carreira no curso de nosso estudo. Três alunas foram escolhidas para participar das autoconfrontações, de acordo com um procedimento que mobiliza dois critérios:

- O acordo explicito das alunas para participar do estudo e de encontros com os pesquisadores;
- Sua prática extracurricular de uma prática física artística.

Nos trechos apresentados, nos centraremos em um grupo de alunas composto de duas sem práticas artísticas fora da escola e duas que praticam de maneira intensiva for a da escola: Mathilde, que pratica dança, e Lucie, que pratica patinação artística.

1. O conceito de Zona de Desenvolvimento Proximal e seu uso na investigação sobre a aprendizagem em EF

1.1 Três dimensões do conceito de ZDP

Nas pesquisas em EF, o conceito de ZDP é fortemente utilizado para defender os procedimentos de ensino que valorizam a cooperação entre os alunos em diferentes níveis. (D'arripe-Longueville & al., 2002) Mais amplamente, nas pesquisas em educação, o conceito de ZDP foi mobilizado em "toda situação na qual, participando de uma atividade, pessoas estão adquirindo domínio de uma prática ou de um assunto." (Wells, 1999, p. 333)

Nós gostaríamos, na sequência, de situar três dimensões do conceito de ZDP.

1.1.1 A ZDP é uma emergência

Comumente, a definição que serve de referência a tais trabalhos é a seguinte: "A distância entre o nível de desenvolvimento real, determinado pela resolução independente de problemas, e o nível de desenvolvimento potencial, determinado pela resolução de problemas sob a direção ou em colaboração com pares mais competentes." (Vygotsky, 1978, p.86)

De maneira complementar, é possível acrescentar que "com a colaboração, a direção ou qualquer outra forma de ajuda, a criança sempre é capaz de fazer mais e de resolver tarefas mais difíceis, que ela não pode cumprir sozinha." (Vygotsky, 1987, p. 209)

Essa definição parece, do ponto de vista de Roth & Radford (2010), ter orientado uma leitura muito simplificada, na medida em que a interpretação que foi feita pelos autores tende a opor individualidade. Uma dessas individualidades é a do professor ou aluno mais capaz, sendo o outro o que está aprendendo. De acordo com Roth & Radford (2010), essa interpretação orienta a uma leitura substancialista da aprendizagem, vista como assimilação de conhecimentos, e sobre o coletivo concebido como conjunto de indivíduos interagindo sem problemas. Para Barker, Quennestedt & Annestedt (2015), seguindo Roth & Radford (2010), é improdutivo pensar a ZDP em termos de posição fixa. Pelo contrário, a ZDP emerge da interação entre participantes que se tornam ao mesmo tempo professores e aprendizes. Em outras palavras, é ilusório pensar que colocar em uma situação os alunos que apresentam uma assimetria de conhecimentos garante a emergência de uma ZDP: "Os aprendizes tentam, mas não conseguem criar uma comunicação coletiva e, portanto, uma ZDP. O novato na situação não consegue exprimir o que deve aprender ou como deve aprender e não se torna um *expert* no que diz respeito à sua própria aprendizagem." (Barker, Quennerstedt, & Annerstedt, 2015)

1.1.2 A imitação de um conceito central para compreender a ZDP

Para avançar mais no conceito de ZDP, é necessário voltar ao conceito de imitação em cuja base Vygotsky elabora do de ZDP. (Chaiklin, 2003) A imitação não é concebida, em Vygotsky, como uma cópia das ações. Pelo contrário, Vygotsky dá uma outra significação à imitação, que implica, para ele, na compreensão das relações estruturais do problema a resolver. Vygotsky utiliza o termo *imitação* para se referir às situações nas quais uma criança é capaz de se engajar em uma interação com outro mais competente para uma tarefa que ela não será capaz de cumprir sozinha. O exemplo que ele dá de aprendizagem de xadrez é esclarecedor: "Se eu não sou capaz de jogar xadrez, eu não poderia jogar uma partida mesmo que um mestre me mostre como. Se eu sei aritmética, mas encontro dificuldades com a solução de um problema complexo, uma demonstração conduzirá imediatamente à minha própria resolução do problema. Por outro lado, se eu não sei matemática avançada, uma demonstração da solução de uma equação diferencial não fará meu próprio pensamento avançar nessa direção com um só pé. Para imitar, deve haver uma possibilidade de passar do que eu posso fazer ao que eu não posso fazer." (Vygotsky, 1934/1987, p. 209)

Em outras palavras, só é possível imitar à medida que a imitação é acompanhada de uma compreensão. Para Chaiklin (2003), a imitação se torna possível (a) à medida que as funções psicológicas ainda são insuficientes para sustentar uma performance individual; (b) são suficientemente desenvolvidas para tal; (c) quando o aluno está em condições de saber como utilizar as ações de um par mais experiente. Nisso, o contexto de imitação é central para compreender o de ZDP.

1.1.3 Uma ou duas ZDP?

Retomando o célebre evento de Vygotsky da criança que desenha, Clot (2008) propõe distinguir duas zonas potenciais de desenvolvimento. Lembremo-nos este exemplo de Vygotsky: o pesquisador propõe à criança desenhar. Ao final de um certo tempo, essa atividade do aluno mostra sinais de saturação. O pesquisador então pede que a criança mostre a um colega como desenhar. A criança retoma o desenho com um interesse renovado. O sentido da atividade mudou e foi relançado pelo pesquisador. Desenhar consiste primeiramente em produzir uma obra, em seguida ela adquire um status instrumental, na demonstração a um par. Com base na distinção realizada por Leontiev (1978), entre atividade, ação e operação, Clot destaca o quanto o sentido, isto é, a relação dos objetivos das ações com o motivo da atividade, evolui. Clot (1999, p.173) sustenta "a tese de uma dinâmica da ação sujeita a duas exigências psicológicas diferentes: o sentido e a eficiência. Cada uma dessas tensões psíquicas se resolve atravessando zonas de desenvolvimento potencial distintas, mesmo que elas tenham em comum dar suporte a um sujeito através da atividade de outro ou vários outros." Indo mais longe, não pode haver, para Clot, desenvolvimento de novos motivos sem desenvolvimento de meios de ação e vice-versa."

Nós tiraremos dessa releitura de Vygotsky sob o prisma dos trabalhos de Leontiev (1978) e de Clot (1999) que não existiria uma, mas duas zonas potenciais de desenvolvimento, e que o desenvolvimento da atividade está inscrito na alternância de um desenvolvimento do sentido e de um desenvolvimento da eficiência.

1.2. ZDP, Imitação, desenvolvimento do sentido na atividade de alunas em um ciclo de dança

1.2.1 A organização do ciclo de dança

Vamos restituir, em primeiro lugar, a organização geral das aulas tal qual elas são implementadas pelo professor. Nas aulas nº 1 e nº 2 do ciclo, o professor mobilizou foto tiradas de diferentes universos da dança e pediu para escolher três fotos para criar uma coreografia coletiva com base nas posturas identificadas. Nas aulas nº 3 e nº 4, ele propõe partir de gestos esportivos trazendo a experiência pessoal das alunas (em sua prática extraescolar ou no cenário da prática de EF), de maneira a poder compor uma segunda frase dançada, que será introduzida na coreografia final a ser realizada pelas alunas.

1.2.2 A imitação no coração das aprendizagens das alunas

Durante o ciclo de dança, as alunas tiveram a escolha de constituir seu grupo. As duas alunas que praticam uma atividade artística fora da escola (Mathilde e Lucie) se juntaram e formaram seu grupo com duas alunas não especialistas. Essa heterogeneidade lhes permite escolher movimentos para a produção da coreografia coletiva final. As duas alunas mais experientes escolhem os elementos a incorporar na coreografia final tendo em vista dois objetivos contraditórios:

- Escolher um movimento que exprima um certo grau de domínio técnico, de maneira a demonstrar sua *expertise* diante da turma no fim do ciclo;
- Adaptar o grau de dificuldade dos movimentos escolhidos às capacidades das alunas com mais dificuldade do grupo:

> Mathilde: Eu escolhi as imagens (suporte da tarefa do professor na lição 3) de maneira que combine bem com a coreografia que nós queremos fazer no fim do ciclo.
> Mathilde: Eu escolhi as imagens para poder adaptar o nível de dificuldade ao grupo. Por exemplo, não escolhemos ir ao chão porque é difícil demais para nós nos levantarmos de uma maneira estética.

Depois de ter escolhido os movimentos, o grupo ensaia diante do espelho da sala de dança, ferramenta que só elas utilizam. O professor não fez referência a ela durante o conjunto do ciclo. No entanto, é uma ferramenta que lhes permite produzir coletivamente a coreografia, ajustando coletivamente o grau de dificuldade. Ao longo do ciclo, as alunas colaboram e mobilizam um processo de imitação para aprender. É a observação da produção delas no espelho que informa as alunas mais experientes sobre a pertinência da escolha dos movimentos dançados, assim como sobre os conselhos necessários para que as alunas menos experientes se apropriem dos movimentos.

1.2.3 Um desenvolvimento do sentido na atividade das dançarinas

Na aula 3, um episódio chama os pesquisadores envolvidos. Quando o professor pede às alunas para escolher entre os gestos esportivos para compor uma sequência dançada, Mathilde e Lucie interpelam o professor:

O professor volta na direção do grupo e faz os gestos de uma manchete. As meninas fazem "beicinho".
Mathilde: Mas a dança é um desporto como os outros!
Professor: Mas sim, se você quiser que a gente parta de outra coisa que não seja a dança para vir na direção da dança, mas bem entendido, a dança é um esporte.
Mathilde: Mas então a gente tem que pegar outra coisa
Professor: Bem, sim, porque a ideia é utilizar tudo o que sabemos fazer. Por exemplo, que que é isso? (imita um arremesso de basquete)
Lucie: Basquete.
Professor: (imita uma manchete)
Lucie: Vôlei.
Professor: Então, viram, coisas simples. Eu mostro isso porque é a minha cultura, mas depois vocês podem escolher outra coisa.

O professor se afasta e retorna porque a aluna E2 o chama.
Lucie: Senhor, podemos usar patinação?
Professor: Bem, por que não? Patinação em velocidade ou não sei o que? Você vê, pra marcar a posição. Mas vocês podem, claro.

Lembremos que Lucie é a aluna que pratica patinação artística. Quando o professor lhe responde sobre esse episódio, ele evoca (de maneira não consciente, ele dirá na entrevista de autoconfrontação) a patinação em velocidade, que é uma prática esportiva e não uma prática artística. Qual é a diferença entre essas duas formas de práticas? O que é que permite diferenciar um movimento esportivo de um movimento dançado? Quando se efetua a passagem? Essas questões são delicadas. Elas são objeto de debate ainda atualmente no meio da dança. (Guarino, 2015) Essa controvérsia, assim como a negociação que as alunas começam com as regras formuladas pelo professor mostra evidentemente que a tarefa não faz sentido sob o olhar do objeto da atividade das alunas. Que objeto é esse?

O objeto da atividade das alunas consiste em demonstrar sua competência diante dos outros alunos da turma. A prática da dança não é inofensiva, desse ponto de vista. Ela engaja as alunas numa encenação delas mesmas diante do grupo da turma. É a partir de então certamente mais o caso na dança do que na ginástica, em que os movimentos são codificados. Nesse sentido, a questão da qualidade do movimento aparece como algo essencial para essas alunas. Nesse sentido, o desafio de inventar uma coreografia a partir das imagens ou de gestos parece sem dúvida difícil demais no lapso de tempo dedicado ao ciclo (7 aulas de 1h). Assim, escolher uma coreografia para apresentar diante da classe e adaptá-la às exigências feitas pelo professor parece menos difícil.

Lucie: Inventar uma coreografia completa é difícil demais em tão pouco tempo. É por isso que eu escolhi aprender a coreografia da Beyoncé no YouTube no início do ciclo.
Lucie: Eu escolho os movimentos de maneira a fazer uma coreografia que eu goste.

Além disso, há as ferramentas fornecidas pelo professor (fichas com verbos de ação para os deslocamentos).

Mathilde: E depois nós nos movimentamos em um espaço pequeno, mas não demais.
Pesquisador: É um critério pra você?
Mathilde: Sim, porque na dança que eu faço fora da aula nós utilizamos muito o espaço da cena. É um critério importante na dança de salão.
Pesquisador: Mas a coreografia da Beyoncé é feita diante de uma câmera, não? Não tem muita utilização da cena.
Mathilde: Sim, por isso que nós não nos mexemos muito.

Através dessa análise, destaca-se que se a questão da qualidade do movimento ou a mensagem da coreografia é esvaziada nas proposições do professor, é paradoxalmente a atividade das alunas que faz ressurgir essas dimensões essenciais. Um outro elemento interessante é que o objeto da atividade implantada pelo grupo está inscrito em um horizonte temporal mais amplo que o da aula: as aprendizagens só ganham sentido na perspectiva de demonstrar suas competências em uma coreografia emprestada em parte de Beyoncé, e conhecida por seus colegas de aula. Consequentemente, é possível dizer que as alunas aprendem a despeito da tarefa proposta pelo professor e não com ela. A eficácia de suas ações só pode ser julgada pelo critério do objeto perseguido. Para parafrasear Clot (2008), a eficácia não é somente a realização de objetivos perseguidos, estabelecidos pelo professor (realizar uma sequência dançada com gestos emprestados de práticas esportivas), é a descoberta, por essas alunas, de novos objetivos (integrar esses elementos a uma coreografia, definida no início do ciclo). Trata-se, para as alunas, de ir além do que pedem os professores, para realizar esse motivo, mas igualmente que sua produção possa estar em harmonia com aquilo que elas consideram critérios de qualidade uma coreografia conhecida pelos colegas.

Lucie: O professor quer que a gente escolha gestos simples, mas nós queremos escolher gestos mais "técnicos" (no sentido de mais difíceis de realizar)
Mathilde: Nós escolhemos a coreografia da Beyoncé porque é certo que todo mundo conhece.

É, enfim, o que chamamos em linguagem corrente a preocupação e a realização do trabalho bem feito, aquele no qual podemos nos reconhecer individual e coletivamente. Vamos mais longe: é porque elas chegam a fazer com o que lhes pede o professor que se dá alternância funcional entre sentido e eficiência de suas ações. Vemos que, longe de impedir a realização de seu projeto, é porque elas se arranjam com a tarefa que a repetição necessária à automatização dos gestos ganha sentido. Dá-se aqui a alternância funcional entre sentido e eficiência descrita por Clot. (1995)

Como observam Griffin & Cole (1984, p. 62), "A sabedoria adulta não fornece teleologia para o desenvolvimento da criança. A organização social e as atividades dirigentes criam um vão na criança, que pode desenvolver uma nova análise criativa... Uma zona próxima ao desenvolvimento é um diálogo entre a criança e seu futuro; não é um diálogo entre a criança e o passado de um adulto." Nesse sentido, a ZDP abre inevitavelmente para um processo criativo. Em oposição a uma concepção tradicional da ZDP, orientada para uma conceitualização de uma zona de transmissão de conhecimentos de um sujeito mais experimentado na direção de outro, os resultados tendem a mostrar que o que se aprende não é da ordem do conhecido, do "já-lá". Não se trata, para as alunas, de reproduzir a coreografia de Beyoncé, mas, pelo contrário, de incorporar o que o professor pediu para fazer no que ela deseja fazer com a coreografia de Beyoncé.

1.2.4 Uma primeira modelização da ZDP aberta pelas alunas

Nesse estágio da análise, é possível modelizar a zona proximal de desenvolvimento (Figura 1).

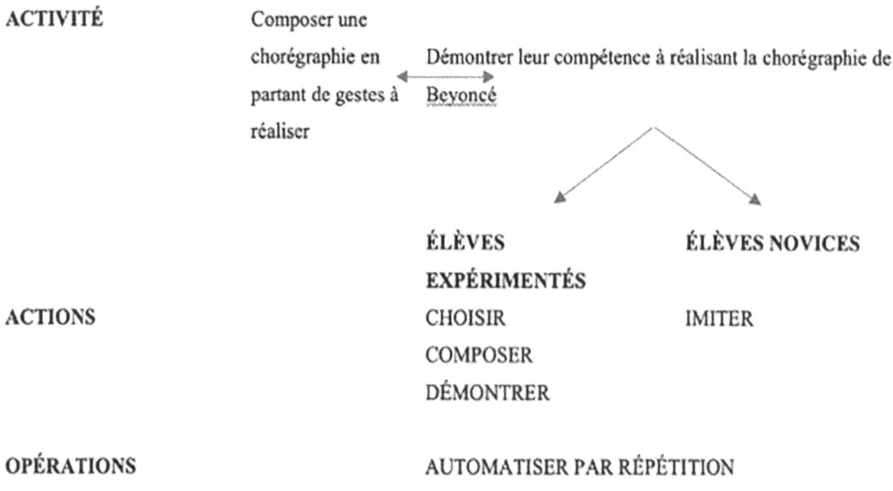

Se percebemos que a tarefa pedida pelo professor entra em conflito com o motivo da atividade das alunas, é necessário seguir a análise, para identificar as contradições entre a atividade de ensino e a atividade de aprendizagem das alunas. É sob esse prisma que poderemos responder a questão das relações entre ensino, aprendizagem e desenvolvimento.

2. As contradições entre atividade de ensino e atividade de aprendizagem como motor da ZDP

Nos desenvolvimentos que seguem, nós reintegramos a atividade do professor na análise, de forma a identificar as contradições entre atividade de ensino e atividade de aprendizagem.

2.1 A atividade do professor

O fato de permitir a todas as alunas realizar uma coreografia coletiva organiza o professor, ao mesmo tempo, no acompanhamento que faz das alunas e no nível da formação dos grupos.

Pesquisador: *Com base em quais princípios você elabora seus grupos?*
Professor: Um: sem mistura. Não é isso que me preocupa mais nesse nível 1. Num nível 2 sim, eu insistiria mais nisso. No primeiro nível, é mais certo que eu poderia ver a capacidade delas de expressão, reprodução, eu tento misturar um pouco os níveis, mantendo um nível afetivo um pouco melhor, para que se sintam à vontade.
Pesquisador: *Por que você mistura os níveis?*
Professor: Para permitir ter um melhor rendimento coletivo. É interessante ter duas alunas em grupo de 4 que vão talvez carregar mais as outras e levá-las a se desenvolver. Então é isso, um dos primeiros pontos.
Pesquisador: *E de repente e assim vai haver necessariamente cooperação?*
Professor: Não, não necessariamente. Porque vai haver o corpo visto pelas outras, isso não é simples, é por isso que eu...
Pesquisador: Porque aqui, se olharmos esses programas, vemos "participa ativamente da elaboração" (nos programas de 2008), poderíamos dizer, salvo engano, que você coloca os alunos em cooperação para que haja uma entrega correta do serviço.
Professor: Sim.
Pesquisador: Mas ela não determina necessariamente o fato de que as alunas participem ativamente, em grupo, da elaboração. Quer dizer que se pode

pensar que se há níveis que são diferentes, as que estão mais à vontade vão na verdade elaborar para as outras.
Professor: Certamente, de qualquer maneira é isso que acontece um pouquinho.

Aqui, vemos que o professor está especialmente lúcido quanto ao fato de que sua determinação dos grupos será um entrave à participação ativa de todas as alunas do grupo em uma elaboração coletiva, destinada a ser vista e julgada pelo conjunto do grupo. No entanto, não são as expectativas para o ciclo, mas sim a competência definida pelo programa – a saber, a *produção* de um projeto artístico – que determina seu ensino. A questão da apropriação, pelas alunas, de elementos simples de composição e interpretação é de fato pensada como recurso, a serviço da produção delas. Em outras palavras, ela é principalmente pensada como um meio de serviço para essa produção esperada, a qual, como uma aquisição, implica que as alunas aprendam a se relacionar com as emoções ou efeitos que querem produzir no espectador. A partir de então, o professor fornece às alunas, através de suportes escritos, a multiplicidade de procedimentos, permitindo-lhes criar um trabalho certamente original, mas que não se inscreve de fato no enquadramento de um *projeto artístico*, isto é, portador de uma mensagem a ser transmitida. Em situação de observação, nós fomos abatidos pela fraca utilização dessas fichas pelas alunas (um só grupo de quatro alunas consultou as fichas em 4 aulas!).

Além disso, a questão da expressão, da qualidade do movimento, não está diretamente em linha com a complexidade que ela introduz no ensino. Daí, o objeto do professor consiste em responder às expectativas do programa através da competência esperada ou da competência visada, sem se interrogar sobre o senso artístico que demanda do professor um nível de exigência mais elevado.

Professor: Sim, mas eu propus (soluções) para os alunos que estavam com dificuldades, que não sabiam como se deslocar, eu propus verbos para se deslocar. Com outros, eu não preciso. Mas eu poderia muito bem, para ver o que eles iam fazer, não dizer nada. Não é a criatividade total, mas entre uma pausa 1 uma pausa 2, é preciso que eles se virem rápido, **é preciso que eles sejam criativos**, mas para mim não era esse obrigatoriamente o objetivo. **Para mim, o objetivo era sobretudo que eles compreendessem, e esse é o objetivo para esse primeiro nível, que dançar pode ser tudo**. Veja você, a gente parte de fotos, quer dizer, de reprodução, a gente parte de gestos esportivos que a partir do momento em que a gente tem um projeto conjunto de deslocamento estético, com objetivo de mostrá-los a outros, e em que há uma expressão do sentimento, da sensibilidade, é dança, e **não há um termo técnico para colocar por trás da dança**.
Pesquisador: De acordo, mas e a questão da qualidade do movimento, da expressão da mensagem?
Professor: Não é meu objetivo nesse primeiro nível.

Nesse trecho, dois aspectos em particular se destacam:

- A dificuldade de identificar o que surge legitimamente de um movimento dançado, que é esvaziado da reflexão um pouco mais adiante, na entrevista, por um objetivo que ele se estabelece: "Eu quero fazer eles compreenderem que todo o movimento destinado a ser mostrado é dança."
- As injunções contraditórias (É preciso que eles [os alunos] sejam criativos.), que mostram bem que o objeto da atividade de aprendizagem a construir não está realmente identificado.

Nesse cenário, existe certamente uma contradição entre o objeto da atividade do professor, que é permitir aos alunos realizar uma coreografia coletiva para responder às exigências dos programas, e o objeto da atividade de aprendizagem dos alunos, que é realizar uma coreografia de qualidade para demonstrar suas competências em relação aos colegas de aula.

2.2 Modelização das contradições entre atividades de ensino e atividades de aprendizagem

Com base na modelização dos sistemas de atividade proposta por Engeström (2001), nos propomos aqui a modelizar as contradições entre os sistemas de atividade de ensino e aprendizagem (Figura 3).

Dois tipos de contradições aparecem:

- Uma contradição interna ao sistema de atividade, entre o objeto da atividade – que os alunos elaborem uma coreografia original – e o fato de fornecer soluções feitas para alunos com dificuldades;
- Uma contradição de objeto, entre alunos e professor.

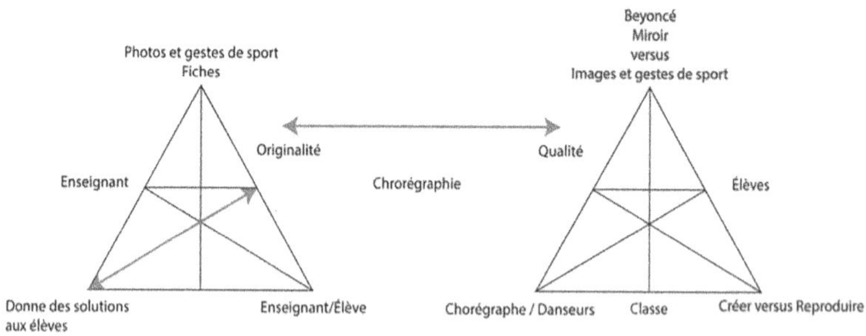

Figura 3: As contradições entre atividade de ensino e atividade de aprendizagem.

3. Extensão do conceito de ZDP nas pesquisas colaborativas sobre desenvolvimento

Que lição tirar desse estudo de caso, para pesquisas que visem transformar a atividade dos profissionais que participam delas?

Nós vimos que a ZDP emerge, entre as alunas, de um conflito entre o que elas desejam fazer e aquilo que professor lhes pede que façam. Esse conflito é percebido de maneira consciente pelos alunos. O conflito emerge no episódio em que as alunas negociam as regras da tarefa formulada pelo professor. No entanto, o professor não percebe de forma alguma a contradição entre sua atividade e aquela processada pelas alunas.

Aqui, é preciso distinguir bem as contradições, dilemas e conflitos. (Engeström & Sannino, 2011) No quadro da teoria histórico-cultural da atividade, os conflitos ou os dilemas são considerados como manifestações das contradições subjacentes. Os conflitos são considerados formas de resistência, de desacordo ou de crítica. Para De Dreu & Van de Vliert (1997, p. 1), "há conflito quando uma pessoa ou um grupo se sente lesado por outra pessoa ou outro grupo, por exemplo, em razão de uma divergência de interesses ou de um comportamento incompatível de outra pessoa ou de outro grupo." Para Engeström & Sannino (2011), as manifestações discursivas dos conflitos podem ser observadas nos desacordos entre os participantes.

Nesse quadro, o desacordo entre as alunas e o professor, que emerge na aula 3, nos parece poder ser a expressão de uma contradição entre atividade de ensino e atividade de aprendizagem das alunas. Esse ponto nos parece particularmente importante, para poder estender a noção de ZDP. Para Eyme (2017, p. 503), "as contradições se diferem dos conflitos ou dos problemas pois elas são apenas sintomas, cuja resolução responde às exigências da situação, mas sem prometer transformações." Assim, transformar o trabalho dos professores participantes de pesquisas colaborativas passa pela confrontação dos mesmos com as contradições entre sistema de atividade de ensino e sistema de atividade de aprendizagem. Em outras palavras, trata-se de, no seio dessas pesquisas, transformar as contradições em objeto de conflito, para permitir que s professores recriem seus sistemas de atividade de ensino. Trata-se assim de estender a noção de ZDP às pesquisas colaborativas que nós conduzimos. Nesse cenário, poderemos destacar a qual ponto as contradições inscritas na atividade conjunta de ensino-aprendizagem constituem uma ferramenta a serviço da abertura de tal zona de desenvolvimento potencial.

Conclusão

A noção de ZDP usualmente mobilizada na literatura relativa às atividades físicas e esportivas leva a uma interpretação tanto comum quanto redutora. Especialmente mobilizada nas aquisições de habilidades discretas ou de ações, ela não se refere à construção e produção, pelos alunos, de sua própria atividade. As alunas envolvidas na prática de dança em EF apresentada nessa sequência estão muito engajadas na produção de sua própria atividade, a serviço da demonstração da sua competência em relação a outros alunos. Elas elaboram essa atividade a despeito das restrições fixadas pelo professor, ou até mesmo em diálogo com essas restrições. Elas não são simples reprodutoras de uma forma cultural, elas são criadoras.

É preciso então ampliar o uso da noção de ZDP, para permitir compreender essa atividade cultural pelos alunos de EF. Ao mesmo tempo, essa ampliação deve permitir vislumbrar o papel criador de contradições na emergência dessa ZDP. De forma complementar, nos parece que essa operação abre caminhos para a transformação do trabalho de professor, com base na superação dessas contradições entre os sistemas de atividade de ensino e de atividade de aprendizagem. Há, portanto, uma necessidade de levar a sério o conceito de ZDP em todos os métodos que visem a transformação do trabalho de ensino.

Referências

Barker, D., Quennerstedt, M. & Annerstedt, C. (2015) Inter-student interactions and student learning in health and physical education: a post-Vygotskyan analysis. *Physical Education and Sport Pedagogy*, 20:4, 409-426, DOI: 10.1080/17408989.2013.868875

Chaiklin, S. (2003). The zone of proximal development in Vygotsky's analysis of learning and instruction. In A. Kozulin, B. Gindis, V. Ageyev, S. Miller (Eds.), *Vygotsky's educational theory and practice in cultural context.* Cambridge : Cambridge University Press.

Clot, Y. (1995). *Le travail sans l'homme?* Paris : La dispute.

Clot, Y. (1999). *La fonction psychologique du travail.* Paris : PUF.

Clot, Y. (2008). *Travail et pouvoir d'agir.* Paris: PUF.

Cole, M. (2009). The perils of translation. A first step in reconsidering Vygotsky's Theory of Development in Relation to Formal Education. *Mind, Culture and Activity,* 16(4), 291-295

D'Arripe-Longueville, F., Gernigon, C., M., Huet, L., Cadopi, M. & Winnikamen, F. (2002). Peer Tutoring in a Physical Education Setting: Influence of Tutor Skill Level on Novice Learners' Motivation and Performance. *Journal of Teaching in Physical Education*, 22 (1): 105–123.

De Dreu, C.K.W. and Van de Vliert, E. (1997). Introduction: using conflict in organizations. In C.K.W. De Dreu & E. Van de Vliert, (Eds), *Using Conflict in Organizations*. Sage: London.

Dyson, B. & Casey, A. (2012). *Cooperative learning in physical education: a research-based approach.* London: Routledge

Engeström, Y. (2001). Expansive Learning at Work: Toward an Activity Theory reconceptualization. *Journal of Education and Work*, 14(1), 133-156.

Engeström, Y. & Sannino, A. (2011). Discursive manifestations of contradictions in organizational change efforts: a methodological framework. Journal of Organizational Change Management, 24(3), 368-387.

Eyme, J. (2017). Engeström ou la troisième génération de la « théorie de l'activité ». In J.-M. Barbier & M. Durand (Eds.), *Encyclopédie d'analyses des activités* (pp. 495-505). Paris : PUF.

Griffin, P. & Cole, M. (1984). Current activity for the future: The zo-ped. In B. Rogoff & J.Wertsh (Eds), *Children's learning in the 'zone of proximal development'* (pp.45-64). San Francisco: Jossey-Bass.

Guarino, L. (2015). Is Dance a Sport? A twenty-First century debate. *Journal of Dance Education,* 15, 77-80.

Jornet, A. (2018). Vygotsky and Marx: toward a Marxist Psychology. *Mind, Culture and Activity*. Doi: 10.1080/10749039.2018.1480635

Kozulin, A. (2016). Foreword: How to reconstruct deconstructions. In A. Yasnitsky & R. Van der Veer (Eds), *Revisionist revolution in Vygotsky studies: The state of the art.* London: Routledge.

Leontiev, A. (1978). *Activity, Consciousness, and Personality*. Englewood Cliffs, N.J.: Prentice-Hall.

Roth, W.-M. & Radford, L. (2010). Re/thinking the Zone Proximal of Development (Symmetricaly). *Mind, Culture & Activity*, 17(4), 299-307.

Rovegno, I. & Dolly, J.P. (2006). Constructivist perspectives on learning. In D.Kirk, M. O'Sullivan & D. Macdonald (eds), *Handbook of Research in Physical Education* (pp.242-261). Thousand Oaks, CA; London: Sage.

SCHNEUWLY, B. (1995). De l'importance de l'enseignement pour le développement. Vygotsky et l'école. Psychologie et Éducation, 21— 25-37.

STETSENKO, A. (2008). From relational ontology to transformative activist stance on development and learning: expanding Vygotsky's (CHAT) project. *Cultural Studies of Science Education*, 3, 471-491.

VYGOTSKY, L.S. (1978). *Mind in society*. Cambridge, MA: Harvard University Press.

YASNITSKY, A., & VAN DER VEER, R. (2016). *Revisionist revolution in Vygotsky studies: The state of the art*. East Sussex, UK: Routledge.

III. PÔR EM PRÁTICA

1.

REALIDADE AUMENTADA (RA), ATIVIDADE DE CONCEPÇÃO E DEBATE DE IDEIAS: CO-CONSTRUIR COM ARTEFATOS OS SABERES TÁTICOS DO JOGO COLETIVO EM EF NA ESCOLA PRIMÁRIA TAIWANESA

Ching-Wei CHANG, Taiwan
Escola Normal Superior de Taiwan (NTNU, ROC)
Nathalie WALLIAN, França
Universidade de La Réunion, ICARE (EA 7389)

Introdução

Na Educação Física (EF) em Taiwan, o trabalho didático em jogos coletivos está em plena mutação e sofre uma dupla influência do ocidente e do oriente. Com efeito, as abordagens vygotskianas começam a penetrar os domínios da pesquisa e da formação de professores, ao encontro das preocupações do campo: o olhar do pesquisador e do praticante tende a desviar das abordagens centradas na aquisição de técnicas corporais, em benefício de uma reflexão aprofundada sobre as maneiras como o praticante co-constrói suas competências, assim como sobre os saberes correspondentes. Abrindo-se às abordagens japonesas contemporâneas, inspiradas em Satô (2012) – que faz menção aos trabalhos de Vygotsky –, a influência do conceito de *comunidade colaborativa de aprendizagem* coloca em contexto um sentido forte e recoloca a noção de saber no coração da dimensão social compartilhada. Enfim, as novas tecnologias integram facilmente as práticas de ensino porque elas fazem plenamente parte da cultura dos alunos taiwaneses. É por isso que o contexto taiwanês é um contexto favorável ao cruzamento de abordagens vygotskianas, com apoio significante das novas tecnologias, como meio de suscitar, entre os alunos, práticas reflexivas. Favorecendo entre eles uma atividade de concepção que autoriza o desenvolvimento da reflexividade e *in fine* a autonomia na tomada de decisões, Taiwan começa uma mutação cultural maior, longe dos preceitos confucionistas, fundados na repetição e correção de erros pela memorização, um modelo prevalecente na aprendizagem tradicional do chinês.

O objeto desse artigo consiste em investigar o laço entre novas tecnologias (NT) e apropriação de saberes táticos em jogos coletivos, do ponto de vista da gênese de uma atividade de concepção do jogador e do uso de artefatos para essa aprendizagem. A ideia sustentada consiste em considerar as condições de uso das NT em uma perspectiva "aumentada". A escolha pelo ensino de jogos coletivos (basquete e handball) na escola primária para um estudo de caso se justifica, por um lado, pela riqueza oferecida por essas atividades coletivas aos alunos, em termos de alternativas de decisão e, por outro lado, pela necessidade de propor aos professores generalistas do primeiro grau ferramentas práticas eficazes de intervenção educativa.

A primeira parte desse estudo consistirá em posicionar as noções de "realidade virtual/aumentada" no contexto do ensino de EF. Depois, o pensamento vygostkiano e satoiano será conectado com a noção de "situação encarnada" [situative embodiement] (Barab & al., 2007) em aprendizagem motora. Em segundo lugar, as modalidades de introdução das NT no ensino recíproco entre pares permitirão vislumbrar condições de uso da RA em EF. Enfim, na situação de jogo complexa, o uso de RA será questionado considerando os efeitos dos artefatos para os alunos. Perspectivas serão formuladas para os estudos por vir, sobre as abordagens didáticas da EF em RA.

1. Atividade de concepção, realidade virtual/aumentada e situação encarnada

Vygotsky afirma que a consciência está associada ao uso de ferramentas e artefatos que operam a mediação com o mundo, distinguindo a espécie humana da espécie animal. O *aumento* da realidade se deve ao fato de que as tecnologias de RA permitem, sob condições, melhorar e enriquecer o real, trazendo uma atenção particular ao contexto. O uso de artefatos introduz a dimensão material da realidade sobre um modo cultural e historicamente situado, sendo a realidade constantemente mediada e reinterpretada pelas práticas: a contribuição da RA é mudar a perspectiva, melhorar a compreensão e a construção das significações, aumentando a realidade através de ferramentas de informação educativas adicionais (Bowker & Starr, 2000): supõe-se que as NT tragam uma mudança qualitativa na relação com o real observado. Assim, em EF, elas interessam especialmente no domínio das condutas motrizes que, em essência, são imateriais, instáveis, situadas e efêmeras – a questão é saber como o jogador age de maneira reflexiva e implementa uma ação reflexiva.

Estimulando a cognição encarnada, a RA ajuda a construir significações a partir da realidade íntima [inner reality], incluindo aspectos contextuais, culturais e sociais: Barab & al. (2007) chamam isso de "incorporação situada" [situated embodiement] na qual "o aprendiz entra na situação nos planos narrativo e perceptivo, em um projeto, endossa uma participação legítima e se engaja em ações que têm consequências." Squire (2010) considera que nessas condições "...o currículo fundado em tecnologias (RA) ativa identidades dos estudantes como solucionadores de problema, mais do que como consumidores de informação conformados." De acordo com Cook (2010), as RA "agem como captadores sensoriais, facilitando visualizações específicas dadas a representar para os alunos de maneira situada."

Na escola primária taiwanesa, a questão da genealogia da consciência ganha importância crucial no contexto do ensino tradicional, centrado na memorização, repetição e correção de erros. Introduzindo o pensamento reflexivo em EF, o sistema educativo opera uma mudança de paradigma que desencadeia no aluno em uma mudança de postura com a qual o contexto cultural não o familiarizou. Essa mudança é radical, mas vital, porque o ambiente natural taiwanês é extremamente incerto (ex.: tufões, terremotos, tsunamis, animais perigosos...) e exige dos cidadãos grande adaptabilidade, longe das normas e procedimentos de segurança experimentados atualmente. A escola primaria é impactada por isso até na formação dos professores, e vê a EF se utilizar com força do paradigma reflexivo inspirado em Vygotsky, mas igualmente em Satô (佐藤学, 2012, 2015) e Okano (岡野昇, 2015). A influência deste último, japonês e firmemente oposto às evoluções do sistema neoliberal, defende uma aprendizagem colaborativa fundada em três princípios: uma filosofia das questões públicas, uma democracia no acesso aos saberes e excelência construída por todos. Permitindo que o aprendiz desenvolva um pensamento reflexivo, ele lhe permite acessar uma forma de autonomia crítica que futuramente autoriza a emancipação. A questão é saber como, em EF, o processo de socialização pelo compartilhamento de saberes é favorecido por uma reflexividade aumentada.

1.1. Jogos coletivos, reflexividade e consciência: um processo dialógico

Em jogos coletivos, a atividade de aprendizagem se inscreve em um contexto situado no seio de um coletivo que opera um processo de co-construção. Na relação dialógica que estabelece com o mundo, com outrem e consigo, o indivíduo opera transformações constantes: em função dos efeitos produzidos pelas suas ações, ele engaja recursivamente uma restruturação de suas intenções e estratégias. Em jogos coletivos, o jogador estabelece uma relação com seus parceiros e adversários em um quadro regulamentar restrito. Com a maneira que ele estabelece o diálogo se inscrevendo no jogo, ele (re)orienta suas ações e intenções: se, por exemplo, ele se faz interceptar pela bola em um passe, ele ou escolherá um outro parceiro, ou evitará devolvê-la na presença de tal defensor, ou se absterá de compartilhá-la, tentando atirar etc. Assim, o jogo se co-constrói ao longo de ações mais ou menos eficazes em relação com os parceiros que também compartilham modalidades de interação significantes.

Mas o trabalho de conceitualização da ação é complexo, escondido e difícil de interpretar, para o professor. Buscando suscitar a reflexividade na ação, o instrutor levará o jogador a "se voltar a si mesmo", mobilizando operações de pensamento ativo e autorreflexivo: a postura do jogador será modificada antes mesmo que ele adquira técnicas corporais elaboradas. Bronckart (2002, p. 27) afirma, a esse respeito, que "estar consciente é poder acessar seu próprio pensamento e agir sobre ele". O "virar o espelho para si mesmo", no sentido lacaniano do termo (Lacan, 1946), só é possível no encontro com esse outro que produz diferença e alteridade. Assim, o jogador se co-constrói no diálogo com outros jogadores, parceiros e adversários, na e pela relação dialética de colaboração-oposição, em situação de enfrentamento lúdico: é sob o olhar do outro, na troca com outro – seja verbal e/ou não-verbal – que se elabora a postura de jogador que toma decisões, e a de aluno que aprende saberes de ação. (Avenier & Schmitt, 2007) Dirigindo um passe a um parceiro mais ou menos habilidoso, distanciado e/ou "marcado", quem está com a bola vai tornar seu passe "pegável" e validar – ou não – a qualidade do outro em função dos efeitos da ação. Assim, o trabalho de conceitualização da ação está orientado pela elaboração de uma reflexividade orientada, que interpreta no contexto e de maneira recursiva o valor pragmático da ação.

No sentido vygotskiano, toda ação apresenta um caráter duplo (Bronckart, ibid, p. 39): de uma parte, uma dimensão histórico-social que inscreve a experiência humana em um *hic et nunc* e, de outra, uma dimensão *meta-reflexiva*, que desdobra a experiência, sob uma postura conscientizada em atos. Esse caráter autorreflexivo do mecanismo da consciência está articulado com as experiências capitalizadas, acionáveis em contexto, que, pela memória, opera uma remobilização dos saberes, longe de uma sedimentação como que provocada por uma repetição orientada à detecção de erros e a redução das lacunas. Na atividade motriz, se coloca então a questão do traço: como vislumbrar uma "retomada" da ação mesmo quando ela é efêmera, imaterial e instável?

1.2. Traço de atividade, debate de ideias e interpretação

Em EF, a questão do "traço da atividade motriz" coloca sérias dificuldades, sobretudo com alunos jovens, para quem colocar em palavras a ação é uma verdadeira prova. Porém, o trabalho de conceitualização da ação exige colocar em palavras e uma "explicação" que mobiliza tantos conceitos (p.ex. levantamento de bola, marcação, disputa de força) quanto formulação de regras para uma ação eficaz (p.ex. "Para passar, é necessário..."), além do uso de um vocabulário apropriado (p.ex. uma falta não é uma infração, para um árbitro; o sinal "caminhar" no não verbal de um árbitro significa "bola do adversário"). De repente, se coloca a questão de propor ao aluno um *traço de atividade* que autorize a retomada de sua experiência de um ponto de vista externalista, certamente, mas cruzando pontos de vista (p.ex. portador, parceiro, adversário, árbitro, espectador) à distância da ação (adiada imediatamente ou postergada para o próximo curso).

Ao autorizar o uso de *tablets* em cursos de EF, o próprio teor do estatuto de jogador se vê modificado: a todo instante, lhe é possível "voltar atrás", ao longo da ação. Considerando que a ação motriz, uma vez registrada e numerizada – isto é, limitada e estabilizada –, é comparável a um texto (Hjelmslev, 1985, p. 85; Wallian, 2015), torna-se então possível aplicá-la à análise textual, tanto de conteúdo quanto de discurso. "A língua significa quando, ao invés de copiar o pensamento, ela se deixa desfazer e refazer por ele. Ela carrega seu sentido como um traço de um passo significa o movimento e esforço de um corpo." (Merleau-Ponty, 1960, p. 56) Além disso, a situação de "debate de ideias" (Gréhaigne, Godbout et Bouthier, 2001) parece, em jogos coletivos, propícia à análise da atividade: a análise discursiva autoriza, sob condições, o acesso ao que faz sentido para o aluno, e ao processo de co-construção de um sentido compartilhado. Essa situação consiste, depois de uma fase de jogo em situação reduzida (4x4 em basquete), em dar um tempo para trocas aos jogadores, em torno de 1) o que se passou e 2) o que há para se fazer para ganhar. Os relatos descritivos e narrativos dos eventos, assim como a argumentação em torno dos momentos marcantes do jogo, permitem extrair as regras de ação eficazes para esse estado da disputa de forças entre as equipes. Vê-se então que a atividade de interpretação – ou semiótica – opera 1) uma descrição em palavras da ação e das intenções por trás dela; 2) uma confrontação argumentada de pontos de vista; e 3) uma arbitragem consentida, sobre o que há para fazer juntos.

A questão da natureza do traço, suporte das interpretações, assim como de suas modalidades de reunião, então se coloca. Como engajar uma abordagem conceitualista, a partir de elementos removidos no jogo e apresentados por interpretação reflexiva em autoscopia? Vamos definir as noções de realidade virtual/aumentada (RV/RA).

1.3. Autoscopia, realidade virtual e realidade aumentada

A distinção entre "realidade virtual" e "realidade aumentada" é operada por Milgram & al. (1994), que as posiciona de acordo com um *continuum* virtual: no intervalo entre essas duas realidades (RA e RV) se situam as realidades mistas (RM), compostas pelo ambiente real da RA, da virtualidade aumentada (VA) e da RV.

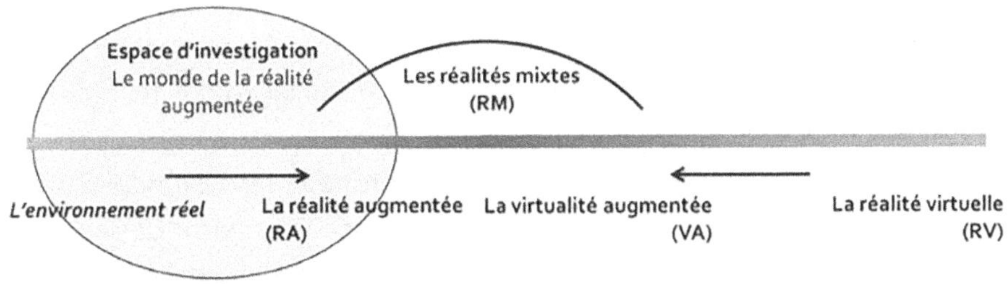

Figura 1. *Continuum* dos ambientes conectados reais/virtuais (de acordo com Milgram & al., 1994)

Este estudo se situa no espaço correspondente à investigação, no mundo, sobre a realidade aumentada: a abordagem dos jogos coletivos, com o uso de *tablets* numéricos para guardar traços da atividade em autoscopia é a aplicação correspondente. Imergindo o jogador em espaço de RS, o dispositivo autoriza a substituir e simular em um certo grau o mundo físico experimentado, com o fim de permitir-lhe suspender o esforço físico em benefício da reflexão sobre e na ação. Esse tempo de suspensão é propício à elaboração de uma reflexividade sobre e pelo jogo, tanto simultaneamente quanto com um ligeiro atraso.

2. Ensino recíproco entre pares, RA e artefatos em jogos coletivos

A tecnologia RA pode, sob condições, autorizar o que Vygotsky designa como "mediação com o mundo": ela representa um contato com uma realidade e permite o desenvolvimento da reflexividade "economizando" o esforço em sentido amplo (energético, emocional, informacional...), pela suspensão da ação. O desenvolvimento da reflexividade no aluno, por outro lado, envolve uma descentralização, para uma reflexividade mais consciente, pois intencionada e, de outro lado, uma liberação da influência – sempre obliterante – da urgência da ação. Operando uma mediação com o mundo experienciado, a RA favorece a interação e a abstração reflexiva.

(Fitzgerald & al., 2012) Assim, por exemplo, formulando a constatação sobre o resultado do jogo e dos determinantes estratégicos da ação coletiva, argumentando sobre o que há por fazer para ganhar no contexto, discutindo posicionamentos mútuos para ocupação estratégica do espaço, o jogador aprende a relacionar a disputa de forças com outrem, a gestão de janelas temporais em relação à tomada de decisão e a otimização dos recursos em função das restrições do jogo.

A RA afeta a maneira como o aluno interage com o mundo físico e representa uma ajuda na construção de interpretações a partir da realidade experienciada. O jogador "entra em uma situação no plano narrativo e perceptual; ele tem um projeto, deve argumentar seu papel e se engaja em ações que têm consequências." (Barab & al., 2007).

2.1. Para uma modelização em etapas dos artefatos de acordo com o processo reflexivo

Várias etapas de construção dos usos da RA na ação surgiram em Taiwan, graças ao dispositivo implementado para coleta de traços de atividade em autoscopia.

Em um primeiro momento, os jogadores focaram em elementos técnicos simples, como por exemplo um arremesso parado para a cesta de basquete. Nessas condicoes, o jogador observador produz um artefato que parte da motricidade de um par em situação autêntica de aprendizagem para autorizar a retomada atrasada.

Figura 2. RA produzindo um artefato de nível 1: a *busca recíproca* de indicadores sobre o traço.

Nessas condições, o dispositivo se inscreve em continuidade com o "estilo recíproco" (Mosston, ???), que estabelece, em uma grade preestabelecida de itens descritivos, a análise do jogador "por comparação de lacunas e por hierarquização". O artefato serve assim como ponto de comparação entre o traço e a referência traduzida em indicadores observáveis em uma ficha de observação. Essa etapa é apropriada para as habilidades motrizes básicas e tecnicamente estabilizadas.

A segunda etapa da construção refere-se a uma leitura orientada dos traços pela indicação na imagem de indicadores comportamentais decisivos e pertinentes. Nesse caso, a interpretação já é realizada por marcadores que direcionam os pontos de atenção para o leitor e lhe permitem compará-los com o trabalho do jogador observado.

Figura 3. RA produzindo um artefato de nível 2: a *busca recíproca* de indicadores sobre o traço.

Nessa situação, o dispositivo parte de traços destinados a serem explicitados, descritos, comentados, comparados e argumentados. O jogador aprende a interpretar a atividade de um par através da comparação com a produção esperada, tal qual apresentada em RA. Os índices pertinentes de interpretação permitem orientar a leitura comparada e detectar o diferencial nos traços coletados. Ainda aqui, são os elementos de motricidade elementar que são realizados pelo artefato e a interpretação é relativamente reduzida e desambiguizada.

A terceira etapa se interessa na busca ampliada de indicadores pertinentes para a ação.

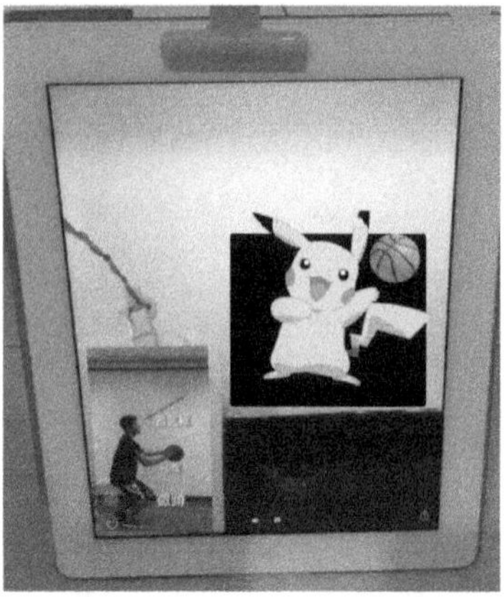

O jogo de oposição pode integrar um atacante excedente, o coringa, que vai entrar no jogo em momentos precisos, desequilibrando as disputas de força que vão se reequilibrar posteriormente. Ao precisar as expectativas com "pulgas" animadas que substituem o jogo do coringa, o artefato coloca o jogador em situação simulada de desequilíbrio à qual ele deverá se adaptar. A "pulga" que perturba o jogo obriga o jogador a se descentrar de seu espaço próximo, em benefício de uma consideração ampliada dos elementos determinantes do jogo e da tomada de decisão.

Figura 4. RA produzindo um artefato de nível 3: a *busca recíproca* de indicadores sobre o traço.

Assim, o professor pode:

1°) oferecer diferentes tarefas de aprendizagem, ajustadas às necessidades particulares;
2°) estabelecer tarefas comuns com dificuldades;
3°) propor um ciclo de aprendizagem apresentando caminhos variados.

A quarta etapa diz respeito à realização da traçabilidade do percurso estabelecido pelo jogador no coração do artefato.

Assim, integrando traçabilidade na busca pelos índices de traço pelo jogador, o dispositivo permite identificar as maneiras de proceder para acesar níveis de complexidade superior. Com efeito, estocando na memória as etapas singulares do percurso, o artefato permite, ao mesmo tempo, destacaro ritmo de progressao, os momentos de latência, as etapas significantes de progresso decisivo, assim como a trajetória global de progressão.

Figura 5. RA produzindo um artefato de nível 4: a *busca recíproca* de indicadores sobre o traço.

A traçabilidade da navegação no dispositivo permite então restituir em tempo real, e para o jogador e professor, a historicidade do procedimento dinâmico de construção de acordo com diferentes escalas temporais; na microssituação de aprendizagem, na escala de um ciclo completo de aprendizagem e mesmo ao longo de toda a escolaridade, no percurso da EF, no quadro de um "caderno virtual de progressão no esporte". Da mesma forma, ela autoriza a extração de uma tipologia de acordo com o perfil do jogador e do aprendiz, útil para diferenciar a intervenção. No entanto, esse procedimento, aplicado às técnicas elementares (arremesso, passe...) e às habilidades simples, requer uma retomada, no jogo, situação de uma complexidade claramente superior. O artefato RA proposto nesse caso toma outra dimensão.

2.2. Os artefatos em situação complexa de jogo

A construção de competências táticas em jogo coletivo de oposição requerer uma leitura interpretativa da disputa de forças, levando em conta a dialética de enfrentamento, assim como as dinâmicas variadas das janelas temporais de decisão. Assim, a interpretação do jogo exige que uma grade de análise seja elaborada, reunindo fatos a montante dos fatos observados, com fins de orientar, através de expectativas focalizadas, o olhar do observador. Neste caso, não sendo o professor do primário que atua em EF especialista nem na disciplina de EF, nem nas atividades físicas de esportes coletivos, é necessário ajudá-lo a construir seu próprio referencial de análise, levando em conta a complexidade da situação do jogo coletivo. O desafio da RA consiste então em orientar a análise da sistemática do jogo, autorizando uma interpretação para a decisão, notadamente para permitir aos jogadores que interajam de maneira transformadora.

O dispositivo P.L.A.Y. (***P**laying games; **L**earning focus; **A**ssessing project; **Y**es we've got it!* [*Jogar jogos; Aprender foco; Avaliar projeto; Sim, nós conseguimos!*]) é pensado para trazer uma estrutura para a RA aplicada em situações complexas de jogo coletivo. Partindo sistematicamente de situações autênticas de jogo, uma parte grande é atribuída à fase ativa de exploração e engajamento motor. O registro das fases do jogo é coletado por um tempo contínuo longo e informações sobre "eventos notáveis" são repertorizadas. (Leutenegger, 2003) Esses eventos notáveis correspondem a momentos-chave nas fases-mães do jogo, assim como às diferentes "configurações do jogo", caracterizadas por Gréhaigne (2007), as quais correspondem aos níveis típicos de construção do jogador. A RA permite, assim, ao fim da análise tecnológica da atividade física esportiva ou artística, passar para uma fase didática, ao longo da qual a coleta de percursos, operados pelos jogadores para construir o jogo no enfrentamento, serve de base para o trabalho de "reconhecimento" desenvolvido na formação dos professores. Ao treinarem para re-conhecer as configurações do jogo, os educadores aprendem a analisar a estrutura típica significante, a partir da qual as táticas são modelizadas em função do nível dos jogadores.

Assim, em uma aula de jogadores de BB (10 anos) em situação de 4x4 emcampo reduzido, o trabalho de "ataque rápido com coringa" é coletado em RA para uma retomada a partir da experiência real vivida pelos jogadores, em tempo quase real.

Figura 6. Contexto de aplicação de RA em situação complexa de jogo 4x4.

Munidos de *tablets* imantados, os jogadores em situação de debate de ideias são levados a projetar nesse espaço representado os eventos passados e as táticas por vir. Argumentando em torno de uma ferramenta de visualização dos posicionamentos e deslocamentos, eles inscrevem a mobilidade dos jogadores em uma dialética fina, própria à abstração, que leva à formulação de regras de ação eficaz, antes de voltar para experimentá-las no retorno ao jogo.

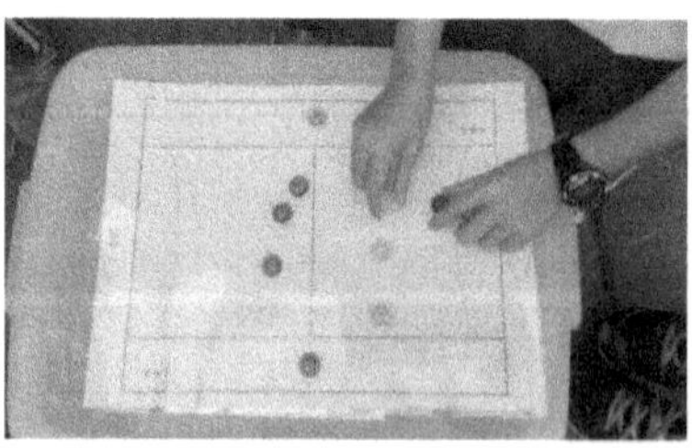

Nessas condições, manipulando peões magnéticos e argumentando sobre alternativas de decisão no contexto, os alunos aprendem a "ler" para antecipar os resultados plausíveis do jogo.

Figura 7. RA produzindo um artefato de nível 5:
a conceitualização formalizada de táticas coletivas

Nessa situação, os alunos em debate de ideias (t = 5') são filmados no *tablet*. Uma vez que eles entram em acordo, graças às interações formalizadas sobre o *tablet* magnético, o retorno à situação de jogo é reposicionado por comparação.

A atividade comparativa entre, de um lado, as intenções compartilhadas e negociadas e, de outro, a realidade do jogo em situação de enfrentamento, é conduzida pelos próprios alunos. Identificando pontos similares e divergentes da ação projetada/real, eles conseguem colocar em palavras significações do jogo construídas em configurações típicas.

Figura 8. RA produzindo um efeito diferencial e contrastante sobre as táticas coletivas projetadas/reais.

A alternância de fases do jogo, de debate de ideias e depois de retomada da interpretação com retorno ao jogo autoriza, não só recuperação psicológica do jogador, mas o estabelecimento de uma reflexividade, orientada pela busca por índices pertinentes para a ação. Esses índices permitem orientar a ação coletiva de acordo com princípios e regras compartilhadas e negociadas – às vezes amargamente – sobretudo em início de ciclo.

Nessa situação de observação ativa, o aluno que registra os traços de ação pertinentes (parte inferior do campo) antecipa sobre os eventos que se desenrolam diante se seus olhos: se "ler é formular hipóteses de sentido quanto ao resultado plausível da ação", o jogador se torna então um intérprete.

Figura 9. RA produzindo um artefato de nível 6; a leitura orientada de táticas coletivas.

2.3. Trabalhar os artefatos para ajudar a abstração da ação coletiva conceitualizada

Os alunos co-constroem, progressivamente, etapa por etapa, configurações cada vez mais elaboradas e significantes. A introdução pontual de regras de jogo modificadas (ex.: introdução de um coringa, limitação do espaço de deslocamento em corredores, proibição provisória de entrar em ataque no campo adversário...) obriga os jogadores a rediscutir o estado da disputa de força e a formulação tática das intenções de jogo.

Com objetivo de visualizar as relações dos jogadores para poder identificar as configurações do jogo, é possível materializar na imagem os posicionamentos dos atacantes/defensores. Esses posicionamentos mudam perpetuamente, conduzindo por alternância o deslocamento da bola para frente/para trás do espaço efetivo de jogo.

Figura 10. RA produzindo um artefato de nível 7:
os deslocamentos/reposicionamentos no espaço efetivo de jogo.

Nesse estágio do uso da RA, torna-se possível munir os coletes de *chips* com GPS diretamente conectados aos *tablets*. O tratamento informático dos deslocamentos reais dos jogadores autoriza a restituição dos eventos notáveis, em torno da problemática da ocupação do espaço, tendo em vista as janelas temporais mais ou menos abertas. (Gréhaigne, 2009) O artefato permite então que o jogador compreenda a ligação entre posicionamento espacial e janela temporal de decisão.

Parece então, no dispositivo de RA experimentado em jogo coletivo, que a elaboração de táticas a partir de situações autênticas de jogo é favorecida pela co-construção de imagens operativas dinâmicas de acordo com os níveis de jogo, levando a uma leitura interpretativa cada vez mais elaborada e orientada por expectativas precisas.

3. Complexidade e efeitos de artefatos: a co-construção do sentido compartilhado em contexto

A RA autoriza a emergência de níveis de abstração e de conceitualização de uma complexidade crescente. De acordo com as formas e usos tomados pelos artefatos apresentados aos jogadores, o nível de complexidade do jogo é restituído em um projeto de leitura orientada. Não contente em "reconhecer" as configurações típicas do jogo, o jogador se torna plenamente um leitor que antecipa, formulando hipóteses de sentido, o resultado da ação, e que valida – ou não – o valor das decisões tomadas de acordo com os efeitos reais. Em outras palavras, a RA permite ao jogador, sob condições, de co-construir sua ação tendo em vista intenções explicitadas e negociadas e efeitos esperados/observados no jogo, coletando, ao longo da experiência, traços do percurso histórico.

Essa dialética corresponde bem às ideias estabelecidas por Vygotsky, que considera que aprender é um processo de socialização, inscrito em uma historicidade, na qual a experiência dá forma à abstração, pela tomada de consciência do jogo com outrem. Mudando de ponto de vista, admitindo a troca de papeis em uma perda de bola, discutindo as interpretações plausíveis dos eventos surgidos no jogo, o jogador constrói, consigo mesmo e com outrem, um diálogo significante através do qual ele se transforma.

A linguagem intervém como um componente fundador da racionalidade do jogador, ajudando-o a colocar em palavras fatos e intenções, a argumentar pontos de vista a compartilhar, a formular proposições a debater, a sintetizar regras coletivas. Debatendo fora do jogo e dialogando no jogo, as trocas se tornam construtivas e produtivas. A elevação progressiva da complexidade das situações de aprendizagem leva progressivamente o jogador a levar em conta não só "mais informações", mas índices hierarquizados de acordo com uma carga sêmica diferencial: aprendendo a priorizar suas decisões, o jogador especula sobre as janelas temporais, arbitrando o urgente e o importante. Se a realidade do jogo não é simplesmente "refletida" na percepção do jogador, ela impacta a ponto de transformar: o conhecimento abstrato é, assim, gerado pela realidade interpretada e debatida em e por uma prática orientada por intenções explícitas. (Vygotsky, 2002, p. 112)

In fine, "não há o pensamento, a linguagem (e a ação). Cada uma das duas (três) ordens, examinadas, se desdobram e lança um ramo na outra... As operações expressivas se passam entre palavra pensante, (ação em pensamento) e pensamento falante (agido) e não, como se diz ligeiramente, entre pensamento, (ação) e linguagem." (Merleau-Ponty, 1960, p. 26).

Conclusão – Quando o pensamento (verbal) se torna acionável e a ação conceitualizante

O trabalho do pesquisador dos públicos de alunos jovens tem de interessante que a linguagem ainda não está totalmente descentrada de um ponto de vista egocêntrico: ela apresenta igualmente um alcance lexical ainda frustrado, limitando a abstração. Com efeito, o jovem jogador tem tendência a considerar sua interpretação como real e o fato de descobrir por si que há outras realidades, através da RA, o leva a considerar – e até a contestar – o ponto de vista de outrem. Aprendendo a colocar em palavras intenções, experiências e impressões, o jogador elabora níveis de abstração crescentes, que autorizam a formalizar seu pensamento para além da própria experiência.

Em uma perspectiva de desenvolvimento e emancipação, os aportes da RA, longe de alienar em uma tecnologia estúpida porque desambiguizante ou demagogicamente estética, podem ser vislumbrados em um moto colaborativo desmaterializado. Com efeito, é a utilização funcional dos artefatos de RA – e de fato seu poder transformativo – que autoriza a transformação: em outras palavras, as condições de utilização da linguagem, verbal no caso dos debates de ideias, não verbal no das ações de jogo coletivo, dão acesso às significações compartilhadas e às conceitualizações elaboradas no seio da comunidade das práticas. As operações mentais estabelecidas se inscrevem em uma variedade de atividades: se exprimir, (se) contar, (se) descrever, (se) expor, (se) comparar, (contra-)argumentar, (se) inventar... Elas colocam em jogo uma abstração fundada em análise, indução, dedução, abstração, síntese, experimentação (Vygotsky, 2002, p. 180), para, *in fine*, compartilhar, jogar junto e ver-se transformado.

Referências

AVENIER, M-J., et SCHMITT, C. (2007). *La construction de savoirs pour l'action.* Paris : L'Harmattan.

BAKHTINE, M. (1929, 1977). *Marxisme et philosophie du langage*. Paris : Minuit.

BARAB, S., ZUIKER, S., WARREN, S., HICKEY, D., INGRAM-GOBLE, A., KWON, E.-J., KOUPER, I. and HERRING, S. C. (2007). Situationally embodied curriculum: relating formalisms and contexts. *Science Education, 91*(5), 750-782.

BOWKER, G., C. et STAR, S., L. (2000). *Sorting things out: Classification and its consequences*. Cambridge, MA, MIT Press.

BRONCKART, J.-P. (2002). La conscience comme "analyseur" des épistémologies de Vygoski et Piaget. In Y., Clot (dir.). *Avec Vygotsky*. Paris : La Dispute.

COOK, J. (2010). Mobile Phones as Mediating Tools within Augmented Contexts for Development. *International Journal of Mobile and Blended Learning, 2(3)*, 1-12.

FITZGERALD, E., ADAMS, A., FERGUSON, R., GAVED, M., MOR, Y., & THOMAS, R. (). Augmented reality and mobile learning: The state of the art. Retrived January 10, 2017, from http://oro.open.ac.uk/34281/

GRÉHAIGNE, J.-F., (2007). *Configurations du jeu. Débat d'idées et apprentissage du football et des sports collectifs.* Besançon : PUFC.

GRÉHAIGNE, J.-F. (2009). *Autour du temps.* Besançon : PUFC.

GRÉHAIGNE, J.-F., Godbout, P. et Bouthier, D. (2001). "The teaching and learning of decision making in team sports", Quest, 53, p. 59-76.

HJELMSLEV, L. (1985). *Nouveaux essais*. Paris : Presses universitaires de France.

LACAN, J. (1949). *Le stade du miroir comme formateur de la fonction du Je telle qu'elle nous est révélée dans l'expérience psychanalytique.* XVIeme Congrès international de psychanalyse, Zurich.

LEUTENEGGER, F. (2003). Etude des interactions didactiques en classe de mathématiques : un prototype méthodologique. In A., Weil-Barais, A., Danis, & M-.L., Schubauer-Leoni (Ed.), *Numéro spécial du Bulletin de psychologie, 56*(4), 559-571.

MERLEAU-PONTY, M. (1960). *Signes.* Paris : Gallimard.

MILGRAM, P., TAKEMURA, H., UTSUMI, A. and KISHINO, F. (1994). Augmented reality: A class of displays on the reality virtuality continuum. *Proceedings of Telemanipulator and Telepresence Technologies,* (pp. 282-292) SPIE Press.

Satô, M. (2012). À la recherche d'une école pour le XXIe siècle. Quelles (réformes scolaires) alternatives aux politiques néolibérales ? *Les Dossiers de l'éducation, 27,* 37-54. [https://journals.openedition.org/dse/447]

Squire, K. D. (2010). From information to experience: Place-based augmented reality games as a model for learning in a globally networked society. *Teachers College Record, 112*(10), 2565-2602

Vygotsky, L.S. (2002). *Pensée & langage*. Paris : La Dispute.

Wallian, N. (2015). Sémiotique de l'agir enseignant en Éducation Physique et Sportive: figures d'action et registres interprétatifs en milieu difficile. Revue *Carrefours de l'éducation, 40*(2), 63-80.

佐藤学(2012)。学校を改革する一学びの共同体の構想と実践。東京都:岩波書。

佐藤学(2015)。21世紀型の体育の学びへ。載於岡野昇與佐藤学編著，体育における学びの共同体の実践と探究（227-234頁）。東京都：大修館書店。SATOManabu

岡野昇(2015)。体育における学びの移り変わり。載於岡野昇與佐藤学編著，体育における学びの共同体の実践と探究（3-34頁）。東京都：大修館書店。OKANO Noboru

2.

ORGANIZAÇÃO DE ATIVIDADES CONJUNTAS E SUA EVOLUÇÃO NA ZONA DE DESENVOLVIMENTO PROXIMAL NO ENSINO DE ESPORTES. O PROCESSO DE TRANSFERÊNCIA DE RESPONSABILIDADE E CONTROLE DA APRENDIZAGEM

Víctor López-Ros, Bernat Llobet-Martí, & Bruno Avelar-Rosa, Espanha
Instituto de Pesquisa Educacional – Grupo de Pesquisa em Cultura e Educação
Universidade de Girona (Catalunha, Espanha)

Introdução

O que professores e aprendizes fazem diariamente na escola, em condições normais e naturais, para favorecer a construção de conhecimento desses aprendizes? Como esse processo complexo de múltiplas interações é articulado em torno de tarefas que precisam ser resolvidas? Este artigo aborda tais questões mostrando como a atividade conjunta entre professores e aprendizes é articulada e desenvolvida em torno de conteúdos específicos por toda a Zona de Desenvolvimento Proximal. Para este fim, dois exemplos concretos de processos de ensino e aprendizagem de dois times esportivos são mostrados, com atenção focada no curso da atribuição de responsabilidade e o controle da aprendizagem e do controle de aprendizagem do professor em relação aos alunos. A análise de sequências destaca a importância dos recursos semióticos usados na interação e também que o processo não é fácil, nem fluido nem linear, e está aberto a eventos imprevisíveis.

1. Sobre a Zona de Desenvolvimento Proximal (ZDP) e a Organização de Atividades Conjuntas (OAC)

O conceito de Zona de Desenvolvimento Proximal (ZDP) (Vygotsky, 1978, 1993) é umas das mais conhecidas noções entre as ricas contribuições de Vygotsky (Daniels, 2001; Mahn, 2015), que atraiu muitos estudiosos e pesquisadores desde o momento em que apareceu. Existe, então, um vasto número de trabalhos na área, desde a década de 80 do século passado até hoje (por exemplo, Chaiklin, 2003; Newman, Griffin & Cole, 1989; Moll, 1990; Veresov, 2017; Wertsch, 1985) Isso implica, além do número considerável de contribuições, na aparição e existência de interpretações nem sempre coincidentes sobre esse conceito. Uma das críticas a respeito de alguns trabalhos sobre ZDP é que eles não consideram nem interpretam o conceito na integralidade do contexto do trabalho de Vygotsky ou a partir de uma perspectiva sócio-histórico-cultural. Então, alguns autores (Chaklin, 2003; Smagorinsky, 2017; Veresov, 2017) apontam a necessidade de rever os preceitos básicos do conceito de ZDP, com a intenção de localizá-lo na perspectiva teórica em que foi concebido. Ainda há controvérsias sobre como considerar a ZDP, assim como sobre as derivações pedagógicas do conceito.

Ainda que a ideia de ZDP apareça em diferentes textos de Vygotsky[1], há enorme consenso em relação a considerar que a definição é especificamente coletada quando Vygotsky escreve sobre as relações entre aprendizagem e desenvolvimento no contexto do desenvolvimento de processos psicológicos superiores, no texto traduzido como *Mind in Society* (1978). O conceito de ZDP foi originalmente definido como: "a distância entre o nível de desenvolvimento real, que se costuma determinar por meio da solução independente de problemas, e o nível de desenvolvimento potencial, determinado por meio da solução de problemas sob a orientação de um adulto ou em colaboração com parceiros mais experientes." (Vygotsky, 1978: 86)

De acordo com isso, a definição de ZDP carrega diferentes ideias subjacentes, as quais são essenciais para seu entendimento. (Chaiklin, 2003; Moll, 1990; Wertsch, 1985) Em primeiro lugar, o conceito de ZDP pode ser

[1] Para uma revisão completa, ver Chaiklin (2003).

considerado dentro da ideia de mostrar, de forma concreta, as relações estabelecidas entre as funções interpsicológicas e as funções intrapsicológicas, no quadro dos processos de desenvolvimento psicológico superior. Essa questão é congruente com a lei genética do desenvolvimento, a qual "enfatizou a primazia da interação social no desenvolvimento humano." (John-Steiner & Mahn, 1996: 192) Em segundo lugar, apesar de alguns comentários criticando uma certa visão reducionista, a ZDP destaca a distância entre o nível de desenvolvimento real das crianças, manifestado na habilidade de realizar uma tarefa autonomamente, e o nível de desenvolvimento potencial, que depende de ajuda externa, estando essas funções ainda não completamente amadurecidas, mas em um processo de amadurecimento. (Vygotsky, 1978) Essa distância mostra as relações de interdependência entre a aprendizagem e o desenvolvimento humano, enfatizando que a verdadeira aprendizagem sempre precede o desenvolvimento. (Vygotsky, 1978) Em terceiro lugar, mostra que a aprendizagem que conduz o desenvolvimento ocorre quando tarefas com um nível de dificuldade mais alto são mais resolvidas do que aquelas realizadas individualmente. De alguma maneira, isso mostra que a dificuldade de uma tarefa envolve o desenvolvimento de funções psicológicas em processo de amadurecimento. Em quarto lugar, considerando a natureza social do desenvolvimento, ela destaca a importância de procedimentos de mediação, que aparecem ao longo dos processos de interação e tornam possível sua apropriação pelo aprendiz. Desses, a linguagem e outros recursos semióticos são proeminentes.

Assim, os processos de interação e comunicação entre aprendiz e professor em torno de um objeto de conhecimento estão no centro do que acontece na ZDP. Essa negociação envolve necessariamente um nível suficiente de intersubjetividade (Bruner, 1997; Cole, 1996; Wertsch, 1985), que permita aos participantes entenderem a mente do outro, situados no contexto da atividade na qual estão envolvidos (considerando que a interação não garante o estabelecimento de comunicação em si).

De acordo com o ponto de vista de Wertsch (1985), na fonte de Rommetveit e colaboradores, "a intersubjetividade existe quando os interlocutores partilham algum aspecto das definições da sua situação. Tipicamente, essa sobreposição pode ocorrer em diversos níveis e, portanto, podem existir várias intersubjetividades." (p.159)

Atingir altos níveis de intersubjetividade requer ajustes contínuos de contribuições à interação, tanto da parte do professor quanto da parte do aprendiz. (Wertsch, 1985; Smagorisnky, 2017) Em outras palavras, professor e aprendiz estão envolvidos numa atividade conjunta, na qual o interlocutor influencia e é influenciado por outro e, portanto, essa atividade conjunta não está completamente estabelecida previamente. (Rogoff, 1990, 1995) A atividade conjunta pode ser entendida como um sistema criado criativa e mutuamente pelo professor e aprendizes (Moll, 1990), os quais são mutuamente influenciados. Nesse sentido, Newman, Griffin, & Cole (1989) mencionaram a ZDP como uma Zona de Construção de Conhecimento, enfatizando que os processos de mudança cognitiva são construídos pelos participantes, isto é, eles não são dados antecipadamente, e mostram um caráter dinâmico.

Os processos de interação entre participantes na ZDP estão localizados em sistemas de atividades mais amplas (Cole, 1996, Rogoff, 1995) e são construídos através do estabelecimento de melhores níveis de intersubjetividade entre eles. (Wertsch, 1985) Tal fato tem a ver, também, com o domínio de recursos semióticos, que garantem entendimento mútuo e adaptação da participação de cada interlocutor na atividade conjunta. (Mercer, 1995; Vila, 1998) Nesse sentido, podemos considerar que os processos de atividade conjunta formam um sistema de interatividade que leva em consideração a participação de cada interlocutor em relação a um conteúdo específico e é parte de um sistema de atividades mais ampla, o qual dá sentido às ações realizadas. (Coll, Onrubia & Mauri, 2008; Cole, 1996; Rogoff, 1990, 1995) Então, por exemplo, uma escola tem propósitos específicos, que permitem entender e contextualizar as atividades realizadas pelos participantes em seu núcleo. Esses propósitos ou razões socioculturais não são coincidentes, por exemplo, com aquelas que direcionam um clube esportivos orientado para a performance. Da mesma maneira, o que acontece em uma aula ou em uma sessão de treinamento só pode ser entendido se o contexto for levado em consideração. Em outras palavras, os processos de aprendizagem e desenvolvimento dos participantes de um contexto específico são condicionados por ele.

Apontamos que a interatividade considera as contribuições dos participantes em relação a um conteúdo específico ou um objeto de conhecimento. Isso significa que os processos de atividades conjuntas estabelecidos na ZDP se referem às relações de influência mútua e interdependência entre participantes, assim como às características do conteúdo ou objeto de conhecimento expresso em determinada tarefa. Essa ideia está incluída no conceito de triângulo interativo ou triângulo didático (Cole, 1996), entendido como a unidade básica das interrelações entre elementos envolvidos no processo de ensino e aprendizagem, e constituído em cada um dos vértices pelo professor, o aprendiz e o conteúdo, respectivamente. As relações mantidas e desenvolvidas pelos três elementos ao longo do tempo são interdependentes e as formas de organização da atividade conjunta através da ZDP não podem ser entendidas se essas influências mútuas não forem consideradas. (Coll et al., 2008) Portanto, o professor mantém uma relação assimétrica com o aprendiz, a partir da sua posição de guia/instrutor. No entanto, suas ações são influenciadas pelas ações do aprendiz, a compreensão da situação, as contribuições para a interação, entre outros, e por características específicas do conteúdo, as quais definem a adequação ou não das tarefas propostas. No caso do aprendiz, sua participação é condicionada pela sua habilidade de entender e resolver as tarefas propostas pelo professor e as características do conteúdo, mas simultaneamente, suas contribuições modificam as ações do professor e podem demandar ou não modificações no conteúdo. Como muitos trabalhos indicam (Daniels, 2001, Frankel, 2012), a influência mútua entre participantes nos processos interativos dentro da ZDP ocorre quando a relação pode ser claramente assimétrica. Finalmente, as particularidades do conteúdo objeto da aprendizagem e as tarefas utilizadas para tal propósito determinam o processo de ensino e aprendizagem e suas características. (Comino, 2017; López-Ros, 2001, 2013) Assim, as características específicas de um conteúdo como, por exemplo, escalada, são diferentes daquelas de natação ou introdução aos esportes em equipe. Por outro lado, se tomarmos o exemplo dos esportes em equipe, começar a usar tarefas de natureza global e tática tem consequências interativas muito diferentes do que se, ao contrário, decidirmos usar modelos técnicos baseados em eficiência da habilidade.

2. Como o processo de Organização de Atividades Conjuntas é articulado durante o processo de transferência de responsabilidade e controle da aprendizagem?

A emergência do conceito de ZDP no contexto anglo-saxão gerou considerável impacto e deu origem a conceitos subsidiários, entre os quais a metáfora do *andaime*, sugerida por Wood, Bruner e Ross (1976). A ideia inicial dessa metáfora apontou que os processos interativos na ZDP podem ser entendidos como a estrutura de um andaime, no sentido de que, no início, existe uma estrutura que guia e sustenta a parede. Depois disso, progressivamente, essa estrutura começa a desaparecer. Da mesma maneira, o processo de orientação do professor no contexto da atividade conjunta seria muito mais intenso no início e, depois, gradualmente retirada. (Mercer, 1995; Vila, 1998) Nesse sentido, a atividade conjunta mostraria modificações progressivas à medida que o aprendiz avança na construção do conhecimento.

Ainda que alguns trabalhos mostrem como a metáfora do andaime pode não representar uma "leitura" adequada da ZDP (Daniels, 2001; Smagorinsky, 2017), ela serviu como referência para muitos trabalhos. (Valsiner, 2005; Van de Pol, Volman, & Beishuizen, 2010) Em termos gerais, e de acordo com a noção de ZDP, o andaime é interpretado como o processo de ajuda sistemática oferecia pelos mais *experts* ao aprendiz, a qual é sistematicamente retirada à medida que o aprendiz se torna autônomo na resolução de uma dada tarefa. Então, o professor age como guia em um processo de atividade conjunta que é, por definição, assimétrico e parcialmente imprevisível quanto ao seu desenvolvimento.

A organização de atividade conjunta (OAC) na qual o professor ajusta a ajuda pedagógica e dá ao aluno autonomia no controle de sua aprendizagem é destacado por diversos estudos. (Coll, Colomina, Onrubia, & Rochera, 1992) Isso coloca a atividade conjunta claramente na transição dos processos interpsicológicos para os intrapsicológicos e enfatiza a importância dos recursos semióticos durante a interação e a interatividade. A revisão realizada por Van de Pol, Volman & Beishuizen (2010) aponta as três principais características do processo de andaime: o apoio contingente, a retirada progressiva do suporte e o processo de transferência de responsabilidade.

A ideia de transferência de responsabilidade também foi coletada por diferentes trabalhos (Coll et al., 1992; Coll et al., 2008) que analisam como a influência educacional é exercida nos processos de ensino e aprendizagem e como ela produz o processo de controle e responsabilidade da aprendizagem na ZDP, também no campo da educação física e esportes. (Comino, 2017; López-Ros, 2001; Llobet-Martí, 2016; Pradas, 2012) Esses trabalhos indicam a existência de dois mecanismos de influência educacional, os quais estão presentes nos processos de ensino e aprendizagem, que requerem dispositivos de ensino específicos e que acontecem na ZDP. Então, os processos interativos que facilitam a aprendizagem na ZDP implicam em: a) um processo de transferência do controle e responsabilidade de aprendizagem; e b) o estabelecimento de um sistema de significados compartilhados cada vez mais complexo e rico. Ambos os mecanismos são inter-relacionados e mostram interdependência mútua, ainda que possam ser analisados focando a atenção em um deles. Isso significa que a atividade conjunta realizada pelo professor e o aprendiz será modificada enquanto o aprendiz se torna mais autônomo. As maneiras como essa atividade conjunta é organizada vai envolver desde maneiras de mostrar maior controle e um nível mais alto de regulação pelo professor, até formas de mostrar uma apropriação e um nível de controle maior pelo aprendiz. Então, é razoável, por exemplo, pensar que as formas de atividade conjunta indicam uma forte presença de aspectos organizacionais e o controle do desenvolvimento terá maior predominância no início do que no fim do processo de aprendizagem. Ou, o período de prática autônoma de um aprendiz de uma habilidade motora específica será maior no fim de uma sequência de ensino e aprendizagem. Esses aspectos vão se manifestar, também, através do uso diferenciado de certos recursos semióticos, assim como pelo estabelecimento de níveis mais altos de intersubjetividade, que vai revelar um universo de significados compartilhados mais ricos (e provavelmente maiores), enquanto o processo de ensino e aprendizagem avança.

Vários trabalhos no campo da educação física e esportes indicam algumas características sobre o processo de transferência do controle e da responsabilidade pela aprendizagem. (Comino, 2017; López-Ros, 2001; Llobet-Martí, 2016; LLobet-Martí, López-Ros, & Vila, 2017; Pradas, 2012) Por conseguinte, eles revelam que esse processo é dinâmico e progressivo, mas não é nem linear, nem fácil (nem fluido). Ao logo da evolução das formas de atividade conjunta, há frequentemente momentos de estagnação, regressão e rupturas. Tais momentos estão frequentemente associados com a necessidade de renegociar significados e atividades, e requerem uma mudança nos níveis de intersubjetividade, para permitir e favorecer o restabelecimento e o avanço do conhecimento compartilhado. Uma análise detalhada revela que tais rupturas ou retrocessos estão associados, entre outros aspectos, com incompreensão e/ou níveis inadequados de contingência, de acordo com a complexidade das tarefas.

3. Examinando exemplos práticos: análise da evolução da Organização de Atividades Conjuntas em duas sequências de ensino de esportes

Para mostrar como a atividade conjunta se organiza e como evolui ao longo do processo de transferência e cessão do controle da aprendizagem, usamos dois exemplos de sequências de ensino de esportes coletivos, com aprendizes iniciantes. Uma sequência corresponde a 4 sessões de uma unidade de introdução ao handball, com alunos de escola primária (11-12 anos de idade), outra corresponde a 11 sessões de introdução ao rugby em um clube esportivo com aprendizes iniciantes (17-19 anos de idade). Ambas as sequências são reais, portanto, mantêm toda a validade ecológica e usam o Modelo Técnico-Tático Integrado (López-Ros, 2016; López-Ros & Castejón, 2005) como modelo de ensino de esportes.

Todas as ações e conversas durante essas duas sequências foram registrados em vídeo e com microfones sem fim. Isso permitiu obter todas as informações sobre o que os participantes fizeram e disseram, e identificar a analisar as formas mais genéricas de OAC. Posteriormente, todas as contribuições dos participantes foram transcritas e analisadas usando uma perspectiva pragmática da análise do discurso.

É possível utilizar diferentes níveis de abordagem para analisar a OAC. (Coll et al., 1992; Coll et al., 2008) Neste trabalho, com o objetivo de obter evidências genéricas sobre o processo de transferência do controle e responsabilidade de aprendizagem através da evolução das formas de atividade conjunta, focamos somente no nível mais geral (ou macro). Descrevemos e analisamos a interatividade entre participantes vendo como ela emerge, que características manifesta e como evolui enquanto o aprendiz progride em sua aprendizagem. A aprendizagem foi corroborada em ambas as sequências (López-Ros, 2001, 2013; LLobet, 2016; LLobet-Martí, López-Ros, & Vila, 2017), mostrando que a evolução da OAC está diretamente ligada à apropriação e à aperfeiçoamento do conteúdo.

Para determinar as formas da OAC, usamos Segmentos de Interatividade (SI) como unidade de análise. Essa unidade foi usada em outros trabalhos (Coll et al., 2008; Comino, 2017; Pradas, 2012) com o propósito de estudar a evolução da OAC no processo de transferência, com diferentes conteúdos e em diferentes configurações. É usada uma metodologia interpretativa, a qual, em primeiro lugar, estabelece os SI que emergem e tornam visíveis as formas de OAC entre participantes. De acordo com o quadro teórico e a proposta metodológica utilizada usada (Coll et al., 2008), cada SI emerge considerando: a) a gama de possíveis ações e coerência com a atividade que acontece; b) a função instrucional que guia a atividade em que professor e aprendiz estão envolvidos.

Como o objetivo é capturar as formas de OAC que emergem, o estabelecimento de diferentes SIs frequentemente requer um processo repetitivo de "ir e voltar", por parte dos pesquisadores, até que a estrutura final de cada SI esteja delimitada.

Cada SI é constituído de diferentes padrões comportamentais dos participantes (Professor – P e Aprendizes – A). Esses padrões revelam as formas concretas que tomam as atividades conjuntas de cada participante no contexto de um dado segmento. Então, por exemplo, um SI com uma clara instrução de organização prática que será realizado na sequência pode implicar que o professor e os aprendizes se envolvam numa atividade conjunta, a qual garante que os aprendizes conheçam a tarefa a realizar e suas condições. Isso pode levar a diferentes padrões comportamentais, por exemplo: 1) (P) explicação, (A) acompanhamento e questionamento, (P) resposta; 2) (P) demonstração e explicação, (A) acompanhamento e questionamento.

Neste ponto, quais são as formas de OAC que podem ser vistas nas duas sequências analisadas, ou seja, o que emerge? Como essas formas evoluem enquanto os aprendizes melhoram em sua "performance"? Como a atividade conjunta é articulada e evoluída e desenvolvida nessas duas sequências ao longo da ZDP?

Na sequência de 4 sessões de handball, encontramos cinco tipos de SI (López-Ros, 2001, 2013), cada um constituído de diferentes padrões comportamentais. Esses SI foram: a) Segmento de Organização de Atividade (SIOA), no qual o professor e os alunos são envolvidos na apresentação das tarefas, assim como nas condições de realização da atividade; b) Segmento de Prática Guiada (SIPG), no qual os estudantes realizam a tarefa (por exemplo, 5 contra 5, mantendo a posse de bola) e o professor oferece ajuda enquanto eles o fazem; c) Segmento de Discussão (SID), no qual o professor e os alunos falam e discutem sobre os eventos que aconteceram durante a tarefa que estão fazendo; d) Segmento de Recapitulação (SIR), no qual o professor e os alunos discutem situações e eventos mas em relação a conteúdos de outras sessões ou aos objetivos da sessão e da sequência (não em relação à tarefa imediata que vêm realizando); e e) Segmento de Transição (SIT), que são os momentos e atividades sem função instrucional.

Nas 11 sessões de rugby encontramos seis tipos de SI. (Llobet-Martí, 2016; Llobet-Martí, López-Ros, & Vila, 2017) Cinco SI são muito semelhantes aos encontrados na sequência de handball, mas nesta sequência destacamos a emergência de um Segmento de Prática Autônoma (SIPA), no qual os jogadores praticam sob sua própria responsabilidade, sem o auxílio de um treinador (que em geral está preparando outras atividades em outra área do campo). Provavelmente, esse SIPA é um bom exemplo da ideia de "atividade", para além da "interação face a face" apontada por Rogoff (1995), na qual a influência do professor existe ainda que não esteja presente.

Ambas as sequências enfatizam que as formas de OAC em situações de esportes desenvolvidas usando um modelo técnico-tático integrado apresente fortes semelhanças em seu nível macro. No entanto, ainda que as classificações de SI sejam semelhantes, os padrões comportamentais não necessariamente coincidem. Assim, os padrões que emergem no SID na sequência de handball não são os mesmos que aqueles que aparecem no SID do rugby. É razoável considerar, como indicamos, que os processos de interatividade no ZDP são construídos no caminho e requerem altos níveis de intersubjetividade e negociação. Essas características destacam sua dinâmica e sua natureza imprevisível.

Como a OAC evolui junto com a ZDP? Que evidências podemos começar a observar? Em resumo, na sequência do handball encontramos uma diminuição do número de SI enquanto a sequência progride. Isso mostra que existem menos rupturas na OAC. Em termos gerais, um nível mais baixo de rupturas na interatividade é interpretado como aumento da fluência do processo de transferência e da apropriação pelos aprendizes. Obviamente, isso requereria uma análise mais profunda que excede este capítulo.

Mais especificamente, parece que o SIOA diminui em número e tempo utilizado, enquanto a sequência progride. Isto é, os estudantes estão se apropriando e construindo o conhecimento relacional aos aspectos organizacionais e funcionais das tarefas, de modo que é desnecessário renegociar as condições da tarefa, as regras de participação e outros aspectos. Isso mostra o processo de transferência, assim como o estabelecimento de um sistema de conhecimento compartilhado. Ao mesmo tempo, os SIPGs diminuem e o tempo passado neles aumenta. Este fato poderia parecer contraditório com os postulados da aprendizagem motora que presumem que maior e melhor tempo de prática envolve mais aprendizado. Nessa sequência, acontece o oposto, o que provavelmente pode ser entendido conectado ao tempo de SID, ou seja, ao estabelecimento de processos de diálogo e entendimento sobre a prática realizada. O aumento do tempo também é evidente no SIR, o que significa que o processo de transferência parece estar relacionado à apropriação do conhecimento sobre as condições para realização da tarefa e também aos processos reflexivos e estímulo ao entendimento sobre a prática, o fortalecimento da relação entre o conhecimento processual e conceitual. Em outras palavras, o progresso feito pela ZDP está destilando mudanças nas formas de OAC em que professor e estudantes estão envolvidos. No entanto, essa evolução aparentemente progressiva dos diferentes SIs é interrompida em uma das sessões (sessão 2). Isso mostra que o trânsito através das ZDP e o processo de transferência não é fácil nem linear e frequentemente mostra falhas e retrocessos.

Algumas das características observadas nas 4 sessões de handball também aparecem em uma sequência muito mais longa (11 sessões), com outro esporte (rugby), que mostra diferentes características e em um contexto diferente (clube), mas usando o mesmo modelo metodológico (o modelo técnico-tático integrado). Então, por exemplo, há um declínio no número de SI à medida que a sequência avança. Também há uma leve diminuição no SIOA e no SIPG, enquanto nenhuma mudança significante é observada no SIPA, SID, SIR. Contudo, uma análise mais detalhada dos diálogos e discussões do SID mostra como, no início da sequência, o treinador criou momentos ou espaços específicos para debater aspectos táticos. À medida que o SID avança, o tempo passado nele é transferido para o SIPG. Isso poderia significar que, quando os jogadores se apropriam de um nível mais alto de conhecimento, o técnico pode dialogar, apoiar e discutir com eles enquanto estão envolvidos no segmento prático. Esse exemplo sugere que alguns padrões específicos de comportamento da atividade conjunta podem ser transferidos entre diferentes SI durante o processo de transferência do controle da responsabilidade de aprendizagem.

Comentários finais

A análise da OAC em processos reais de ensino e aprendizagem pode nos oferecer uma visão mais precisa do que acontece em condições normais quando professores e aprendizes se movem através das ZDP. Um aspecto que parece fundamental está ligado à capacidade de ajuste do suporte pedagógico em cada momento, considerando que tal ajuste só faz sentido em um quadro de intersubjetividade que facilite uma comunicação permanente. A evolução das formas de OAC nos permite entender como o suporte pedagógico se articula no contexto de uma unidade inseparável configurada por professor, aluno e conteúdo. Longe de ser capaz de prever completamente o desenvolvimento dessa atividade através da ZDP, parece que uma parte importante do processo não é fácil nem fluída e requer negociações permanentes. O processo de ensino e aprendizagem na ZDP mostra uma natureza dinâmica e interdependente e deve ser observado considerando sua complexidade.

Referências

CHAIKLIN, S. (2003). The Zone of Proximal Development in Vygotsky's analysis of learning and instruction. In A. Kozulin, B. Gindis, V. Ageyev, V. & S. Miller. (Eds.) *Vygotsky's Educational Theory in Cultural Context.* (p. 39-64). New York: Cambridge University Press.

COLE, M. (1996). *Cultural Psychology. A once and future discipline.* Massachusetts: Harvard University Press.

COLL, C., COLOMINA, R., ONRUBIA, J., & ROCHERA, M.J. (1992). Actividad conjunta y habla: una aproximación al studio de los mecanismos de influencia educativa. *Infancia y Aprendizaje, 59-60*, 189-232.

COLL, C., ONRUBIA, J., & MAURI, T. (2008). Supporting learning in educational context: the exercise of educational influence and the analysis of teaching. *Revista de Educación, 346,* 33-70.

COMINO, J. (2017). *L'organització de l'activitat conjunta i la seva anàlisi en el procés d'ensenyament i aprenentatge de l'equilibri dinàmic en l'educació física escolar*. Universitat de Girona. Tesis doctoral no publicada. Girona.

DANIELS, H. (2001). *Vygotsky and Pedagogy*. London: Routledge Falmer.

FRANKEL, K. (2012). Coping with the double bind: Bidirectional learning and development in the zone of proximal development. *Learning, Culture and Social Interaction, 1*(3-4), 153-166.

JOHN-STEINER, V., & MAHN, H. (1996). Sociocultural approaches to learning and development: a Vygotskian framework. *International Psychologist, 31* (3/4), 191-206.

LLOBET, B. (2016). *Analysis of the interactivity in a teaching and learning sequence with novice players: the transfer of learning responsibility and control.* University of Girona. Unpublished doctoral thesis. Girona

LLOBET-MARTÍ, B., LÓPEZ-ROS,V., & VILA, I. (2017). The analysis of interactivity in a teaching and learning sequence of rugby: the transfer of control and learning responsibility. *Physical Education and Sport Pedagogy,* DOI: 10.1080/17408989.2017.1341472.

LÓPEZ-ROS, V. (2001). *L'organització de l'activitat conjunta en l'ensenyament escolar dels esports col·lectius*. Universitat de Girona. Tesis doctoral no publicada. Girona.

López-Ros, V. (2013). La organización de la actividad conjunta en la enseñanza escolar de los deportes colectivos. In Castejón Oliva, F.J., Giménez Fuentes-Guerra, F.J., Jiménez Jiménez, F.J., & López-Ros, V. (Eds.) *Investigaciones en formación deportiva* (pp. 41-64). Sevilla: Wanceulen.

López-Ros, V. (2016). El "modelo integrado técnico-táctico" de enseñanza deportiva. Origen, contextualización y características metodológicas. *eJRIEPS, 38*, 63-91.

López-Ros, V., & Castejón, F.J. (2005). L'ensenyament integrat Tècnic-Tàctic dels esports en edat escolar. *Apunts. Educació Física i Esport, 79,* 40-48.

Mahn, H. (2015). Classroom discourse and interaction in the Zone of Proximal Development. In N. Markee (Ed.) *The Handbook of Classroom Discourse and Interaction* (pp. 250-264). New York: John Wiley & Sons.

Mercer, N. (1995). *The guided construction of knowledge. Talk amongst teachers and learners.* Clevedon: Multilingual Matters Ltd.

Moll, L. (1990). Vygotsky's zone of proximal development: Rethinking ints instructional implications. *Infancia y Aprendizaje, 50-51,* 157-168.

Newman, D., Griffin, P., & Cole, M. (1989). *The construction zone: working for cognitive change in school.* Cambridge: Cambridge University Press.

Pradas, R. (2012). *L'organització de l'activitat conjunta I el pensament del professorat sobre l'acció docent en educació física escolar.* Universitat de Girona. Tesis doctoral no publicada. Girona.

Rogoff, B. (1990). *Apprenticeship in thinking. Cognitive development in social interaction.* New York: Oxford University Press.

Rogoff, B. (1995). Observing sociocultural activity on three planes: participatory appropriation, guided participation, and apprenticeship. In Wertsch, J., Del Rio, P., & Álvarez, A. (Eds.) *Sociocultural Studies of Mind* (pp. 139-164). Cambridge: Cambridge University Press.

Smagorinsky, P. (2017) (In press). Deconflating the ZPD and instructional scaffolding: Retranslating and reconceiving the zone of proximal development as the zone of next development. *Learning, Culture and Social Interaction.*

Valsiner, J. (2005). Scaffolding within the structure of Dialogical Self: Hierarchical dynamics of semiotic mediation. *New Ideas in Psychology, 23,* 197-206.

Van de Pol, J., Volman, M., & Beishuizen, J. (2010). Scaffolding in Teacher-Student interaction: A decade of Research. *Educational Psychology Review, 22,* 271-296.

VERESOV, N.N. (2017). ZBR and ZPD: Is there a difference? *Cultural-Historical Psychology, 13*(1), 23-36.

VYGOTSKY, L.S. (1978). *Mind in Society: The development of higher psychological processes.* Cambridge MA: Harvard University Press.

VYGOTSKY, L.S. (1993). *Obras escogidas, II.* Madrid: Visor.

VILA, I. (1998). El espacio social en la construcción compartida del conocimiento. *Educar, 22-23,* 55-98.

WERTSCH, J. (1985). *Vygotsky and the social formation of mind.* Cambridge, MA.: Harvard University Press.

WOOD, D., BRUNER, J.S., & ROSS, G. (1976). The role of tutoring in problem-solving. *Journal of Child Psychology and Psychiatry, and allied disciplines, 17,* 89-100.

AFTERWORD

Carlos Eduardo GONÇALVES
University of Coimbra, Faculty of Sport Sciences and Physical Education, Portugal.
Serge ÉLOI
Universidade Paris-Leste, França.

Reading the texts in this book leaves us with a handful of questions and evokes the paragraph that is mandatory for any academic work: "suggestions for future studies". As previously mentioned, Vygotsky did not study motor and sportive learning and his ideas and theoretical foundations require empirical validation. However, it is necessary to be aware of the obstacles that arise. Vygotsky is not an easy author, and his works present an intellectual density that imposes increased attention. Furthermore, many of his articles are not available in good translations for those who do not know Russian. It was not by chance that Lebed and Bar-Eli (2014) applied Vygotsky's concepts to Sports Science in a particularly pertinent manner, for they have read the original versions.

The types of existing risks are basically two. First, the access to Vygotsky through secondary sources or unsuited translations may lead to imprecisions on what he actually intended to state (Santos & Morgan, 2019). Second, there is opportunist use of Vygotsky's thought, detached from his humanistic and pedagogical proposals. Tegmark (2017) offers an elucidative example of this second skew. In the early 21st century, academic interest in the area of Artificial Intelligence began to pay attention to social contexts, that means, to learning through interaction, not only with the physical world, but also with other intelligent agents. Such change has been inspired by the late adoption of Vygotsky's Activity Theory, enthusiastically welcomed by several groups that research about the relations of humans and computers. Vygotsky's understanding about social and cognitive development has been proved to be useful to analyze and to perfect the multi-agent system: to create an intelligent population, instead of a solitary individual. However, the deformation of Vygotsky's view is patent within the current boom of interest in multi-agent systems in deep learning, which takes the form of generation of opposing networks in which two neural networks compete with one another. It is unlikely that contemporary experts in deep learning have ever read or even heard of Vygotsky.

It is for these reasons that the authors who contribute to the volume herein are aware of the importance that Vygotsky's works may have in the development of research about sports learning, but also know the difficulties that come up in the design of studies and in the choice of methodologies, facing the absence of a solid body of literature.

Thereafter, a close link between theory and practice is imperative. The precise comprehension of the concepts proposed by Vygotsky, to avoid making more of the same. Contrary to what a reckless reader may hastily conclude, Vygotsky is not constructivist – we can even consider him as anti-Piaget –, he does not have a stadial conception of human development and rejects any kind of positivism or determinism. His way of thinking is always dialectical.

His views on learning, as a constant process of reorganizing higher nervous dynamics, always socially implicated, poses important methodological challenges that are not reducible to the schools of thought that currently dominate contemporary Sports Science. This is where the researchers brought together in this book were mostly defied.

As a well-known example, the present focus in the importance of decision-making in the competition situation, in which the idea of creativity is the alpha and the omega in the path to success, is approached by Vygotsky as a facet of imagination learning that must be a responsibility of those who teach.

The meaning of the Zones of Proximal Development, the importance of the teacher/coach, the use of artifacts and signs as stimulation tools for higher nervous processes and for imagination, represent fascinating perspectives for Sports Science, in a moment of theoretical uncertainty and scarcity of research anchored in human beings in their social environments.

It is up to contemporary Sports Science researchers to extend and develop Vygotsky's instrumental theorization, in its application in sportive and artistic practices nowadays. That is both a difficult and captivating challenge.

References

LEBED, F. & BAR-ELI, M. (2014). *Complexity and control in team sports*. Oxxon, Routledge.

SANTOS, M. & MORGAN, K. (2019). Developing creative team games players: from jazz to sport coaching. *International Journal of Sports Science & Coaching*, 14(2), 117-125.

TEGMARK, M. (2017). *Life 3.0: being human in the age of artificial intelligence*. London, Allen Lane.

POSFÁCIO

Carlos Eduardo GONÇALVES
University of Coimbra, Faculty of Sport Sciences and Physical Education, Portugal.
Serge ÉLOI
Universidade Paris-Leste, França.

A leitura dos textos neste livro deixa-nos com uma mão cheia de perguntas, evocando o parágrafo obrigatório de qualquer trabalho académico: "sugestões de futuros estudos". Como foi referido anteriormente, Vygotsky não estudou a aprendizagem motora e desportiva e as suas ideias e fundamentações teóricas necessitam de validação empírica. Mas precisamos de estar conscientes dos obstáculos que se levantam. Vygotsky não é um autor fácil e os seus escritos possuem uma densidade intelectual que obriga a redobrada atenção. Para além disso, muitos dos seus artigos não estão disponíveis para o publico não conhecedor russo, e em traduções de qualidade. Não é por acaso que foram Lebed e Bar-Eli (2014) que aplicaram de forma particularmente pertinente os conceitos de Vygotsky a questões das Ciências do Desporto, porque o leram no original.

E os riscos existentes são fundamentalmente de dois tipos. Em primeiro lugar, o acesso a Vygotsky através de fontes secundárias ou de traduções truncadas, o que pode levar a imprecisões sobre o que Vygotsky exactamente quis dizer (Santos & Morgan, 2019). Em segundo lugar, o uso oportunista do pensamento de Vygotsky, desligando-o dos seus propósitos humanistas e pedagógicos. Tegmark (2017) dá-nos um exemplo elucidativo deste último enviesamento. No início do século XXI, os interesses académicos na área da Inteligência artificial começaram a prestar atenção aos contextos sociais, ou seja, à aprendizagem através da interacção não só com o mundo físico, mas também com outros agentes inteligentes. Esta mudança foi inspirada pela adoção tardia da teoria da acção de Vygotsky, que foi entusiasticamente acolhido por vários grupos de pesquisa sobre a relação dos humanos com os computadores. O entendimento Vygotskiano sobre o desenvolvimento social e cognitivo provou ser útil para a análise e aperfeiçoamento de sistema multiagentes: criar uma população inteligente, em vez de um indivíduo solitário. Contudo, a deformação da visão de Vygotsky, é patente na actual explosão de interesse em sistemas multiagentes em *deep learning*, que assume prioritariamente a forma de geração de redes adversárias em que duas redes neuronais entram em competição uma com a outra. É improvável que os especialistas contemporâneos em *deep learning* tenham alguma vez lido, ou sequer ouvido falar, de Vygotsky.

É por estes motivos que os autores que contribuíram para o presente volume estão conscientes da importância que o conhecimento de Vygotsky pode ter no desenvolvimento da pesquisa das aprendizagens desportivas, mas também sabem das dificuldades que se levantam no desenho dos estudos e na escolha das metodologias, face à ausência de um sólido corpo de literatura.

Por conseguinte, é imperativa uma ligação estreita entre teoria e prática. A compreensão precisa dos conceitos propostos por Vygotsky, pois então estaríamos a fazer mais do mesmo. Contrariamente ao que um leitor imprudente pode apressadamente concluir, Vygostki não é construtivista – podemos mesmo considerá-lo como anti-Piaget -, não tem uma concepção estadial do desenvolvimento humano e é alheio a qualquer tipo de positivismo ou determinismo. O seu modo de raciocínio é sempre dialético.

A sua visão da aprendizagem como um processo constante de reorganização das dinâmicas nervosas superiores, sempre socialmente implicada, coloca desafios metodológicos importantes e que requerem desenhos de investigação alinhados com os conceitos teóricos., que não são redutíveis às escolas de pensamento actualmente dominantes nas Ciências do Desporto contemporâneas. Foi aqui que residiu o principal desafio para os pesquisadores reunidos neste livro, dado que a obra de Vygotsky abre vias de pensamento que não são redutíveis aos modelos propostos pelas escolas dominantes nas Ciências do Desporto.

Como exemplo bem conhecido, o presente enfoque na importância da tomada de decisão em situação de competição, em que a ideia de criatividade é o alfa e o ómega no caminho para o sucesso, é tratado por Vygotsky como uma faceta da aprendizagem da imaginação que deve constituir uma responsabilidade de quem ensina.

O significado das Zonas de Aprendizagem Proximal, a importância do professor/treinador, o uso de artefactos e signos como instrumentos de estímulo dos processso nervosos superiores e da imaginação, representam perspectivas fascinantes para as Ciências do Desporto, em momento de incerteza teórica e de escassez de pesquisa ancorada no ser humano no seio do seu contexto social. Cabe aos pesquisadores contemporâneos em Ciências do Desporto prolongar e desenvolver a teorização instrumental de Vygotsky na sua aplicação às práticas desportivas e artísticas dos nossos dias. Trata-se sem dúvida de um desafio tão difícil como cativante.

Referências

Lebed, F. & Bar-Eli, M. (2014). *Complexity and control in team sports*. Oxxon, Routledge.

Santos, M. & Morgan, K. (2019). Developing creative team games players: from jazz to sport coaching. *International Journal of Sports Science & Coaching*, 14(2), 117-125.

Tegmark, M. (2017). *Life 3.0: being human in the age of artificial intelligence*. London, Allen Lane.